Measuring Time —
by an hourglass

Kitty Crockett Robertson

All essays first appeared in the *Ipswich Chronicle* and were collected
and edited for this publication by Betsy Robertson Cramer

© 2008 Elizabeth J.R. Cramer
All Rights Reserved.

No part of this publication may be reproduced, stored in a retrieval system, or transmitted, in any form or by any means, electronic, mechanical, photocopying, recording, or otherwise, without the written permission of the author.

First published by Dog Ear Publishing
4010 W. 86th Street, Ste H
Indianapolis, IN 46268
www.dogearpublishing.net

ISBN: 978-159858-682-4

This book is printed on acid-free paper.

Printed in the United States of America

"The spinning wheel of the seasons turns ever faster. Already the shadows are long early on the marshes and the heavy dews and the crickets mark the fall that comes too soon, too soon. ..." from Kitty's *"A Golden Signal of Summer's End"*

Measuring Time — by an hourglass is dedicated to all who remember and cherish

Poem for Adèle
SORT OF A POEM FOR ADÈLE ROBERTSON, B. 1901

One thing I like about Kitty Robertson
is she always looks as though she has come fresh
from some exhilarating tussle
with the weather—a blizzard,
or an hour under the big hot marsh sky
with the greenheads.

                      I see her, mostly,
standing in front of the post office
so I associate her with the trees there
when they are in bloom. She
always seems in bloom.

                      On the radio
her voice of amused indignation breaks
into a startling crackle, like somebody
stepping on a strawberry box. In print
she gets better and better; more
and more herself.
Town conscience and rememberer,
she tells us where we live.

                      She tells us
to cheer us up and shape us up but mostly (I
feel) she wants us to enjoy the lame
direct and if necessary contentious contact
with reality she enjoys.

                      The Bible
suggests that three score and ten
is a correct allocation but in Kitty's case
it clearly isn't enough.

                      —John Updike

*written for Kitty on her 70th birthday; published in
the Ipswich Chronicle, Ipswich, Massachusetts.*

FOREWORD to the first edition

My mother, Adele LeBourgeois Crockett Robertson, known to all as Kitty, was born in Ipswich, Massachusetts, on August 4, 1901. She was the oldest child and only daughter of Dr. Eugene Crockett and Elizabeth LeBourgeois Crockett The family's home was at 298 Marlborough Street, Boston. She attended various schools and Radcliffe College, escaping on winter vacations and during the summers to Ipswich. In the early Depression days, she made the town her home and tried to run the Crockett property as a working self-sufficient farm.

The times and probably the scope and quality of the land were not right for such farming. In 1936, she met and married my father, William A. Robertson, after his return from Admiral Byrd's second Antarctica Expedition. I was their only child. While my father was at sea on the Murmansk runs during World War II, my mother worked at the Robinson Shipyard and at the Sylvania Factory, both in Ipswich.

For several years after the war, they fished out of Annisquam on the 40-foot dragger, *Kelpie*, designed and built by my father. The fishing life with its long hours, heavy work, and forced togetherness was not mutually agreeable and so again there were changes.

At the age of 50, Kitty began a career of newspaper work as a reporter, first on the Ipswich Chronicle, then on the daily Lawrence Eagle-Tribune, and back again for the Chronicle. She also reported Ipswich doings for several local radio stations. Money was nearly non-existent and my father, instead of painting full-time as he preferred, worked at a variety of non-painting jobs until he died in 1968. Except for much later vacation travels, the only pause in Kitty's newspaper work was from 1975-78, during which she served as elected Selectman for the Town of Ipswich. Her defeat at re-election was a "shift of the wind" that allowed her to return to observing and reporting.

The essays in *Measuring Time — by an hourglass* were all written for the *Ipswich Chronicle* under a weekly deadline which she sometimes described as "agonizing." They cover a period of about 15 years; the last, "Montreal Express; Voice of Times Past" was completed on the morning of February 7, 1979, several hours before her sudden death. The columns were exceptions to the immersion in the present that is the reporter's life and for my mother, I think, they integrated the past with the present, kept it alive, gave it a continuity in a busy life of meetings to cover, news stories to write, telephone calls to answer.

Chronicle publisher Bill Wasserman and his editor then, John Curran, encouraged her to write about what she often scornfully referred to as "the good old days". The selection presented here is a result of their encouragement.

I have tried to make the selection less a representative collection of all that my mother wrote–the number in Measuring Time is probably less than 15 percent of the total number of Chronicle columns–than a picture of what she saw and felt about growing up in Boston and especially her life in her beloved Ipswich, which she called a "microcosm" of the world. To retain the immediacy, I have limited editing to the removal of only the most obvious time references in essays that in some cases were written years apart. Although she and I began collecting her columns years ago, the project was not completed while she was alive. I sorted over again after her death and, therefore, the selection is my own. I regret if anyone's particular favorite has been omitted.

I am very grateful to William S. Wasserman, Jr., publisher of the North Shore Weeklies, Inc., parent organization of the *Ipswich Chronicle*, for his continued support of this book, for permission to reprint the columns, and for his permission to reprint John Updike's "Sort of a poem . . .", written for the occasion of Kitty's 70th birthday. I believe that Updike's words capture and preserve my mother's spirit and enthusiasm. I also credit the typing skills and editorial assistance of Kory Waymen, San Jose, California, who helped me in making a whole out of many isolated pieces.

Many in Ipswich and elsewhere have encouraged me to put together the columns but I am particularly appreciative of the patience during long hours of conversation, the overcoming of my doubts and hesitations, the suggestions of Ipswich friends, Mary Conley (Mrs. John F. Conley), Jack and Sharon Josephson, Oliver Coolidge, and Nancy Thompson, who also has volunteered to undertake the distribution of this book.

My special appreciation goes to Edward D. Baring-Gould, Santa Barbara, California, whose friendship, support and encouragement over the years since my mother and I first began to assemble the essays have helped make this book possible. I feel sure that my mother would agree that part of the dedication of Measuring Time should be shared by him as well as by all who love Ipswich, its land, its people, its waters.

Betsy Robertson Cramer
Ipswich, Massachusetts
June, 1981

A note to the second edition:

Thanks to Nancy Thompson's wonderful distribution efforts, the first edition of *Measuring Time* sold out quite quickly. Over the years there have been many requests for a reissue of Kitty's reflections on her life. About ten years after her death, I read my mother's earlier manuscript that became *The Orchard, A Memoir*.

After *The Orchard* was published, a process for me of about four years, I heard that people preferred *Measuring Time*, saying there is a universality in each of the short essays. Too close, still, I can't tell, but I have found in this recent effort that they touch me, reminding of my own very different childhood and of the sweet scents of Ipswich marshes and fields we shared.

Going line-by-line, word-by-word over the typo-filled scans of the prior edition was an immersion in a past that is long gone, as irretrievable as the *Kelpie* and my own childhood. But as each of our pasts remain alive in our memories, so I feel are Kitty's memories of Boston and, especially, her beloved Ipswich, sparkling and evocative, even timeless. I do feel truly privileged to be able to make available *Measuring Time* again.

Betsy Robertson Cramer
Santa Barbara, California
April, 2008

CONTENTS

Poem for Adèle by by John Updike v
Foreword vii

CHILDHOOD
A Family of Inveterate Dreamers .2
The Inner Eye: The Art of Seeing Things 5
Measuring Time by an Hourglass 8
Fog Horn 11
Train 14
Home: "Over the river and into the woods..." 17
Spring in Ipswich, General, and Grandma 20
Thoughts on Long-ago Birthdays 23
Mr. Patterson 26
Lighthouse 30
The Choate House 33
Testing Ben Franklin's Theory .36
Oasis of Cranberries Among the Dunes 39
Reminiscences of the "Great Dune" 42
Riding the Revere Beach Cyclone 45
Changing Aims of a Former Duck Hunter 48
Gunner 51
No Place for the Oriole's Hammock 54
Of Spirits, Nymphs, and Hamadryads 57
The Great Red Oak is Dead 60
Reflections on the Magic Sheet of Crystal 63
And in Horse and Buggy Days .66
Coasting 69

SPRING
Spring — Always Different, Always New 76
Grandma 79
Dandelions 82
Tears Among the Spring Peach Blossoms 86
Thunder 89
Hayfields 92
Decoration Day 95

SUMMER
Welcome, Summer! ... More than Ever 100
Summer Begins 103
Idle Hands 106
In the Long, Lovely Days of Summer 109
A Native Knows About Greenheads 112
Haying was a High Point 115
After a Bang-up Fourth, Quiet Summer Stars 118
Summer Birthday — An August Event 121
Once on a Perfect Day in August 124

BOATS
Sailboats 130
River Bottom 133
Quietly, the Little Boat Slips Along... 137
Kelpie 140
A Mad March Day off Gloucester 144
...And Only We Who Were Lost 147
Kelpie Proudly Continued on Course 150
Beware the Deep, Cooling Sea 153
October Tides 156

AUTUMN
Sailing Days Dwindle Down 162
Initials 165
A Time for Apple Picking 169
Autumn 172

The Devil Walked Abroad on Halloween 175
Making Allowances for the Devil 178
Visit to a Haunted House on Halloween 181
A Raffle Ticket to Thanksgiving 184
Melancholy Walk in Gray November 187

RUMINATING ON FAMILIAR THINGS
The Times They Are a-Changin' 192
A Fleet of T-Bones 195
Who Will Feel Nostalgia for the Seventies? 198
Energy Crisis: A Blessing in Disguise? 201
Lights Out: A Sunday Storm 204
Memories While Cleaning out an Attic 207
Only the Memories Aren't for sale 210
Ike Belonged to a Different Age 213
Adele LeBourgois, What's in a Name? 216
So What's New about Nudity? .219
A Golden Signal of Summer's End 222
Ruminating on Familiar Things 225
Orchards 228
Montreal Express: Voice of Times Past 231
Seals 234
There is no Escaping the Omens 237
Failure: Only a Shift of the Wind 239
My Bed: Like a Boat on a Foggy Sea 242
The Montreal Express is Early .245

WINTER
Winter Back Then 250
Winter Breakfasts 253
The Good Old Days 256
Skating 259
Christmas in Boston 262
Christmas Memory 265
Winter Stars 268
Home 271

Portrait by Charles S. Hopkinson, 1904

CHILDHOOD

... I had an hourglass when I was a little girl, blown all of a piece, two crystal cones separated by a narrow neck through which the grains of sand could trickle one by one from the filled cone to the empty cone, marking in this visible way the passage of time. And when the bottom half was filled with a tiny perfect Fujiyama of sand, you had only to turn it over, and once again, time started running second by second, grain by grain. ...

A Family of Inveterate Dreamers

I come from a family of dreamers. I mean dreams at night. The idle thoughts and imaginings indulged in by children, swinging in a hammock or lying flat on the grass under a tree with moving leaves, those were known as "wool gathering" and not to be indulged in if there was a grownup around to order activity and useful accomplishment. How many of those long thoughts were interrupted by commands to pick the berries, tidy up the bedroom, or bail out my sailboat after the rain!

All those lovely possessions, my boat, my horse, and my bicycle, had inherent in them the seeds of duty, a concept strong in the days of my childhood. The boat had to be painted, caulked, puttied, and the sail unfurled and dried after rain to prevent mildew. The horses had to be exercised, not ridden when I wanted to, but when they needed to be, and the bike had to be put under cover and dried off after rain.

Only in my bed at night, and especially in the time between sleep and waking, was I free of all these obligations, these duties, and all those boring things that must be done. Now, right now.

My mother was the great dreamer and as she grew older, though not old by modern standards, her dreams as recounted at breakfast more and more concerned her childhood on the Louisiana plantation. It was through these dream tales, rather than the more standardized stories that began, "when I was a little girl," that I painted in my mind the unforgettable picture of the child galloping her pony through fields of waist-high sugar cane and across the short grass of the three mounds that in the flat country gave the plantation its name of Belmont.

The "pretty mountains" were actually salt domes containing in their bowels a black fortune of oil. But no one knew it then or cared, and it was not till a half century afterwards, long after the family fortunes had collapsed and the plantation had passed into other hands, that the oil wells were pumped among what had been the fields of cane and rice. Always through my mother's dreams ran the Mississippi that flowed behind its earthen levee in times of flood, higher than the roof of the house. The passing riverboats, bound upstream for St. Louis or down-stream to the Delta, were above eye level of the child on the second story gallery of the pillared house. Once she was rowed out and across the broad yellow river by old Jock, a gentle black man who had been born a slave on the plantation. Fifty years later, reliving the experience in her dreams, she still felt the shadow of that old terror.

And in the end, in a time of flooding like this spring the great river fingered the weak spots in the levee and finally, in one great yellow burst, breached the dike and poured across the fields and across the rosewood floors of the house. The family perched on the roof were eventually rescued by men in a boat.

I do not know if my mother was old enough to remember, or whether her dreams were based on what she had been told, but they were vivid enough for me to remember for 60 years and even to make a part of my own dream experience.

I, too, am sometimes haunted by her dream picture of the aftermath of the flood with the fields carefully tended for 100 years, growing up to scrub willow and tangled vines. The Mississippi made itself a new channel, and from the levee for many years, it was possible to see the pillars of the house above the yellow tide of the river.

Small wonder that my mother, so intrepid about most things, was always afraid of the water. To her, the Castle Neck River was akin to the Mississippi of her childhood, and my father's crazy catboat brought back terrifying memories of that row with Jock on the big river. My father was reckless and impatient and I remember what must have been one of the last sails with both my mother and my grandmother. I was just a little kid, and the Mississippi was a dream experience without reality, so I thought it was fine when the wind blew squally after a calm start. The boat yawed wildly, heeled over so far that the water slopped in over the rail and the long boom's tip dragged in the water.

My father noted with annoyance the tense, pale faces of his passengers and their hands clutching the weather rail till the knuckles were white. But I laughed and shouted with delight, so afterwards I was invited to go on boating expeditions, some of which were very close calls, indeed. My mother and my grandmother were left at home to worry.

Now in the too short hours that I spend in my bed, I continue the old dreaming habit, compounding my own life's experiences with those of my mother and even my grandmother. And even in that mélange of Louisiana and Maine and Ipswich, I am aware in a curious way that I am only dreaming. I shall wake up and the dream will fade away in the course of the day's doings, but not entirely. There is always something left, a soft haze of sadness for people and times that live only in my dreams.

The Inner Eye: The Art of Seeing Things

I learned the art of seeing things and of total recall from my father. Faced all his life with the threat of blindness, he began in middle age to cultivate what he called his "inner eye" and in order to keep it fed with impressions, he studied with intense concentration the world around him. When we worked with pruning saw and shears in the orchard on winter afternoons, he studied the apple buds and how they lay close to the twig, folded tight, protecting the green heart of the spring leaf against the cold of winter.

Or the triple bud of the peaches. In these were hidden the deep pink flowers that would precede the leaves when the warm winds blew and the snows melted. The tiny things he observed with his nearsighted eyes from inches away, staring and staring, impressing their every detail on his inner eye. The vast sweeps of distance, of sky and marsh and sea, to him were blurred and seen through a perpetual mist, but to my sharp, young eyes, they were clear in detail. I practiced looking, training the inner eye, so that lying in bed at night or even now, years later, I can recall faces and even whole scenes from years ago.

How differently each of us sees the world around us was brought home to me when I watched my husband painting, the magical gift of bringing the visions of the inner eye to canvas or to paper. It was mysterious and fascinating to watch Bill work, combining what he had seen and what he had so deeply felt. It is one thing, I remember thinking to store up impressions for one's own interest, to be able to evoke them for one's own delight, and quite another to share them, to communicate them to others.

I thought of this on a bright afternoon of snow and wondered whether it would be possible to bring a measure of this delight to people who, for one reason or another, could not see. Perhaps somewhere, someone lies ill in the sterile surrounding of a hospital room or is nagged by the miseries and frustrations of being old, or suffers from such grief of loneliness that all the world is dark.

Look through my eyes for a little while and may what you see bring you the joy it brings to me.

This little house is almost a boat when the tide is high, the winter tide that feels its way through the tumbled ice of the marsh almost to the foot of the pine that is all wracked and bent by fifty years of north wind blowing. It is an intimate small marsh between two rounded hills, and
now its varied grasses that I saw change from emerald to russet are covered with ice cakes. In between are pools of water, arctic green, and at eye level, I see two pairs of ducks, swimming and tipping and feeding. Another pair, perched on red legs, is on the ice cake, sleeping. They are safe there.

Under the pine tree are tracks. It was not till I saw Bill painting that I was aware of how blue are the shadows of snow. The little blue tracks are those of rabbits that played there last night, and there are the leaping tracks of a squirrel. The neat sharp paw prints of the fox that I heard barking his shrill wild cry as I lay abed are also there.

No tracks of people or even of dog on this little expanse of snow between the house and the pine tree, this miniature bit of the great wild world. The birds have long since eaten the last scarlet berry from the alder bush and the stems are black . . . someone once said there is no black in nature . . . he hadn't seen the alder against the snow!

There is a scattering of pine needles on the snow and a little drift of oak leaves stripped by the roaring wind of yesterday, but today, it is calm, the high clouds of ice crystals hardly move across the sky, and the snowflakes, still not locked together by the weak sun, lie as quietly as they fell.

The camera's eyes held by a skilled hand, could, I suppose, bring you all this in its lovely detail, and sometimes the cold glass eye can almost see what the eye of the artist sees. But in the vitals of the camera, there is no stirring of delight, no quickened heartbeat when the deer walks down the hill, stepping delicately and clipping a tender twig from an old apple tree.

But in the inner eye, this deer joins all the others, running swimming, staring with his big soft eyes, frolicking in the sun, or sleeping under a tree. It becomes part of the feeling of deer—even of the one seen long ago from a canoe on the edge of a Canadian river with the forest beyond. And the pine tree, hardly moving this calm day, in the inner eye is drenched with rain, lashed by wind, or sheathed in ice. Among the needles, there is even a tiny bit of salt, all that is left of the tears shed when we buried there our little dog and placed a lichened piece of granite to mark the spot.

What my inner eye sees, I can not really share with you, because its vision is transformed by feelings and memories that are mine alone. But if reading these words stirs your own memories and recalls feelings that you thought you had forgotten, I shall be happy.

Measuring Time by an Hourglass

I had an hourglass when I was a little girl, blown all of a piece, two crystal cones separated by a narrow neck through which the grains of sand could trickle one by one from the filled cone to the empty cone, marking in this visible way the passage of time. And when the bottom half was filled with a tiny perfect Fujiyama of sand, you had only to turn it over, and once again, time started running second by second, grain by grain.

In the room with the yellow roses on the wallpaper, shaded by the trailing branches of the elm tree, and overlooking the sweep of broad marsh and the shining river, I used to sit with my hourglass, hypnotically staring at the running sand.

There were days and days when the hourglass lay untouched in my treasure box, along with such talismans as the huge marble to ward off the lightning the crumbling, chocolate brown bone found on the gravelly beach of Hog Island where an eroding bank occasionally exposed what was said to be an Indian burial place, an arrowhead or two, a single lead soldier, a hussar with feathered shako and fur cape on a prancing steed, an oyster shell found on the beach which surely must have washed in from very far away. Each of these things had its use, its magic.

Moving soundlessly on bare feet over the Philippine mating that covered the wide board floor, I skipped in and out among the objects laid out ritually on the mat. This was an exercise learned from a picture in one of my books of a girl dancing in and out among some eggs without breaking one, I forget why.

I tried it with eggs first, but I was too clumsy. Several eggs were broken, the mat was smeared, and I was punished.

What started as a game of skill, gradually became a sort of witchcraft sorcery with whispered incantations and imprecations directed against the enemies of the moment, my parents, my teachers, my erstwhile friends.

After an afternoon spent working my spells, I was both disappointed and relieved to find my intended victims in the best of health. But when, by working with the big-marble, rubbing it, rolling it, muttering over it I called up a thunderstorm out of a clear sky, I decided to give over the magic, it was too dangerous.

It was a most terrible storm, the thunderheads boiling up from behind the green cone of the linden tree on the windless, muggy afternoon. First, there were the rumblings in the distance. I felt the hairs on my neck begin to prickle and stopped working with the marble. But the storm kept coming. The sky grew greenish dark, the edges of the cloud torn and ragged and running every which way. I could hear the rain corning and the wind. Suddenly, there was a tremendous flash and crash. Clutching the marble, I dove under my bed, and huddled close against the wall, eyes squinched tight, but even through the lids, I could see the terror of the lightning.

When the storm went rumbling off out to sea, I crawled out and peering out through the small panes of the west window, I saw a branch of the linden, splintered, and already the leaves were withering.

After that, I quit the magic business because I did not really want to kill anyone, no matter how angry I was, and if I could call up a storm like that . . . well anything could happen.

But the hourglass, that was a gentler exercise, a secret solitary kind of experience, soothing and somehow comforting.

Sometimes, I came home dog-tired after doing my chores, hoeing and weeding in the scorching sun, chasing after the cows in the farthest corner of the pasture. Or there had been games which I was determined to win and so often lost. Or after rowing all the way down to the spindle buoy at the mouth of the Essex River, I had caught no fish at all, not even a bony little cunner, and I had so greatly wanted to surprise my father with a nice mess of fish I had caught myself when he came down from Boston.

It was then, after a day of disappointments and frustrations, that I tiptoed up the back stairs, opened the thin, old paneled door soundlessly, and from the treasure box, fished out the hourglass.

Lying on my stomach on the cool matting I stroked the smooth glass, then carefully turned it over. The grains of yellow sand began gently running building up the little mountain, till finally the last one had joined the others.

Over and over again, I turned the glass, watching hypnotized and soothed, until I dozed and wakened to find that time was standing still.

Long since, the hourglass has vanished with those other talismans, the lead soldier, the magic marble, the shells, and the Indian bone. Time moves forward from a larger glass, the bowl of the sky, the changing phases of the moon, the progression of the seasons. And now, there is no way to stop it. Inevitably, it moves until at last we sleep.

Fog Horn

Somewhere along the rocky Cape Ann shore, there is a fog horn. All one snowy day it sounded, a melancholy cry softened by the hills and marshes that lie between. When I was a child, I used to hear the horn as I lay in bed in my room with the yellow roses on the wallpaper and the
southwest windows open on a foggy night.

The sound troubled me — it was not loud, but it was insistent, a warning against those vague terrors that haunt children. I switched my pigtailed head back and forth on the pillow or burrowed under the covers, trying to shut out the sound of the horn and at the same time to exorcise those fears . . . fear of the end of the world, of fire, of being abandoned, of death, of evil faces peering in the window . . . the foghorn and the imaginings all became entwined in the nightmares, dispelled only by a bright dawn when the fog horn was at last silent, and the clear sun rose over the dunes and the marshes.

The late snow on a recent day was the ghost of winter, the inexorable foghorn was the ghost of a vanished childhood; the old fears had faded like the roses on the wallpaper and finally vanished, leaving only their shadows.

I read once, somewhere, that every thought and every experience made little tracks in the brain, and as so often happens, the words made an indelible impression: a whole maze of tracks, some shining and new, others grass-grown and rusty, and over them the tiny train of memory ran, paused, and ran again. It took the sound of the foghorn to fuel the little train, helped on its way by my idle posture at the window, watching the snow falling, falling.

First, there were the admonishing voices out of the past: "What are you doing sitting there in your pajamas? — daydreaming, when it's time for breakfast, time for school, time to feed the hens, to bring the cows in from pasture?"

Or the teachers' voices: "Kitty Crockett, do you hear me? I shall move your seat from the window if you don't pay attention." I was not seeing the bricks of the Boston schoolyard; instead, the little memory train was running back to summer Ipswich. I was not being fresh to the teacher when I laughed aloud: I was only remembering when I was a knight in armor, riding bareback on our huge, dappled gray farm horse, Sugar.

Thrust through the back of my sneakers were two long pins, spurs, not to stick him with, of course, but because knights always wore spurs. Sugar stopped and snorted in the Goodales' driveway when he saw the doctor coming out from the orchard with a basket of cherries; I was a knight "pricking across the plain" — I pricked Sugar with a pin to make him go. He reared up on his hind legs and I slid down his rump, flop on the grass. Sugar galloped off down the road and into the barn, while I walked home, stopping at the mailbox to take off my spurs and jettison them into the poison ivy.

Then there was the time when I gathered up about a dozen newly hatched baby chicks, put them into a tin cracker box, and rode off on my bike to show them to my friends. A game of hide 'n seekers going on when I arrived, so I left my box for awhile to play. When at last I opened up the box, all the chicks were dead, suffocated. I came home howling with the box of dead chicks, bawling for Grandma. She did not scold or anything, just took me up to her chamber where I sobbed for awhile against the rough stuff of her black dress. Then, she gave me a piece of gingerbread, told me a story, and afterwards, I went out and gave the chicks a really splendid funeral, burying them in the graveyard next to Fritz the canary, Oscar the goldfish, and the fieldstone that marked the resting place of Nixie, my first and best loved dog.

My father dug the hole for Nixie's grave, and he cried almost as much as I did, the silent tears of grownups, when the first shovelfuls of earth mingled with Nixie's grizzled black curls. There is quite a long sketch of memory track for Nixie, who used to take turns with me riding in and pulling the wagon with spokes, "Express" written in flowing letters along the varnished sides.

Grandma tripped over Nixie in the entry and broke her leg. Nixie got skunked regularly every spring and wiped himself on my bed. Nixie chased Flyer, the cat, into the top of the elm tree so it took ropes and ladders to get him down. Nixie brought home a whole ham from someone's house, we never knew whose, and when no one claimed it, we had it for dinner. It was only slightly tooth-marked. Nixie was Shere Khan or Bagheera from The Jungle Book. Nixie allowed himself to be dressed in Grandma's bonnet and shawl. . . . The memory train stops long and often at the station marked "Nixie."

The beloved people and animals of my childhood are gone. Even the country looks different first, the bayberries, then, the blueberries, and finally, the red oaks have taken over the pasture land.

But when the sad-sounding foghorn blows in the snow or fog of spring, the memory train starts to run, a melancholy journey sometimes, back to the time when Ipswich was the world, or at least the only part of it worth knowing . . . and loving.

Train

It was an event of my childhood to ride the train from Boston, a tremendous journey for a little girl, escorted on Friday nights after school through the teeming North Station, placed in the care of an elderly conductor with a down Maine accent, boosted up the high icy steps into the warm car with its windows already frosted.

I was warned against leaning my pigtailed head against the red or green plush of the seats because of "nits," the eggs of lice, left there by dirty children. If I was thirsty, I was to wait until I got home and not to drink the water from the tank and faucet at the end of the car. Hopefully, I would not need to go to the bathroom on the train — but this was one of the most interesting experiences: when you flushed the toilet, a little trapdoor opened, and there was the roadbed and the cinders rushing by below. I spent much time and wasted much water, entranced by this fascinating sight.

I waved to my mother outside on the platform and arranged myself with apparent self-possession, but inside, I was always quailing daunted by the thought that I was on the wrong train, that I would be delivered to some far away strange place in the middle of the night. As often as I dared, I asked the conductor if this were the train to Ipswich, but I was never reassured entirely until we reached the tunnel at Salem and plunged down into the exciting darkness with clouds of steam billowing past the windows and a choking smell seeping through the cracks.

No journey since, by steamer or train to faraway places, ever has had quite the thrill of those weekly excursions home to Ipswich and the farm. The huge engine, a dragon breathing fire into the winter twilight, gobbled shovelfuls of coal from the tender. It gasped and trembled, waiting for the call, "Bo-o-oard." Then, the driving wheels spun on the track, the funnel belched smoke and hot cinders, the cars racked and bucked, and suddenly, we were moving smoothly out onto the maze of tracks, past the signal houses, the roundhouse with its switching engines, the gray granite and bars of Charleston prison where I always shivered from my mental picture of men in cages like animals.

We crossed the river, past the chemical company with its huge pile of sulfur that seemed to have an inner yellow light in the gathering dusk. The afterglow of sunset turned the Lynn marshes all red and gold. At last the train was rushing through the country, and at last it spoke. The wild cry of the dragon, whoooo, whoooo, who who, made all the little hairs on my body stand up and sent shivers down my spine. I snuggled down in the corner of the seat and hugged myself with delight and fear, forgetting the nits in the plush, forgetting everything but the fire-breathing creature that I was riding through the night. I came out of my trance at the Salem Depot and watched the people hurrying along the platform and steel-wheeled carts piled high with freight and mailbags.

Even with the tunnel behind us, I was beset by a new fear. Perhaps the train would not stop at Ipswich but would continue right on to Newburyport or even Portsmouth, New Hampshire. Or perhaps I would suffer a sudden paralysis and would stay chained to my seat. In my mind's eye, I could see my grandmother on the Ipswich platform, looking anxiously for me, while, as in a nightmare, I could not move, even wave, or speak but was carried helplessly away, far away to New Hampshire.

"Hamilton-Wenham next," the old conductor said matter-of-factly, and then I began stirring in my seat putting on and taking off my coat, picking up and putting down my suitcase, sliding my arctics up and down the hot steam pipe, slipping my hands in and out of my mittens; this was all a ritual, necessary to carry out so that when the train stopped for me, I would be ready.

As we rounded the last bend, I was at the door. The engine cried out for the crossing two long, two short; we were slowing down past the mill, past the gates. There was the depot, all its windows lighted, the potbellied stove, the ticket office. The train jolted to a stop with a steamy sigh and there was grandmother on the platform!

"Ipswich. Leave no articles in the car," said the conductor. He opened the door and the cold air came streaming in. I was down the steps, hugging my grandmother. She did not know that I almost went to New Hampshire, that I might have been on the wrong train, that I might not have come at all.

There was the long drive home, old General trotting briskly towards the barn and his hay and oats . . . there was the chat about familiar things: a new calf, a hawk in the chicken yard, a deer that followed the cows back from pasture. And then the warm kitchen, supper, and bed.

But, as I was dropping off to sleep, I heard far away a train slowing for the crossing . . . whoooo, whoooo, who who . . ., such a melancholy sound, but no matter, I was safe and snug in my own bed in the room with yellow roses on the wallpaper.

Home: "Over the river and into the woods…"

"Over the river and into the woods to grandmother's house…." This song I felt was written for me when I jumped off the high step of the steam train at the Ipswich depot, and there was the one-horse sleigh and grandmother waiting. Two whole beautiful weeks to spend at the farm, not just the usual weekend which was over almost before it started.

In distant perspective, like the sharpened view through the wrong end of a telescope, I can see back through the years the old depot, its steep roof edge fringed with icicles. The snow, held from sliding off the roof by little hoops of metal, melted slowly in the weak sun, and so there were always icicles, too high to reach and break off and suck.

There in the cleared patch of hard-packed snow was our single-seater cutter with chestnut Fairfax or bay General in the shafts. All our horses were restive as the train puffed and steamed, but grandmother kept a firm mittened grip on the reins, only nodding to me over her shoulder as I came running up with my little suitcase, piling in, working my feet down into the hay in the bottom and snuffling in the buffalo robe.

As we swung smartly around, we heard the train whistle blowing for the Liberty Street crossing and then we went jingling down Market Street just as the lights were coming on in the early winter twilight. How many, many times through the years have I made this four-mile trip home from town, in sleigh or democrat wagon, on horseback or bicycle, in Model T and various cars, old wrecks or shiny, almost new . . ., but never was it so wonderful as with Grandma, coming back to the farm after imprisonment in the city.

The snow in town was packed hard by many runners, but once we made the swing onto Argilla Road, the tracks thinned out. The little horse, Fairfax, perhaps, settled into his collar, snorted and tossed his head till all the harness bells jingled and then began his fast mile-devouring trot with the bells on the shafts keeping the rhythm. We were in the real country now, the woods of Heartbreak Hill to our left screened us from the wind. To our right were the open fields fringed with trees behind which there was the last of the afterglow of a winter sunset. It was when we came out into the open that the wind caught us, blowing across the marshes, picking up a little whirl of drift powdering the horse's coat and the hairs of the robe.

"Look," said Grandma, "the moon." It was rising almost full, the December moon swinging above the trees of the marsh islands, not bright enough yet to dim the stars but beginning to cast its silver track across the levels where the last high tide had caught and frozen.

The icy wind, unbroken in those days by trees along the road, followed us all the way home. It was all open land, pasture where the snow lay level or scurried in the wind to fill the road five feet deep between the snow walls. In the heavy snows of January and February, we would abandon the drifted road and drive through fields where the snow had blown away, but on this December night, the road was still passable.

It was when we swung east at Northgate, the halfway mark, that Fairfax, thinking maybe of oats in the warm barn, quickened his pace, and we fairly flew along all the bells jingling, the sleigh runners rustling and our breath and the horse's also steaming out behind us.

We rumbled over the planks of the bridge where the wind whipped cruelly across the miles of marshes, and then we passed into the sudden lee of our own hill. A sharp turn between the snowy lilac hedges and then into the yard where Fairfax stopped with his nose against the closed doors of the barn.

I, stiff and half frozen, scrambled out to roll back the doors, then closed them behind the sleigh. By lantern light, we unhitched. I filled the measure with oats and forked some hay into the manger. Fairfax began munching. The cows lying down in their stanchions breathed long sighs; the barn was warm and sweet with hay and homely smell of the animals. I often used to think when I had been naughty and then punished that I would move in with the animals, learn to talk their language, like Mowgli in The Jungle Book, until someday perhaps, I would turn into a horse able to kick up my heels and roll in the pasture or be a dog and run barking after rabbits in the fields.

But with Grandma, I was never naughty or punished, and so I went happily with her into the house where the old iron kitchen stove was nice and hot and the air was sweet with the pot of beans cooking.

After supper, we cracked nuts on the hearth. The wind hooted in the chimney and whistled around the old house. I leaned my cheek against the rough stuff on Grandma's black dress, and I listened drowsily to the familiar stories of when she was a little girl down Maine. I put on my pajamas by the fire and scurried up to bed with my candle. Grandma tucked me in and heard my prayers: "God bless Grandma, Father and Mother, the cows and the horses and the little children everywhere, and make me a good girl, amen."

The moonlight lay in small-paned squares on the floor. The big elm tailed its fingers across the roof. Trees cracked in the frost. An owl hooted. I heard the sea . . . I was home.

Spring in Ipswich, General, and Grandma

As a little kid, a prisoner in the Boston winter, I knew when it was spring.

It was the day when, for the first time, the afternoon sun shone through the bay window of our Marlborough Street house and made a bright spot on the wall, just below the watercolor of boats on a European beach. I loved that picture. It made me think of home, of Ipswich, and it was appropriate that the spring sun touched it first. Even though the sooty remains of my snow fort were still not entirely melted in the curbed patch of muddy front yard, it was spring all right, and I had figured out the days, hours, and minutes to the beginning of spring vacation.

I wondered a thousand times if Grandma would remember that it would be the 3:30 train on Friday and whether she would be at the Depot with General and the democrat wagon, or whether the engineer would remember to stop at Ipswich. It was my recurring fear on these solitary train journeys, that someday the train would go whizzing right through Ipswich to deposit me all alone on some strange and empty platform far to the north and then go rushing off again.

I started putting on my coat and mittens after we passed the Salem tunnel and sat rigidly with my nose pressed to the windowpane as the old down-Maine conductor called out the stations, Beverly, North Beverly, Hamilton and Wenham, and finally, "Ipswich, leave no articles in the car." I was at the door when the train rounded the curve and whistled at the mill. The conductor had to hold me back on the high step till the train sighed to a full stop. And there was the democrat wagon, right beside the depot, and Grandma keeping a tight rein on General who even at an advanced age liked to pretend he was afraid of trains.

It was only in his late years that General demeaned himself to pull a carriage. He was my father's saddle horse in the Spanish War, and in my imaginings, I pictured my father and General right beside Teddy Roosevelt at San Juan Hill, racing through the smoke of battle and my father standing in the stirrups and waving a sword. Actually, neither of them heard a shot fired in anger, and most of their war service consisted of galloping up and down the beach at Swampscott with the caissons of old Battery A. Before being retired to the farm, General did carry my father in parades on Commonwealth Avenue and once lay down and rolled in a mud puddle right in front of the reviewing stand. "I never was so humiliated," my mother said.

But this day of school vacation, with his war days far behind him, General was on his good behavior. He trotted smartly down Market Street and snorted and tossed his head as we swung round the turn of the Argilla Road, then settled down to an easy trot for the long country miles ahead.

There were few signs of spring on that long ago March afternoon. The marshes shorn by the winter's icy knife and the sodden fields bore not a blade of green. Shrunken drifts still dripped in the lee of the old stone walls. But overhead, the sky was soft pink as the sun swung low over the bare trees. Grandma was silent on that ride, I remember, a companionable silence, and every now and then, she turned and smiled to me, her blue eyes faded behind her steel-rimmed glasses. Once when a flock of red-winged blackbirds flew overhead, calling and laughing she squeezed my hand and I squeezed back and snuggled up against her, rasping my cheek against the rough wool of her coat.

It was only when we reached the bridge, and the wide marshes opened out on either side, that Grandma told me how the hens were laying again, now that spring was here, and that Daisy's calf would be born any day now, surely during the week that I was home. The blackbirds were singing again high in the elm branches, and there was the old square house snuggled down in the saddle of the hill. The summer southwesters blew through the front windows, but the winter northerlies roared in the tall chimneys and slapped the trailing elm branches against the roof. You cold hear the wind overhead as you stood by the kitchen door on a blustery day.

I rolled the barn doors back, and General sedately stepped in with the carriage. Fairfax, my mother's saddle horse, whinnied and stamped in his stall, and all the cows, lying down, turned their heads and watched us with their big soft eyes. The barn smelled deliciously of summer hay and the warm sweet breath of the cows. I should spend many hours of vacation there in the hayloft, reading in my favorite nest under the dusty cobwebbed window, while the spring rain pattered on the shingles overhead.

After supper, snuggled under the covers on the cot in Grandma's room as the fire in the fireplace died down to coals and ashes, I listened drowsily as she told me one of the stories that always began "When I was a little girl down in Maine . . . ."

Of all the times spent with Grandma, the hours when she told me stories, consoled me when I came crying and punished, held me without speaking and rocked me in the rocking chair on the day that Nixie the dog died — all those memories so vivid still — there was no time that we were more close than that spring vacation, the year I was eight.

Did we know, did we feel, that it was to be our last? Why else did I cry when getting on the train, and looking through the window, I saw that she had her hand over her eyes as she turned away?

Thoughts on Long-ago Birthdays

Some say that we are conditioned for our journey through life by the time and the place where we enter this world. The astrologer must know the hour, even the minute, the day and the year, before he can determine the celestial influences that shape his subject. The zodiac sign, the phase of the moon, the position of the great stars in their courses, predetermine the life of the squalling infant — or so it has been believed for centuries.

It was a bold man who said, "The fault, dear Brutus, is not in our stars, but in ourselves, that we be underlings." Oh, unhappy thought, only ourselves to blame.

More likely, it seems, is the school of thought that seeks to lessen the trauma of entry into this world from the dark shelter of the womb. The infant is shielded from the glare of daylight, loud noises, sudden motions, and is eased gently into life without shock or fear.

These thoughts float through the mind on the eve of yet another birthday.

I was born in the room in the old square house that overlooks the marshes, the same room that was mine all through my childhood, where the southwest wind whispered in the leaves of the great elm outside, and there were yellow roses on the wallpaper. My mother had a miserable pregnancy that hot summer, and she received little consolation from her doctor, our neighbor Dr. Townsend, the naturalist. In fact, when I began to signal my arrival, he was nowhere to be found, somewhere out in his canoe with his binoculars, watching the birds. He appeared in time to do the honors, but not many years later he gave up the practice of medicine to concentrate on the field of his real interest.

Perhaps because I interrupted him, or because I was such a naughty willful child, I was never one of his favorite people. When I was fresh and saucy to him, he looked at me over his glasses and muttered that I was "one of his mistakes." Mistake or not, I am grateful to him. I have enjoyed my life.

Second only to Christmas were the birthdays of my childhood. August 4 was my day. The first rays of the sun, gilding the elm leaves, brightening the yellow roses, found me wide awake and a whole year older, a year nearer to what seemed the magic situation of being "grown up."

Lying in my bed in the quiet house, I dreamed of a time when there were no chores to do, no school, when no one told me when to go to bed and when to get up, what to eat, what to wear, to wash my face and brush my teeth, not to talk with my mouth full, not to shout in the house. I had not reached this happy state of freedom, but it was one day nearer, my birthday.

And of course, there would be presents and a party.

I went to other children's birthday parties, a fancy paper tablecloth, creamed chicken and peas, ice cream and a cake with candles. At each place, there was a "favor," which when opened revealed a paper hat, which you were supposed to put on and what I most hated, a snapcracker, which when pulled exploded with a bang and made your ears ring. Everyone was dressed up and there were sissy kinds of games like "pin the tail on the donkey."

My parties were different. They began with a hayride to the beach with all the neighborhood kids invited. Wild with excitement, I showed off, how I could drive the horses, how I could jump off the wagon, how I could run into the water with my clothes on. Even the best behaved children soon forgot their manners, and my mother found the whole thing very trying.

When finally the day ended and I was in my bed, still sandy and with my pigtails still wet, I heard my mother downstairs, groaning about the party to my father and wondering what she had ever done to deserve such a child. I wondered myself, sometimes.

Just when I decided that no one loved me, and I must try to do better, there would be a really splendid present. There was the birthday morning when from the breakfast table I saw a strange man leading a haltered horse up the driveway towards the barn. I called it to my father's attention, and he said we had better go and see about it. And there, standing on the barn floor, I was introduced to Hardy, my very own horse, and I cried.

"You never know with kids," my father told my mother. "I guess maybe she didn't like the horse."

"I do too, I love him," I shouted down from upstairs, "and we'll ride for years and years." And we did.

Many tides have ebbed and flowed under the canal bridge since those long-ago birthdays: childhood, youth, grownup years, old age. And there is an accumulation of presents stored in the attic of memory, laughs, and even a few tears.

Mr. Patterson

Scattered across the surface of the salt marsh are a multitude of islands, some so small that they support only one or two red oaks, a spring fur of shadbush and high bush blueberries, others of several acres, miniature forests where the soil is soft and sour from rotting leaves.

When I was a child, I used to know the island where pink lady slippers grew, and I knew the sunny slope, golden with dog tooth violets sprouting from their spotted leaves. Some of the islands had names: Pine Island, where there were no pines in my lifetime; Cross Island and Dean's Island in Essex, reached only in my boat; Eagle's Nest Island, dominating a whole string of lesser islands north of Sagamore Hill; Seeby's Island, occupied long ago by a family of that name.

These spots of marsh-surrounded land, once so familiar to my bare feet, remain almost unchanged through the passing years, while not far away, trees and houses have sprouted on the once bare upland pastures. Even the island oaks do not seem to have grown much in 50 years, and there are few young trees in the underbrush. The oaks in the abandoned pastures, seeded by island acorns, have far outstripped them in size.

I was told that the islands were there before there was any salt marsh and that they were piles of boulders and glacial clays mixed with gravels left when the ice sheet melted. To me, however, the marsh was always there, and the islands were scattered by giants who played on the marshes long before I did: it was they who planted the little gardens of wild flowers and saplings.

I had my own plot of ground to cultivate, and seeing that the weeds preferred it, I pulled up the flowers and encouraged wild pink morning glories and cinquefoil, daisies, and goldenrod. At the edge, I planted a seedling elm, no more than three inches high. I am made to realize how time has passed when I see it now, a great big spreading tree. In the same way, I preferred to think that the giants planted the island gardens of flowers and saplings in the marsh.

It was not until I was much older that the grownup tales of a river of ice sweeping down from the Arctic, covering all the country, seemed as real or reasonable as my own imaginings of the giants and the elves who once inhabited the creeks and marshes and islands of Ipswich.

In this crowded organized world, I wonder if today's children have room in their lives for imaginary companions. During my summer wanderings, I conversed constantly with a friend who was always there to share my pleasure and my pain. He climbed with me in the apple tree or hid with me in the hayloft.

Sometimes he suggested that I answer when I was called or warned me that if I did as planned, punishment was sure to follow, or he would suggest out-of-bounds places to go and things to do. It was his idea that fresh eggs from the henhouse made the finest mud pies, and he advised me to keep quiet during all the speculation as to why the hens had stopped laying. When my grandmother discovered a great cache of broken eggshells, he stood beside me and was amazed as I was.

This companion, this wise and pixie creature, bore the unlikely name of Mr. Patterson. He was not a grownup, not a child. Unseen — I think he was, because I can't remember what he looked like, although I can remember vividly the features and voices of human companions of the time. He spoke to me — but not through the ear and not with tongues. I spoke to him in human speech, carrying on long conversations to the displeasure and dismay of listening grownups; he warned me that this talking aloud could be dangerous, and so, when we were together and there were people around, I only whispered.

I don't know where he came from or where he went. Mr. Patterson simply disappeared when I no longer needed him, coming back only rarely when I was sick or lonely, and finally, not at all; it was a gradual kind of parting one without pain.

Some years later, when we were having breakfast on the stone porch, a splendid chestnut horse came trotting into the yard. On his back was a man in Western gear, leather chaps and wide-brimmed felt hat. The horse wore a bridle with silver trimmings and a tooled leather saddle; the man carried a six-gun in a holster. Greeted as "George" by my father, the man dismounted and joined us for a cup of coffee.

"Say 'Good morning' to Mr. Patterson," my father said, and I choked on my mug of milk. Was this some kind of horrid grownup joke? This man with his seamed sunburned face and grizzled thinning gray hair, what did he mean calling himself "Mr. Patterson"? — yet he seemed to know me very well. He said he had often seen me out on the marshes or in my boat. Had he perhaps been with me? I did not dare ask.

I sat and stared and wondered while he and my father talked on and on about nothing much, as grownups do. Finally, Mr. Patterson got up to go out to where Tommy, the horse, was standing anchored to the ground by trailing reins. It was Tommy who finally broke the ice between us. My Mr. Patterson never had a horse like that, one who could shake hands, lie down and play dead, or allow his master to shoot the six-gun across his back as he lay on the ground.

This Mr. Patterson lived in a little house on Seeby's Island; he even had a wife and daughters, one only a bit older than me. He taught me to shoot the six-gun, to scull a boat with only one oar, to shoot a shotgun, and to scull a sneak box up to an unsuspecting flock of black ducks . . ., all sorts of useful things like that. Mrs. Patterson and the girls preferred their house on Chestnut Street in Salem, and they did not come too often to the camp on the island.

I had a very special feeling for Mr. Patterson, why not? — and sometimes I caught myself wondering if he knew more about me than he pretended. I was quite at home in the low-ceilinged little house that once belonged to the Seeby family, a scatterbrained bunch, he always said. The house was surrounded by homemade sheds, Tommy's barn, and all sorts of Rube Goldberg contrivances which seemed to me fascinating and just right.

George Patterson is long gone, the little house on the island burned, the oak trees that sheltered it are weak and scarred, but as I walked there not too long ago, I found one of Tommy's shoes in the grass, and I remembered.

Lighthouse

Down at the beach, the moving sands alternately reveal and cover a pile of broken bricks, all that is left of the Ipswich Lighthouse. This beacon in the sand, once far from the edge of the tide, was a matter of great interest to the few tourists of the day. Artists painted it, a structure whiter than the sands around, and the photographic firm, Smith and Russell, took a famous picture which I well remember and which was made into a postcard. Visitors, who enjoyed the gaieties of the Post Hotel at Grape Island and the Bluffs, stopped in town after their weekend ride on the steamer Carlotta and brought copies of this postcard of the lighthouse surrounded by grass-crested waves of sand.

The lighthouse tower, built in 1837, still exists, but the living quarters for the keepers and their families recently burnt to the ground. I remember my father telling me when I was a small child that Captain Ellsworth, then a very old man, had told him that in his youth, the tower was so close to the water that the keeper could talk from the balcony to fishermen in their boats.

My father told me also that when he was a little boy and summer camping in a cottage on Fox Creek with his uncle and his cousin Willard, whales were seen quite frequently off the bar. I did believe the story about the lighthouse because it was confirmed by the keeper, father of my friend Stanley Gunderson, but whales . . . no! Much later, however, while fishing in the *Kelpie*, we saw many whales, or blackfish, spouting not too far offshore, and I was ashamed to think I had suspected my father of telling a "wrong story."

When I was a little girl, it was a long hot walk through the soft sand to the Gundersons' cottage and equally far or further from the tower to the edge of the sea. In the space of 75 years, the sand had built out more than a quarter mile. There were cranberry bogs, dunes with their gray-green of poverty grass, gold-flowered in June, and even the beginnings of a pitch pine forest — all between the lighthouse tower and the sea.

Now all this has been washed away; the winter storm tides come close to the old ruined foundation, and if this continues, passing boats may once again be within shouting distance of the lighthouse cottage.

The graceful tapered tower, built of brick and then whitewashed, marked the channel changing course; a little buildup known as the "bug light," was built on the edge of the dunes and was used by mariners as a range light, lining it up with the flashing light of the tower.

The bug light had to be moved every few years, but, even so, it too could not keep pace with the constant changes in the channel. Judging by the wreckage that comes to light deep in the dunes, the broken timbers and treenail fastenings, quite large vessels came in here to Ipswich once upon a time, guided by the tower so carefully tended by Mr. Gunderson and his predecessors.

Mr. Gunderson, who sailed in square riggers from the ports of Sweden when he was young, was constantly trailed by two children, his son Stanley and me. We "helped" carry the empty oil cans back from the bug high and the tower. We watched as he endlessly polished the French lenses of the lamp, handing him the soft cloths and the chamois that he used for the finishing touches, and, finally, passing the long spouted brass oil can of the finest whale oil that was used for the mechanism that was as delicate as a Swiss watch.

The arrangement of lenses focused the light of many candles in the earliest days. The lamp used oil and needed constant trimming of its wicks. Every hour, all night long, Mr. Gunderson visited the light to make sure that it was burning brightly, that no trace of smoke had clouded the lenses and that the intricate brass wheels and gears kept it still turning, casting a reassuring light to guide any vessel that might be trying to thread its way into the port of Ipswich. Even in my day, the ships were few and far between, but the old sailor in his faded blue uniform and peaked cap of the lighthouse service knew well the anxiety of the captain and the crew trying to find the Ipswich bar channel in a northeast snow storm. Many missed — but not because the light had gone out.

Once, fishing in the *Kelpie* not too far off the bar, we hooked and hauled on deck a huge rusty anchor, the wooden stock long since rotted away. We imagined that it was lost by some old coasting vessel trying frantically to claw away from the Ipswich bar with its smother of breakers. It had been too snowy or too foggy, probably, to see the guiding lights and so, like many others, the vessel was lost.

It was a rare treat of my childhood to be allowed to spend the night with the Gundersons during winter visits to my grandmother . . . to curl up all cozy and warm under the eiderdown quilt in the spare room, while outside the storm roared and the sea sounded so much closer and louder than at home. I remember waking to hear Mr. Gunderson go out to tend the light, and in my memory's eye, I can see him still from the window, as he made his way across the dunes to the tower, muffled in his pea jacket and with the sailor's roll to his walk.

His son Stanley and I had great fun. I was the only friend of this lonely inarticulate boy, and I happily joined in the games he made up for himself, propelling a sled across frozen pools with a sawed-off pitchfork as if paddling a canoe, or rafting on the flooded bogs of spring or playing tag up and down the circular iron staircase of the tower, or chasing round the balcony at the top.

. . . Many's the time I wished my father had been a lighthouse keeper!

The Choate House

The other day, for the first time in quite a while, I set foot on the shores of Hog Island, because a friend and sailing companion wanted to see from close up the old house that is the ancestral home of the Choate family. The house, built in 1725, has been restored, and the little patch of front lawn is mowed. The ancient pear tree in the yard has a crop of green pears, and there is water in the well.

But the house is boarded up tight, so it is impossible to see the so well-remembered huge fireplace, the panelling and the wainscotting and the wide board floors. The only tenants now are an animal family, probably raccoons, who have chewed their way in through a back door. Tracing along the granite foundations, I noted the cellar window, not sealed up, through which a skinny child of long ago was able to slither, to spend there many solitary summer hours up in the attic reading the books of Rufus Choate's library, thrown helter-skelter on the floor.

I cannot remember how old I was when I first entered the old house via the narrow basement opening. I was probably about twelve. I had sailed and rowed my yellow dory past the south shore of the island many times, had eaten my lunch under the basswood tree, and had explored the forlorn collection of tumbledown summer cottages of a little colony that had clustered around the old house and had been occupied around the turn of the century.

There was nothing much of interest — a snake sunning on a rotting porch; the remains of a man's bathing suit, moth-eaten with cap sleeves and faded stripes; a collection of mouse-nibbled ladies' magazines with pictures of wasp-waisted creatures too dainty to be true, and here and there a pointed shoe tip peeking daringly from under a frilled skirt.

In the midst of these faded remains of past summer gaiety, the old house stood in somber dignity, turning its back and looking out across the bright waters of Essex Bay toward the Gloucester Hills. I clattered quite easily in and out of the cottages, but around the old house, I walked nervously, finding the sound of the wind in the branches of the elms and pear tree eerie, jumping at the squeak and bang of a loose shutter. The upstairs windows were not shuttered. I always expected to see a face looking out through the small panes.

It was not till after a long time of cautious reconnoitering (and a little older and bolder), that I plucked up my courage to slide in through the cellar window. It was like taking a dive into cold water: once you are in, you are committed to swim gaspingly to shore. It was quite a drop to the cellar floor where I stood palpitating and festooned with spider webs, and for a long moment, I stood stock-still, half expecting to hear feet shuffling across the floor overhead. The only sound was the wind, muffled in the trees outside. It was semi-dark and very cool in the cellar. Step by step, with pounding heart and pausing to listen, I made my way to the stairs and then on up into the house.

The ground floor was disappointing. Fragmented sunshine coming in through knotholes and cracks in the shutters revealed everything, even the design of faded roses and ribbons on the cheap wallpaper that covered the fireplaces. It had been, I learned afterwards, a sort of community center for the cottage colony, and the decor was appropriate: there was even a dirty tattered carpet on the floor.

From the front hall, the staircase with its simple balustrade and midway landing led up to the second floor. Here, there were no shutters on the windows, and with the sun pouring in through the panes of old wavy glass, it was impossible to be afraid. I felt welcome and at home in the low studded rooms, bare and stark as they were. I moved to a window and opened it, letting in the sweet southwest wind. Leaning on the sill, I looked out at the yellow dory tugging at her anchor line down below, and then my gaze moved out across at water and hills that seemed as wide as the world.

Upstairs was the attic with its huge central chimney, the adze-marked ceiling beams and wide, wide floorboards. There were two windows, one at either end, and to their light, I carried books selected from the piles where they had been thrown and settled myself down, back to the wall, to read.

Once I was familiar with them all. The law books, even though they bore Rufus Choate's signature in fading ink and Spenserian handwriting, I found not very interesting.

It was in the Choate House attic that I first read Prescott's *Conquest of Mexico*, hating the Spanish Conquistadores and weeping over the fate of the Indians.

For lighter reading there were the words of Charles Dickens, published in pamphlets, chapter by chapter. It took several days to match them up, all the David Copperfields, the Nicholas Nicklebys, and the Oliver Twists, enough reading for the whole summer and more.

I was greatly entertained by a collection of tracts left probably, by some blue-nosed Choate, describing in abundant detail with lurid pictures what happened to people who smoked tobacco, drank rum, and failed to go to church. The poor drunkard lay in his corner like a heap of rags, but the Devil was splendid with his pitchfork, horns, and lashing tail. I was so taken with him that I sneaked this booklet home, the only thing I ever took from the house. I used to take it from its hiding place and feast my eyes, shuddering with delight.

For several years, I visited the Choate House regularly; ...really, I felt I lived there. I knew it when the rain thundered on the attic roof, when the birds sang in the trees outside, or when the soft fog came smoking in over the dunes, and the old house then was the only solid thing when the rest of the world disappeared.

Occasionally, I brought with me the true friend of the moment and did the honors of the house, but none of my friends found it as interesting as I did. After running up and down the stairs, looking out the window, peering down the well, they would turn to their boats and sail away, leaving me alone in my castle.

When the new owner started fixing up the house, I abandoned it forever. I did make sure that they heard about the books. Before anything was done, however, someone followed the workmen in and took all the books away, and with them, unknown I'm sure to the taker, went part of my secret childhood life.

Testing Ben Franklin's Theory

I wonder if the writers of scientific books for children achieve quite the effect they expect when they produce the facts to explain the natural phenomena. At least for children reared on fairy tales, myths, and imaginings as I was in those distant pre-TV days, science was grafted onto an already existing body of knowledge.

Take thunder. Every child knew that the tremendous rumbling and rattling were the wheels of Thor's chariot, or the crash of the balls in some celestial bowling alley, or the angry voices of the gods raised in dispute. All of which was a matter of choice of the moment.

And so when I read in the *Heart of Oak Reader, Book 4* for children 10 to 12, a schoolbook, but good reading all the same, the story of Ben Franklin's discovery of the true nature of lightning it was just another fairy tale to me. It was, however, worth exploring there was that much fact about it.

And so on a sultry day. when the black thunderheads came piling over the horizon, I took my big box kite out into the newly shorn hayfield.

In the picture, Ben was wearing knee britches which brought him down to the childhood level. All the boys wore them, usually with one buckle broken and one pant leg dragging. There was something in the story about a key. I didn't quite understand that, and also there was a bottle in which to catch the electricity. The bottle was easy, there was an assortment in my room which contained leaves and caterpillars, which might turn into butterflies, or polliwogs (deceased), or pebbles, and bits of quartz.

The key was quite a problem. Examining the picture I could see that there was nothing like that in our house, and the only one was in the lock of Mrs. Sprague's goodies closet and that only present when she was. Still, it was no great thing to slip out the key when Mrs. Sprague bustled about the kitchen stove preparing the lunch, and when she discovered it missing I was long gone. I had every intention of returning it, once its scientific use was over.

Even though there was a perfectly good precedent for the scientific experiment, I had leaned from experience that the less consultation there was with adults, the less trouble there was likely to be. So I carried the box kite with its mile of string wound on a reel the bottle, and the key, out the side door, round under the linden tree into the west field out of sight of the house.

The clouds were piling up in the north; thunder was rumbling. The wind had died down, and the greenheads and midges were not long in discovering the scientist. Except for their buzzing everything was deathly still, except for the robins hollering for rain.

There was no breeze to launch the kite but it would come, I thought, watching the clouds swirling and tumbling overhead.

I attached the key to the tail of the kite. In the picture, the lightning was forking from it in a most exciting way. Presumably, the electricity would follow down the string and somehow it would go into the bottle, just how I was not sure. but it would be handy just in case.

The thunder growled louder now, and lightning stitched the bellies of the clouds. With first breath of the thunder squall, I ran with the kite and launched it into the air.

The wind was fluky, and the kite dipped and soared, tugging at the string as I fed it out from the reel, higher and higher. I could no longer see the key, but the kite, a tiny red square, seemed close to the blackest of the scudding clouds which opened to discharge a lashing torrent of rain. Soaked to the skin, I was too excited to be frightened, playing the kite like a fish in a sea of strange green light.

Suddenly, there was a most tremendous crash, a flourish of stars before my eyes, a tingling and then darkness.

When finally I sat up in the soaked grass, my head was splitting with such an ache as I still remember. The storm had gone growling off toward Gloucester, so I must have been out for quite a while, but I was not burned or anything.

Beside me in the grass, the kite string lay limp, and picking myself up rather unsteadily, I followed it till I came upon the ruins of the kite. The red cloth was torn and the sticks were scorched. The key to the goodies closet was gone, and I could not find it in the grass. Later, Mrs. Sprague grumbled and fussed because she had to have another lock put on the closet door. Somehow, she said, the key had gotten lost. Listening, I wondered if it could have melted. I felt sickish the rest of the day and wondered if Ben Franklin had suffered similarly.

I never was tempted to try again, and besides, a good box kite was not so easy to come by.

Oasis of Cranberries Among the Dunes

On one of those lovely warm Indian summer days last week, I took a long walk on the beach. The tide was out, the sea glassy calm, the sun bright, and with me was my frolicking dancing dog the most perfect beach companion. As we neared the point by the Essex entrance, the tracks of other strollers thinned out, and cutting into the dunes, there were no people tracks at all, only deer hoof prints, the hand prints of a raccoon, and the delicate lace work of a mouse or mole.

Deep in the dunes, there was a little cranberry bog, hidden away behind a thicket of bayberry and poison ivy. I only spied it by accident from a dune top, and I like to think I was the only human visitor to this secret place. The vines were lush and still green; only the tips were touched with the scarlet of autumn, and there were masses of berries, deep crimson where the sun had touched theme pale lettuce green underneath. Squatting down among the vines. I quickly filled both big pockets of my jacket, eating quite a few of the reddest and ripest, rejoicing in the wild tart taste, so well remembered.

Carl Woodbury, his father Loring, and who knows how many Woodburys before them, harvested the cranberries every year as part of their farm produce, picking clean the big bogs that lay between the lighthouse and the pine groves. But they didn't bother with the little bogs far down the beach, and these were part of the wild plenty of Ipswich, along with the strawberries in the fields, the high bush blueberries, the fox grapes, and the barberries, each in their season.

Living off the country like an Indian was one of the delights of my day-long wanderings in those long ago summers. I seldom took anything from the house except a few kitchen matches, it was a matter of pride not to take more than three; if I could not make a fire of dried poverty grass and sun-blanched twigs with those, so much the worse, I would eat my clams and mussels raw. Water could be dug in the low places of the dunes, a foot or eighteen inches down. It was sweet and warm and sandy tasting.

Secreted in a pitch pine grove far down the beach was my cooking kettle, chipped gray enamel with a rusty cover, a treasure from the dump behind the barn, and a rusty tin cup. They were all I needed, and I like to think that I could have stayed away from home for days and weeks, living off the country, and no one would ever find me. I thought about it often in the bright daylight, particularly when I had been punished at home and had gone off in a rage, stomping and muttering and vowing to myself that I would not come home again till tomorrow, or next week, or perhaps never.

What grownups called my "ugliness" faded away as I shipped the oars or hoisted the sail of the yellow dory to row or sail with the outgoing tide to a favored anchorage near the grove with my utensils. I forgot it entirely as I dug with my hands a kettle of clams, or washed and picked over enough mussels for a good lunch, and picked the cup full of whatever berries were in season.

Or sometimes I worked my way to the spindle buoy off Wingaersheek and caught a few cunners, bony scaly little fish, but very sweet and good. And after I had eaten when I got hungry, it might have been 11 o'clock or three o'clock, I had no watch and didn't care, I sat under a pine tree and whittled, or dreamed, or sang and whistled, or imagined myself Robinson Crusoe or one of the family of Swiss Family Robinson, or an Indian child, or a prisoner escaped from a pirate ship who had swum ashore and made a new home on a lonely beach.

But when the tide turned and began running in, and the sun was low down over the shoulder of the island, I began to think about home. I knew even at my ugliest and most resentful that I would never stay out all night. I was terribly, pitifully afraid of the dark. I thought no one knew of this weakness of mine, but I guess my family must have known. That's why they never worried and were always sure that when it began to grow dark, there I would be hurrying up the driveway to the kitchen door.

This was a real primeval fear of mine, I think. I was terrified of the shadows cast by my candle on the wall, and waking in the dark I saw all sorts of horrors in the dark corners of my room which in daylight proved to be only my clothes flung overdue back of a chair. Even when I was quite grown-up, I felt the old chilling sensation of something following me upstairs, the long dark staircase of our house in Boston. So, I was only a daylight runaway, my free life prescribed by the rising and the setting sun.

Lying flat on my back in the little bog the other day, on the soft bed of moss and springy vines with Christy panting like a steam engine after all her running, I found that I could quite well remember how I felt and I was quite surprised to find that I could no longer jump up but had to clamber to my feet and slowly lay out a line of tracks, across the dunes, along the shore, all the way home.

Reminiscences of the "Great Dune"

Sailing along the inside beach this summer, I have noticed that no trace remains of what in my childhood we called the "Great Dune." Unlike the dunes around it, the Great Dune was innocent of anchoring vegetation, and it was surprising that it endured as long as it did. The product of the summer southwesterlies, it sloped gradually on the southerly side and was steep and soft on the north, stretching all the way from the bay to the ocean beach, an expanse of fine sand, ripple-marked by the wind. There was not one blade of grass, not one beach pea vine, nor green leaf. It was like a Sahara sand dune, needing only a string of camels or a band of Arab tribesmen silhouetted against the sky.

I imagined I was one of these as I rode my horse, Hardy, across the Great Dune to the ocean beach. Leaving the yellow dory anchored in the bay, I made my way barefoot over sand so hot that it burned even feet toughened by a shoeless summer.

Dr. Townsend's camp was in a grove near the Great Dune, and the shingled roof, just visible, was the only sign of human presence in all the jumble of dunes and groves and cranberry bogs. Only occasionally, I saw in the distance a clammer or two rowing with the tide or a sea clammer prodding the offshore bars. For the most part, it was my solitary world, shared occasionally with a companion, but most usually enjoyed alone in the company of my imaginings.

Only once a year, on the Labor Day weekend, did I see the Great Dune at night, as one of a vast company of neighbors, kids, and grownups, some even quite old, perhaps fifty of them, gathered for what was known as the "Sleeping Out Party."

In the unsophisticated days before the first war, no one had a motorboat, and the families made their way in sailboats, rowboats, and canoes, piled with blankets, baskets of food, cooking pots and kettles, and extra clothing brought by the prudent remembering the chill and the dew of the September night. All of us children were wild with excitement for days before the great event.

For the sake of peace and quiet in the family, I was allowed to make my way by myself in the yellow dory, carrying my own gear, while my father sailed the rest of the family in the catboat and sailed himself home again. He said he saw no reason to sleep on the hard sand unless he had to, and he arrived in the morning to bring the family home, cheerful, rested, and full of jokes, when everyone else was cross and exhausted.

I always made the familiar journey hours ahead of everyone else and picked out the best mooring place and the best campsite, and chopped and piled the driest wood, and laid the family fire, feeling very efficient and important.

I was there on the beach to greet the first arrival, running back and forth with the gear, enjoying the commotion and noting which grownups were already cross and bossy and to be avoided. My mother was not one of these, and however properly she behaved at home, she was one of the gayest, and I could hear her laughing in the catboat when it was still quite far away.

After supper and the singing round the communal campfire, the more unfortunate younger children were rolled up in their blankets. But the rest of us had resolved to stay up all night and to see the sun rise out of the sea in the morning.

And so, one by one, we slipped away from the fire, out into the darkness under the stars.

The familiar contours of the Great Dune were mysterious and terrifying. For once, I did not want to be alone. Stepping cautiously across the cooling sand, I advanced like a wild animal, stopping to listen and to look. Something, a bird?, made a sudden noise in a grove of trees, and I stopped dead, feeling my heart thumping and I stood breathing hard for a long moment before moving on again towards the ocean beach. I began to run, but feeling that something was running after me, I stopped and whirled around. There was only the sand, silver with dew and starlight, and I did not run again.

Finally, there ahead was the ocean beach and stumbling through the tangle of pea vines and sharp grasses, I joined the other children running and shouting along the fringes of the little waves. I never would admit, even to myself, that I had been so afraid. All night long we ran and played, while the stars moved across the sky, and finally, there was an arch of light in the east and then the bright rim of the sun. Only then did we return to the campground where dew and sand-encrusted rolls of blankets were beginning to come to life, and there was the fine hungry smell of bacon frying.

There were times when it rained in the night, and once a thunderstorm rolled in from the north and we cowered in our blankets, while the rain poured down and the lightning lanced the clouds and illuminated for glaring seconds the expanse of the Great Dune and the lashing nervous trees of the grove. Breakfast was a disaster: the wet wood would not burn. We ate soggy bread washed down with raw eggs.

And then there was the night when the fog rolled in, smoking along the water, blotting out the anchored boats, and I was glad to hear my father shouting and laughing in the catboat and to move home with the east wind, hearing but the creaks and thumps and voices from the other boats, but not seeing them.

The Great Dune has vanished quite away in one last action, smothering the grove of trees and burying the broken timbers of Dr. Townsend's camp, and with it has gone all but the memory of quiet water, empty sand, and the voices of children, thin and piping from a great distance like the whistling of the shore birds on the beach.

Riding the Revere Beach Cyclone

I was quite sad when I saw depicted the fire-twisted ruins of the Cyclone at Revere Beach. There, I thought, has gone another landmark along the path to growing up.

It only added to the glamour that Revere Beach was off-limits for respectable people, particularly girls, and my family waged a losing battle to make me respectable.

My first acquaintance with Revere Beach came by daylight as we drove along the shore road to Ipswich, going home for a spring weekend. My father and mother, conversing in the front seat, agreed that it was a very vulgar place, a blot on the landscape, a ruin of what had once been a pretty beach and salt marshes, much like those at home. But I had eyes only for the amusements, the gay stucco arcades with popcorn machines and tempting great wads of cotton candy, poisonous pink and so delicious. We never stopped for any.

And there was something called "The Tunnel of Love" and shooting galleries with nodding rows of ducks moving past, and little cars spinning and bumping with people shrieking and colliding. Towering above it all on spidery girders, the Cyclone. I craned my neck to see the cars with their passengers, small in the distance like beads on a string.

Slowly, the pairs of cars crawled up the steep incline to the top and then with dizzy speed came roaring down, and even from the road, I could hear the screams of the passengers. I must, I must ride on the Cyclone. I would too, but I knew better than to mention it.

None of the children that I knew had ever been to Revere Beach, and so I had to wait until I was old enough to have "boyfriends" who would do anything or almost, to please me. But even so, it was difficult to find anyone who wanted to take me to Revere Beach. It was quite a responsibility to take a girl there with all those sailors and all.

Finally, I acquired a boy, disapproved of by my family because he was "wild" and had a motorcycle, but by this time, I was old enough to manage my own affairs. Perched on the back of the motorcycle, weaving in and out of the Boston traffic, I suggested that we go to Revere Beach, and no sooner said than done.

Never to be forgotten was that first sight of Revere Beach by night. The whole sky lighted up, a Ferris wheel turned in the spotlight and along the midway, the voices of barkers, the crack of rifles in the shooting gallery, the laughing crowds of sailors and girls, and pervading all, the delicious smell of popcorn roasting and hot dogs grilling. I had my eye on the Cyclone towering above the roofs and the crowds.

We chained the motorcycle to a lamppost. We made our way along the sidewalk, jostled and jostling. I won a funny hat and a stuffed dog in the shooting gallery, and lost the hat on the Whip where the cars switched and swerved on their tracks. It was the thing to scream and clutch your escort, so I did, but I was not really frightened.

Then there were little individual cars, blue and red and yellow with bumpers all around, and the thing was to bump into other people. I enjoyed that and being cornered and bumped by a whole crowd of sailors. There was also a fight before I was extricated.

I was not quite ready for kisses and fumblings in the Tunnel of Love and was quite relieved when the shabby little boat, which had carried us through a whispering and murmuring darkness, finally emerged into the glare and racket of the midway.

I laughed uneasily and said, "No, I don't want to do it again," so we moved on to the hall of mirrors where the floor and ceiling were crazily slanted and our reflections were grotesque, immensely fat or skeleton thin. Here a sailor grabbed me and tried to get me to drink out of his bottle, and again there was almost a fight, the whole scene distorted by the mirrors.

Finally, there we were at the Cyclone, shelling out our quarters for the ride and taking our place in the front car of the first train. When all were aboard and strapped in, the car moved slowly out and began to crawl up the first rise, higher and higher above the rooftops. Then it picked up speed, faster and faster, and suddenly the bottom dropped out.

Below us there was nothing, a vertical drop ending with a series of bumps that threw us violently against the straps, then a switch to the right and a switch to the left, catapulting us sideways. Both of us were too paralyzed with fear to make a sound, but from behind came a wave of screams. Riding the wave, we sailed swiftly along a high level plateau to another precipitous drop. I felt the cargo of popcorn and hot dogs shifting up into my throat and clamped my teeth to hold it down.

Far below, I could see the white ovals of faces all looking up; then there was another drop and we were rolling to a stop. We were too battered and shaken to get up right away, and I heard myself saying hoarsely, "That was great." But I did not want to try it again, not right away.

I was addicted to the Cyclone after that, learning when to stiffen my spine to keep my head from snapping back, when to relax, until, gradually, the thrill was lost. The end came when I had a drunken partner, and after the ride, he said, "When do we start?"

Changing Aims of a Former Duck Hunter

On the recent northeaster when the storm tide flooded the marshes, I watched a flock of black ducks feeding not fifty yards from the window where I stood leaning my forehead against the cool glass. They had found shelter almost under the branches of the pine tree, a new little cove of quiet water, where for a few hours they could dip and preen and doze all unaware of the watcher at the window of the little house. I was so close that I could see the sheen of the feathers, the bright round eyes, and I could hear even above the roar of the storm their sociable whisperings or an occasional squawk, as they chased each other, playing.

As the tide turned and the sodden grasses began to emerge, they moved further and further away out to the wind-whipped water, and finally, they flew away to seek another sheltered place.

I was amazed to think that once upon a time, the sight of a flock of ducks so close by would have sent me racing for my shotgun. I would have crawled on my belly in the wet grass, maneuvering into position for a shot. It was not considered sporting to shoot them sitting on the water, so when I stood up and they took frantic flight, I would fire both barrels. Perhaps, one would fall, somersaulting to the ground in the only awkward motion it would ever make.

Then I would run out, ignoring the icy water, to retrieve my prize with hardly a qualm, picking up the bundle of torn and bloody feathers.

How could I have been so bloodthirsty, and when did I change, and why? I really don't remember when I began to lose interest in my shotgun, so that it stayed for weeks and months untouched in its case, and finally, I gave it away to my brother and never went hunting again.

I was about 12 years old when I saved up the $20 for my double-barreled Ithaca. With my summer's savings earned in dimes and pennies picking berries, I went to Iver Johnson's in Boston. The salesman kept a watchful eye on me as lingered and yearned over the racks of guns.

As always, I was immediately drawn to the most expensive, the Damascus steel barrels, engraved with ducks and pheasants, with the carved black walnut stocks. The price tags were in the hundreds of dollars, and finally, I moved to the cheaper ones. The salesman almost fainted when I picked out the one I could afford and shelled out the money in two's and one's and silver — $20. He must have had kids of his own, because he gave me free a simple canvas case so I could carry the gun home inconspicuously on the streetcar.

My mother had almost given up hope that I would someday turn to the things that girls were supposed to like, dolls or a doll carriage, instead of the succession of jackknives, footballs, baseball bats, or hockey sticks. These were all I ever wanted for Christmas. She was really stunned when I came home with a shotgun, but my father only laughed and said he would give me lessons in how to use it properly.

There were many months before the hunting season. Almost every night, sitting in the wicker chair with the owl cushion with the green glass eyes, I assembled the gun, ran the ramrod with the oily rag through the already shining barrels that had never yet been fired. The blue steel was polished till you could see your face in it. Then, setting up the owl cushion on the bureau, I took careful aim, pulled the trigger, and said in a whisper, "blam, blam."

None of this had prepared me for the first time I fired the gun. I had purchased a box of shells at Goodhue's Hardware Store, which I had secreted under the clothes in my bureau drawer along with my collection of cigarette pictures of baseball players and other measures.

I waited for a time when the coast was clear, slipped two shells into the chamber, and headed for the barn. The cows and horses were out in the pasture, but the rooster was in the hen yard near the fence. I disliked the disagreeable bird who had pecked my bare legs till the blood ran. He gave me a bold and sneering glance through the wire. It would not be sporting to shoot him standing there, so I stamped my feet and hissed at him. He only stood his ground. I shouted, "Blam, Blam." He did not move.

I pointed the gun into the air, but unfortunately I pulled both triggers. There was an ear ringing explosion, and the recoil knocked me off my feet. As I lay on my back, heels in the air, the silly hens ran squawking in all directions, but the rooster stood motionless, grinning, I thought. I would have gladly shot him dead, but I had no more shells.

So I went to the house, rubbing my aching shoulder, carefully cleaned the gun, and put it in its case.

I did not tell my father that I had already fired the gun when he gave me my first lesson. He fired clay pigeons for me, until I got quite skillful.

Then began the long wanderings, along the beach after shore birds, across the marshes after ducks, and the happy days spent building a blind on a point in the river where I crouched watching the cold dawn coming and waiting for the ducks to fly by in range.

The older boys in the neighborhood were great gunners, and once or twice, they asked me to go along with them. But I soon found that I was expected to do the dirty work, row the boat, set out the decoys, and I seldom had a chance to shoot myself. And when I did and brought down a flying bird, they did not like that very much either.

So mostly I was alone. Gradually, I began to realize that I was happier just carrying the gun and not shooting it. More and more, I was repulsed by seeing the birds come tumbling down, or worse, crippled, trying to fly and swim away. More and more, the gun stayed in its case, while I fussed around the blind, weaving the marsh grasses through the wire until it was a thing of beauty, standing till the high tides of winter swept it away.

No one commented when I went out without the gun and there were fewer and fewer birds at the family table. The phase passed, and I turned to other things.

Gunner

I suppose to hear me now that no one would believe that once I was a most ardent hunter, or "gunner" as we used to call it. When I heard from my bed the first early shots that signaled the opening of this season, I remembered how long ago I used to sit on the stone porch of the old house, oiling and re-oiling the blue barrels of my 12 gauge shotgun, acquired with so much sweat for $20.00, my summer's hoarded earnings.

I can only say in justification for myself that our town's most famous naturalist, Dr. Charles Wendell Townsend, began his interest in birds by hunting them; he had a great collection of bird skins in a cabinet in his dining room, water birds, and songbirds too, alas. Most of the doctors on "Doctor's Row" were gunners in the early years of the century, including my father, who shot from the left shoulder on account of his blind eye and brought home many a mess of fine black ducks for our table.

There was no age limit for child gunners in those days, and my hunting companion and I must have been about 12 or 13 when we were allowed to hunt alone. The older boys shunned us, particularly shunned the despised girl, and so we were thrown on our own resources. We had our own sneak bow with a sculling hole in the stern.

It leaked, and even the mulch in the bottom did not keep our tails dry. Although it was a one-man craft, it was big enough for two skinny children and their weapons.

Beginning in August when the marsh grasses began to turn, we commenced work on our blind. Some years, it was on the oak point overlooking the pond. Other years, it was out on the broad marsh on the edge of a little creek, a rickety structure of stakes, brushy chicken wire, and interwoven grasses, built long before the season so that the ducks would get used to seeing it innocently there. That was our theory, and it was our late summer occupation, rowing dory loads of material to the site, wrangling over the construction. When it was done, and feeling very proud, I could see it from my bedchamber window if I rested my head on the sill.

In those days, there was even an open season on migrating shorebirds, and with no qualms at all we built a sand blind far down the beach, bordered it with grass and let fly from it at skimming beetlehead plover, yellow legs, snipe, even sandpipers.

But already then, I felt a twinge of grief to see nothing but a heap of torn feathers on the sand, where seconds before, there had been a tiny warm body borne swiftly, magically on long wings in the sunlight.

It was the same with ducks. I enjoyed it most when it was still too dark to shoot, and we could hear their strong wings whistling overhead as they sought the safety of the sea, while the dawn was only a crimson bar of light over the dunes. I loved building the blind, caulking the leaky boat, planning strategy, tamping the marshes, and oiling the slick barrels of the gun with that stuff which smelled like bananas. I felt a tremendous thrill when a duck would come barreling down to the decoys, and our guns roared. The bird tumbled over in the air and fell plunk on the ground.

But then would come the moment of truth when the warm limp body was in my hands and the blood was on my fingers. I never admitted how I felt when I stood looking down at it, smoothing the iridescent outer feathers and thick undercoat of down that protected the bird from the Arctic cold, but not from flying lead: no, not from that.

I have tried to remember when it was that I became so sickened that I gave the whole thing up and gave my gun away. I think it was after I shot the rabbit in the field and that quiet timid little creature screamed aloud. I never knew a rabbit had a voice until that terrible shriek when the lead from my gun tore into its soft body.

The all time finish for me was the annual murder of the half-tame deer that used to take place down this way before the town was closed to hunting.

The invasion was by meat hunters who did not need the meat, and they would be in a frenzy such as I have never experienced in my bloodthirsty days. They arrived by car, dressed in the latest in hunting gear, stepped out or walked a few steps off the road, and would bring down a deer, or fawn, it didn't matter—though it was nice to have a rack of home over the fireplace. The deer might be walking, rarely usually standing there, and looking from those big soft nearsighted eyes. You didn't have to be a woodsman or a tracker to shoot an Argilla Road deer: just a car, a gun, and a red hat were enough!

No Place for the Oriole's Hammock

The summer hurricane of 1954 felled the two great elms that for more than a hundred years had shaded the old square farmhouse where I was born. The moving branches outside the small-paned window were perhaps the first things that my eyes learned to follow in this world.

All through my childhood, the unforgettable shapes of trunk and branch, tree and leaf were as much a part of me as the house itself. In my bed that used to be my grandmother's, in the square front chamber overlooking the broad marshes, I saw the hot red summer sun rise among the leaves, or the full moon turn the trunks to silver, or the snows of winter outlining each bare twig and branch.

Kneeling with my chin on the windowsill, I was at eye level with the oriole's nest and part of the life cycle of those gorgeous birds.

The male, bright as a flame among the leaves, singing the female, crouched over the eggs. I could see her eye, a shining spot among the dun-colored feathers. I watched the egg shells pitched over side when they were no longer useful, and the ugly reptilian little creatures with open beaks. There came a time when the hammock nest was crowded. Then one day the fledglings were standing on the branch spreading and folding their weak wings. And the flight, a flapping glide to the lilac bush, a struggling return to the branch. Then, almost within hours, they were gone, vanished.

The elm leaves fell, the orioles' hammock filled with snow. Among the bricks and chimney pots of winter Boston, I used to think of the orioles in some topical forest or other and wondered if, like me, they were longing for spring and Ipswich.

The hurricane, the spinning wheel of savage gale and lashing rain, came ripping out of the southeast, long after I, like the orioles, had left the nest. But I was never far away, and all that afternoon, I felt a malaise, a perception of disaster. When the wind slackened and only the rain still poured down, the warm, tropical rain, I went out to the road and looked up the hill toward the old house.

The three great trees, the two elms and the giant linden, were a landmark at sea. Lined up this way and that way, they indicated the bay ledges of the feeding cod and haddock or the flat ground of the yellowtail and blackjack flounders, or the pass through the bar for the little boats returning. Now, on this August afternoon, a vicious squall boiling out of the whirling clouds had changed all that. The elms were gone. Only the linden, a broken dark green cone, remained.

Leaning against the wind, I hurried up the road, and warm salt and warm fresh water poured down my cheeks as I contemplated the disaster. The trees, as their supporting roots were torn from the earth, had settled slowly down and lay along the roof that sagged under the weight, the branches mixed with the bricks of the shattered chimney.

Broken branches, broken roots, stripped leaves, bricks and clapboards all jumbled around an immense hole of torn sod and the clutter of the old white rosebushes and flowering currants that for a century had nestled close to the trunk.

Through streaming eyes I tried to see the orioles' nest in all the devastation, but I could not.

Twenty years ago, almost, but the trees still live in my dreams or the reliving of childhood that comes just before the onset of sleep. Often since I have thought, watching the Ipswich elms sickening and dying, inch by inch and leaf by leaf, that I would rather our trees had died as they did, in the prime of their life, still rich and green, victims of a natural force, a cataclysm of storm.

Over and over, through the years in my journeyings through Ipswich, I have watched the elm trees die. It seems hard to imagine that some beetles arriving in a shipment of elm logs from Holland to New York could cause such devastation and so quickly. The virus must be carried on the feet or the feathers of the birds, how else could the trees in front of the old Choate House on Hog Island have contracted the disease, separated as they are from the nearest trees by miles of creek and salt marsh?

The elm that trailed its branches over the Italian Garden at Castle Hill, and during the pauses in the music we could hear the singing leaves, nothing could save it. The giant that was a seedling when High Street and Town Farm Roads were Indian trails, perhaps, was years in dying. Only a few remain of the green arch of High Street. Downtown, now so stark and bare, was once tree-shaded too. Elm skeletons stand in the one time pastures, now growing up to woodland.

This year, when all the rain has made our trees heavy with leaves like the trees of the English countryside, only the elms are sick. With heavy heart, I watch the great trees on the Southside withering away. One will be dead before autumn, the other may not leaf out come spring.

The treasured trees around old houses, the roadside elms that still shade the highways of Ipswich, all, it seems, are doomed. There are young trees which may be saved by new knowledge or treatment, but none of us now living will see them again in their splendor. Few there are who remember the chestnut forests of my childhood.

The oriole will have to find a new place to swing his hammock when there are no more elms.

Of Spirits, Nymphs, and Hamadryads

The tales from Greek mythology and the naughty doings of the Gods and Goddesses were favorite reading in my childhood. By the light filtering in through the cobwebbed windows my nest deep in the hay of the loft or in the natural crooked branches of the Porter apple tree, I read of Zeus dallying with the girls or unleashing his thunderbolts, stately Juno, Apollo whipping across the heavens in his chariot, Diana, the huntress, and all the intrigues and jealousies that made them so much more human and understandable than the Christian hierarchy of saints and prophets . . . although these too did have their moments, particularly in the Old Testament. Still, I did not take the Bible with me to the hayloft.

What appealed to me as a child, and in fact still does, was the identification with nature, the spirits, the nymphs and the hamadryads in the waters and the trees, particularly in the trees. I heard myself in the great elm that trailed its long branches over the shingles of our old house, groaning in the bitter winter night or singing in the summer southwesters; and when I climbed to the top of the huge linden, I was kin to the spirit of the tree and not afraid. I fancied laughing faces among the leaves. When the great tree burst into bloom, was it the bees I heard or the hamadryads humming in contentment?

When the elm fell and lay prostrate in the hurricane, years ago, I felt a terrible stab of pain to see the leaves withering and the roots torn from the earth. The linden too lost several great muscled branches, and surely it was blood, not sap, that I saw oozing from the wound.

And so it is not strange that the feelings from the springtime of life return in nature's springtime when the hamadryads wake from their deathlike sleep, and all the tiny leaves are green.

In the quarter century that I have lived in this little house, I have transferred my feelings from the linden and the vanished elm to the birch tree that now is flying all its trailing little flags of flowers. Soon they will fall, to be followed by the green shade of summer, and finally by the great burst of gold that it becomes every autumn, late, after all the other leaves have fallen. I have trembled when the white branches bend under the load of ice in winter, fearing it would break or when the flexible trunk creaks under the sudden blast of the thundersquall and all the leaves turn their pale sides up in terror. But the long roots spreading as wide as the tree is high have a firm grip on the earth, and some of the tendrils have enmeshed me too, so that I know in my superstitious moments that when it falls, so shall I.

We built this house beside the birch, then a vigorous young thing, too close perhaps, because now the long branches tap at the windows and finger the shingles of the roof where once they only provided a welcome pool of shade in the side yard.

Unlike me, the birch is not a native of these parts. It is a refugee from Farmer Brown's plantings of Castle Hill where he set out a sort of arboretum of exotics like the mottled bark plane trees that shade the avenue and the groves of red pines and larches. Most of the ancestral birches are gone now, a few skeletons remain, and on the ground the fallen trunks are turning back to mould. I hope I shall not see my lovely birch suffer such a fate and the hamadryads having to leave it to find a new home.

There is a new younger birch growing strong and true beside the barn, and here and there in the fields, there are young whips and saplings, the immortality of the birch, the continuity of its life — and mine.

Wandering outside in the spring of the year, I see and recognize the descendants of the trees I knew as a child. Shagbark hickories march down the hillside from the parent tree, now old and broken with hollow trunk beloved of squirrels. And there are groves of red oaks all grown from the acorns of the giant pasture oak. When I was a child, a tree surgeon called to treat a broken limb, told my father and me that it was more than 500 years old. The Indians, I remember thinking, may have sheltered in its shade, and perhaps the Indian children too had their swing from one of the sturdy branches. I wonder if they also felt sick and giddy after an afternoon of swinging so that they had to lie down in the long grass and watch the clouds passing slowly by overhead.

In the woods, the new woods that have grown up where the pasture used to be, there are wild apples, cousins to the rose and all thorns and twisted branches, grown from seeds from the old kitchen orchard dropped long ago by the birds. The old trees, even the Porter apple with its reading branch, are long gone, but they have left these cantankerous descendants that still blossom pink and sweet in the underbrush come spring. And there are cherries, now veiled in white, hard and sour fruits, much loved of the birds that feast on them long before they are ripe. The parent cherry stump, along with the mulberries and the ancient pear, have vanished like childhood.

The hamadryads, so the Greek folk tales ran, perished when their home tree died, but they still live in the birch and the linden and in my memory, their special immortality.

The Great Red Oak is Dead

An obituary for a tree? Why not? It was a living thing. For centuries, the vital sap flowed in its veins. Now it lies dead, the giant limbs broken on the ground, the huge trunk rotten at the heart, and all returning to the earth from which it came.

The great red oak stood alone in the grassy field in a wide pool of shade. On roasting summer days, the cows lay there to chew the cud, and with them, the child, pigtailed head against soft flank, rested, dozed, dreamed. A myriad of polished leaves stirred in the summer breeze, white clouds floated.

There was a nest of owls, somewhere high up in a hollow branch. I never found it, but at night I heard them calling and sometimes at dusk saw them coming out to hunt, sailing in widening circles on silent wings.

It was almost seventy years ago or so that my father began to worry about the health of the tree, and as to be expected, when someone is sick, you call the doctor. The tree surgeon arrived, complete with the bag of tools.

I tagged along behind, interested to see the medical examination of a tree. No temperature was taken, but the tree doctor slivered little samples of wood with his sharp knife, picked a leaf or two here and there. He carefully examined the great trunk, and then he shook his head. There was, it seemed, not then, not now, no cure for old age.

The tree doctor, my father and I, at a respectful distance, sat in the shade to discuss the prognosis. Another fifty years of life at most. I was relieved, a half century seemed an unbelievably long time to live. My father, though, was disturbed. He had a different view of time. He asked if there were not something to be done.

"No, nothing" said tree doctor. "I would only be lying to you and wasting your money if I said there was."

The two doctors discussed the condition of the patient. The tree doctor said the tree was 500 years old, give or take a few years. It was, then, a sapling in Indian times, part of an oak forest that the white men found when they arrived. Somehow it was spared when all the other trees were cut for the carrying timbers of the house and barn, for frames of ships perhaps, for firewood.

The tree doctor pointed out that sometime, perhaps several times in the course of its life, the tree had been blasted by lightning. That was why it had grown wide but not tremendously tall, not like the linden from whose top branches you could see the ocean and the sails of ships on the horizon. The lightning had smashed the crown of the tree and in its surge to ground had rent the trunk all the way down to the roots.

The tree had done its best to heal the wound, had grown a fold of wood and bark to cover the scar, but the tear in the living flesh was too deep.

Through the centuries, the summer rains and melting snows had penetrated and rotted the tree at its heart. Someday, in a summer hurricane or winter blizzard, it would fall.

And so it did, but not in a spectacular gale of wind. Just quietly on a still autumn night, the great tree crumbled, fell, and died.

Guided by some extrasensory perception, I felt impelled to visit the tree for the first time in years, and so I came upon the corpse, still warm. The leaves, just beginning to bronze, were withering and the squirrels were making merry among showers of acorns. There, torn from the trunk was the crooked branch from which had hung my swing. I searched to see if there remained even one fiber of the stout ropes: not one, and long since, the furrows the grass dug by my heels had disappeared. But even on the ground, I recognized the shape of the branch once so familiar, as I lazily drifted back and forth with a push of my heels.

No place like a swing for a dreaming child, the smooth wooden seat, warm on a cool day, cool on a warm day, the creak of the rope, the rustle of the leaves, and in August, the shrilling of the locust that sang the beginning of the end of summer.

The tree doctor had linked the tree in my mind to the Indians, and swinging, I thought of them. Perhaps, Indian children had a swing there, or climbed in the branches looking for the owl's nest, or gathered the acorns to use in their slingshots as I had done.

Standing beside the fallen giant, I felt a chill of mortality, until I saw all around me the new forest, the children and grandchildren of the great tree, reverently clustered.

Some are big trees now, thick, sturdy trunks, shapely branches, an abundance of acorns ripening for winter. Will there be one still standing in 500 years, and will some child have a swing there or perhaps a tree house in the branches?

I hope so, and if I can, I shall come back to see.

Reflections on the Magic Sheet of Crystal

After the first hard freeze and before the snow, black ice forms on the rivers and ponds. As I passed by the pond the other day, there it was, a magic sheet of crystal, and I longed for young legs and old skates to feel once again the wind in my face and to hear in the frosty air the ring of my skate blades on the surface, clear as crystal and transparent as glass. Perhaps it is better, these days, to skate in memory where feet are never cold nor ankles aching.

My first skates were a clamp-on model with a heel bolt that fitted into heel plates on my boots, and clamps in front that tightened around the sole with a key. Woe to the child who lost the key: it meant walking home across the frozen ground in stocking feet. After one such misadventure, I wore my key around my neck on an itchy string.

I must have been 12 or 13 when my feet had almost reached their not inconsiderable size that I received from Santa Claus a pair of "shoe skates," boots and skates all of a piece. I was dismayed. They were "fancy skates," and I had yearned for hockey skates or even racing skates with long blades; but never one to look a gift horse in the mouth, I made appropriate noises of gratification.

Sitting on my bed, I examined them, the edges razor sharp, the curved front of the blade with teeth to help push off to a running start, the boots, black leather reinforced with rawhide lacings. After all, they were pretty nice, and I guessed I could play hockey on them.

I put them on, there in the bedroom using lots of socks for padding since they were large enough to grow into. I took my hockey stick and puck from the closet and made a few practice shots against the wall; yes, they would do.

My mother, who spent many years hoping that her ugly duckling would turn into a swan had chosen fancy skates. It was one more try to make of her gangling daughter, a young lady, a graceful creature. There was the dancing school dress she brought from Paris, silk crepe with little flowers and ribbons. I had hysterics when I put it on, and somehow it got torn, shredded beyond repair before I ever wore it in public.

With the skates went fancy skating lessons at the old Boston Arena, but I fell down, clowned, tripped up the other children and even the instructor, and finally, it was judged to be hopeless. Happily, I went back to hockey, which I played rough enough so that the boys accepted me in spite of my peculiar skates.

Those skates were the only ones I had in all my life, although three pairs of boots were worn out and replaced. As my feet grew more than was anticipated, I could only wear one pair of thin wool socks, and so my feet were always cold.

In Boston, I skated on the frog pond on the Common, fine rough games of shinny with tough kids from the West End and on the Charles River Basin. The winters must have been colder and the air cleaner, because I remember skating all the way across to the Cambridge shore and skate sailing with a borrowed triangle of cotton cloth and bamboo sticks.

It was great, leaning against the wind, flying over the ice, raising the contraption over my head, checking the speed, and heading off the other direction. In later years, the ice soon got all gritty with soot from the coal fires and the factories, and the skating was good for only a short time after the big freeze and before the snow.

The nearest I ever came to being a fancy skater was when the policeman from Station 16 on skating duty on the river undertook to teach me something he called "Dutch Roll." I greatly admired Officer Callahan with his fine red Irish face, as he Dutch-rolled up and down among the skaters, making long sweeping strokes on the outer edges; but I could only do it on one foot, the left one.

But best of all was skating on the pond in Ipswich. The pond was conceived by old Dr. Goodale. Gravel from nearby pits was piled across a narrow neck between two hills, damming up a few acres of salt marsh which, fed by springs and rainwater, made a pretty little pond.

At first, it was very shallow and dotted with muskrat houses fashioned of bulrushes, a great place to sit and rest and ease the aching ankles. Through the clear black ice, you can see the water lily roots and leaves and schools of goldfish, descendants of many an emptied aquarium. We made fires on the ice to warm ourselves at night as we skated by the light of the full moon, the children who played together in the summer, but who seldom saw each other in winter, except on the pond during winter vacations from school.

I walked down to the pond the other morning and shuffled out a few paces over the ice as smooth and clear as a sheet of glass. Where were my skates, where was my youth? Long gone, but the memory is as fresh and green as ever. With that, we shall have to be content.

And in Horse and Buggy Days . . .

Beside the barn there stands a small shingled building the only survivor of the outhouses of my grandmother's day, the henhouses and chicken houses and the tool shed. The hens, even the rooster, so swollen with male pride, were poor relations condemned to live apart in chilly quarters where the water froze in their pans at night. They laid few eggs in the wintertime, and no wonder, they spent much of the short dark days roosting huddled together with heads under their wings.

The barn was reserved for the cows and the horses and the summer's hay piled to the rafters, with rooms for the tools and the grain, this last room being wired to keep out the rats. It is more than forty years since there have been animals or hay in the barn, and longer than that since the sagging shingled building has had an occupant.

Before the days when the Frenchified word "garage" joined the language, this shed was known simply as the automobile house. Built first to accommodate a "horseless carriage," one of my father's early extravagances, it was later enlarged by extending it into the barnyard and adding a false front, so that it would house the 1910 Packard with its real leather cushions. This splendid vehicle could make the trip from Boston to Ipswich in two hours when conditions were right, navigating the Newburyport turnpike in clouds of dust.

My mother had the annoying habit of shutting her eyes and letting out little shrieks, as my father steered skillfully between the cows of a herd on Topsfield Road. She even said at the end of the journey that she liked it better when they rode the horses down from Boston, stopping overnight at an inn somewhere along the way.

But when it was my turn to ride in front beside my father, I thought it was great when the speedometer needle touched 40, downhill, and the car leaped and swayed and bounced like a sailboat in a tide rip. The Packard for all its power was helpless in the snow of winter and the mud of the Argilla Road in spring and so after one last freezing ride home to Ipswich for Thanksgiving, the car, drained of its vital juices, spent the winter immobilized on blocks in the automobile house.

The cutter sleigh and the two-seater were dragged out from their summer quarters, the hayseeds and moth eggs were brushed off the seats, the buffalo robes were hung on the clothesline and beaten, the horses were taken to the blacksmith to be sharp shod. Even in Boston the same procedures were followed, and everyone waited for the snow.

It seems, looking back, that it always snowed before Christmas. At least from my bed in the room with the yellow roses on the wallpaper, I could see that the trunk and branches of the elm tree were frosted and could hear the wind in the chimney and the swish and tapping of snowflakes against the small panes of the window.

Even a few inches of snow, allowed to lie undisturbed, packed only by the runners of sleighs and bungs, made for splendid sleighing and then before it was worn down to bare ground, it snowed again and yet again, building up a highway, ice-based inches deep, that even the rains of the January thaw could not destroy.

The Boston streets, like the Ipswich streets, were hard-packed snow. The delivery pungs whirling along with fast stepping horses and jingling bells, or heavy hauling coal and wood with powerful horses and squealing runners, packed the snow till it was smooth as a dance floor.

Here in Ipswich, once past Northgate, there was only a narrow track with snow still soft. Our fast horse, Fairfax, picking up his feet like a hackney pony, kicked the powdered snow into fine dust to frost the hairs of the buffalo robe, Grandma's glasses, and my knitted stocking cap and scarf. Where the snow had drifted deep between the stone walls, we left the road through pasture barways and followed the tracks across the open fields.

It was wonderful to go jingling down the Argilla road from the depot, school, and the city left behind. Two wonderful vacation weeks of helping Grandma with the animals, feeding the silly hens in their cold house, breaking the ice in the horse trough, and sliding on my sled down the pasture hill clear out onto the icy marsh once a trail was broken.

I had hardly a glance for the Packard in the automobile house. Even its shiny brass, and glass, and glittering paint, the wooden spoked wheels with the red centers did not interest me. It was a dead thing sitting there. It was the horses with their flying hoofs and jingling bells, snorting, tossing their heads and pulling against the reins as they headed home to the barn — they were alive.

But the Packard, that expensive toy was a symbol of changing times, and old Henry Ford in his bicycle shop was preparing a tin lizzie for everyone and a brave new world.

Coasting

These days, a sled is just another toy that spends much of its time in the garage, too often relegated to a dusty corner with the unused doll buggy, the rusting red wagon. Up front are the skis and poles, and instead of a bike or a sturdy wooden wagon marked EXPRESS in bowing gold script along the side, or a Flexible Flyer, that newest and most glorious of sleds, most of today's children dream of owning a motorbike or a mechanized KART, or even a snowmobile on which they can roar over the snow.

In my childhood, in that long ago simpler time before the first world war, I used to lie abed and dream of someday owning the biggest-sized Flexible Flyer, big enough for three children to sit behind the steersman or for a man to lie at full length. I grew past sled age without ever possessing one of these magnificent things, but I shall never forget the Christmas when the medium-sized Flyer stood beside the fireplace. How glorious was the shining varnish and the red-painted runners; what a work of art, that dark blue flying eagle picked out with gold.

As a drowning man is said to see all his life fly by in kaleidoscope, so did I, in that split second of awe see myself flying down the pasture hill, bashing down the steep slope of Sagamore between the barway in the stone wall, skimming across the ice of the pond, clear to the other side.

With a sled like that, even Boston in the winter might be bearable: there was the little hill on the Common where all the "toughies" were with their loaded snowballs, and there was the back side of Beacon Hill where the bolder spirits went flying down across Cambridge Street.

Those were the days when people with autos laid them up for the winter. All the traffic on Cambridge Street was pungs, loaded with all sorts of goods, and these could be avoided by a skillful child's belly bumps on a Flyer.

Before Santa brought the Flexible Flyer, I was quite content with a little old-fashioned sled, looking like something out of a Currier and Ives print, straight runners curved up in front, hand grips along the sides — girls were supposed to sit on a sled, since lying flat was unladylike.

I was never ladylike, and besides, how could you steer sitting upright? It was only by dragging a foot in the snow that you could direct your course zigzag down the hill, the snow flying in a plume behind, and all the rubber wearing off the sole of the arctics, so that come spring they leaked even more than usual.

My possessions always had a life and personality of their own, interwoven with mine. Even the smallest was alive. I wept when my white cotton sailor hat blew overboard and drowned, and I saw no humor when my mother intoned, "Little Nat lost her hat, sailing on the bay." Grownups, I thought, had no feelings. I felt a twinge of disloyalty when I saw the little old sled gathering dust in the barn, its paint faded and cracked.

Once loved, the old sled was no match for the shiny new Flexible Flyer, but still, I tried to think of it, lonely and abandoned when I set forth into the fresh snow that fell so providentially that Christmas night. The new clothesline was stiff in my mittened hand, and I walked to the front of the house where Argilla Road sloped gently down to the causeway and the bridge. I clasped the sled to my belly, took a few running steps, and flung myself down the hill. How smoothly the Flyer glided on its bright steel runners, how responsive it was to the touch of the steering bar!

Easily, I was able to avoid the fresh pile of steaming horse buns, to zigzag in and out of the pung runner tracks. What a wonderful sled, all glittering new. As I pulled it up the slight rise to the bridge, I sang one of those songs that used to well up from my heart, strings of words linked together, sometimes rhyming sometimes not, set to a droning kind of tune.

I paused to lean my ear to the telephone pole at the bridge, a ritual listen with a shiver of delight to the mysterious singing of the vibrating wires, and then I continued on across the field, along the edge of the pond and up the steep slope of Sagamore, all pastured smooth and treeless by the cattle. Here and there, an errant boulder poked its granite face up through the snow or a prickly juniper crouched under a snowy tent.

The only tracks were the matched pairs of a rabbit or the lacework pattern steps of some bird searching for juniper berries. It was cold after the snowfall and entirely still. In the far distance, a dog barked and faintly came the whistle of a train, whooo, whooo and two short hoots, blowing for a crossing somewhere to the north. Occasionally, the surrounding silence was broken when the belly of the pond rumbled as the ice froze deeper or a tree cracked with frost. I stood at the barway halfway up and rested, my breath steaming in the frosty air. Then on and up, the snow squeaking under my arctics and the sled runners whispering, curling up a little frill of snow like the bow wave of a boat.

At last I stood on top of the round dome where the wind had scoured a bare spot to reveal a patch of frosted moss and lichen. The hill was steeper than I thought, the barway smaller. My foot and runner tracks faded into a great distance. After turning the sled around, I hesitated for a long time. There was no one to see if I walked down partway and started from there, just this first time. But I would know and the sled would know that I was a coward, and so, without thinking anymore about it, I gave a running push, and I was off.

For the next flashes of terrifying speed, I would have given anything to have been puttering around on my old sled. This one was like a wild horse plunging down the hill, faster and faster, the runners whistling my eyes streaming in the wind. I jolted breathless over a bump, missed a rock by inches. The stone wall loomed ahead, where was the barway? With a wild swerve, I made it and continued ever faster down the last open slope and out across the pond.

For a long moment, I lay trembling with excitement and fear. I might have been killed if I had hit the wall. The snow could have come and covered me and the shattered Flyer, and no one would have found me till spring, just a little bag of broken bones inside my knitted leggings.

I turned this picture round and round in my mind for some time, filling in the details of what everyone said, "What a nice girl was Kitty Crockett and what a shame." Overcome with grief, I stumbled blindly to my feet and headed for home.

"How was the coasting? How did your new sled go?" my grandmother asked. I could not answer, I only burst out crying.

"There," she said, and, "There." How could she know that I was almost dead in the snow?

She asked me no questions . . . just gave me a hot cup of cocoa and told me a new story about "When I was a little girl . . . ."

Kitty and Hardy, Crane Beach, approx. 1917

SPRING

... The cows were out to pasture in the green fields, the birds were singing, everything was coming into new leaf; red of the oaks and maples, greeny gold of the poplars and hickories, and then the great linden with its heavily muscled branches, brilliant emerald green with leaves clear to the very top. ...

Spring — Always Different, Always New

I should not want to live in latitudes where the climate never changes, a land of eternal summer. How wonderful to see the spring come to New England, to Ipswich, always different, always new.

It begins with the drip, drip of the melting snow on the roof in March. It quickens with the song of the first song sparrow, and how that brave little voice lifts the heart to ecstasy. And then there is the full laughing chorus of the redwings and a new voice of recent years, the lilting bubbling song of the cardinal. All winter I have fed him and his timid little wife on expensive sunflower seeds, and now he rewards me: he sings and perhaps makes his nest in the broken trees of the old orchard.

There are setbacks and disappointments. April snow, the raw east wind of the still cold ocean, the drift of fog past the budding oaks of the marsh islands, but every day the sun swings higher. The mourning doves begin their melancholy cooing earlier, and with the sunrise, the bird songs swell into a paean of joy.

Lying in my bed beside the open window, I anticipate the shrilling of the clock that starts my day with moments of pure joy, the joy of being alive in one more spring.

As far back as I can remember, and that's a very long time, I have loved best the spring of the year. Children have their rituals to follow, and among mine were shedding my shoes and stockings at the mailbox and running barefoot through the fields. It was not always comfortable. My feet were soft from a winter shod in leather, and I felt every pebble, every sharp twig and thorn with a wince of pain. Come summer I should run over hayfield stubble and sharp gravel with nary a twinge, but there was a bitter sweetness to the pain of the first day when bare feet were in contact with the warming earth.

My first unshod excursion took me along a familiar route through the block north of Grandma's garden, the old Indian midden where broken and rolling clam shells of ancient feasts sweetened the soil and made it rich. I paused for the annual search for an arrowhead or a flake thrown up by the frost. Most of them had been picked up long ago by the generations that had tilled this bit of land.

Then a close scrutiny of the asparagus bed, too soon for even one green spear to show above the ground. There was someone else waiting too: the woodchuck emerged from his winter sleep, lean from a long winter of short rations and eager as was I for something green and fresh. He whistled and dived into his hole when he saw me. I lingered by the mound of fresh turned earth, hoping that he would come out again and all the while, he was watching me from his back door, his eye bright among the grasses.

Then onward along the southern slope of hayfield, looking for the first dandelions. How delicious those bitter greens after a winter of carrots and turnips, parsnips and potatoes.

"Spring tonic," my grandmother said, and she would have liked to dose me with sulfur and molasses to clear the blood of all those winter poisons, a ritual when she was a little girl down Maine.

Unscientific, unnecessary in those enlightened days sixty years ago, and so I was spared.

My wandering steps brought me at length to the edge of the marsh where windows of mulch sheared from the thatch banks by the ice had been driven ashore by the gales of winter.

The mulch was thick and soft, smelling faintly salty and so I sat down in it, picking through for treasures, the shell of a baby horseshoe crab or a mussel shell, the inside polished to iridescence. Then I laid me down, snuggling in the softness with the clouds moving by overhead, half expecting to see some tangling in the upper branches of the island oaks. The sun was warm, the sky the soft blue of April, and so I dozed and even dreamed a little.

Rousing from my catnap, I continued on my way, because there was a destination for my wanderings.

The marsh island floated in a sea of grass, surrounded by a maze of creeks and channels. From the north side at marsh level, it slanted upwards to quite a rise of ground, then fell away to a steep slope to a gravelly beach and the marsh.

Here was spring journey's end. All through the mat of fallen oak leaves, there were the spotted leaves of the dogtooth violets, and there nodding on slender stems the yellow flowers, like tiny lilies, trout lilies. Nowhere else in the periphery of my wanderings did these flowers grow. To me, they were rare and magical almost as exciting as the one pink lady-slipper I found in the pine woods of the dunes, only one and only once. Or the bottle gentian like a bit of sky fallen beside the dusty road. This too, only one and only once.

But the dogtooth violets came up every year in this sheltered place. Careful not to step on them in my bare feet, I crouched down to admire them from a toad's eye view. And suddenly, they were blurred for my eyes had filled with tears: they were so beautiful, so rare.

The ritual included picking just two, and one leaf, to take home to Grandma.

It is years since I have visited the island slope. I am afraid to, really, I am afraid the dogtooth violets are not as beautiful, as magical as I remember.

But they are still there, I know they are. And anyway, they still bloom in my memory on the south slope, in the sun.

Grandma

On one of those crystal-bright days that are our reward after a long cruel winter, I took my knife and ventured forth into the fields for a mess of dandelions. By this time of year, the products of the root cellar have become pretty sad: the potatoes limp and sprouting, the carrots withered, the cabbage jaundiced, and the last of the Russet apples wrinkled and dry. Dandelions, my grandmother told me, purified the blood after a winter diet that saw few fresh vegetables. The fresh green leaves were a welcome sight as they pushed up through the fog of last year's grass.

I do not know whether children today with all their manufactured diversions have time for the rituals that governed the lives of children long ago. In more leisurely times, there was room for idle imaginings and ancient superstitions fed on a diet of fairy tales, procedures to avert evil and to ensure the fulfillment of wishes — more reliable than prayers, though these did no harm, certainly, and might make assurance doubly sure.

Each season, particularly spring, the time of quickening and of freedom, had its convention. The laying aside of shoes was a sign, and so it would be in bare feet that I gamboled behind my grandmother through the greening fields in the search of dandelions.

I thought of this the other day as I sat on the step with my basket and knife preparatory to setting forth. I could have found plenty of dandelions right around the house, but there had to be still the ritual, the little adventure, even though I kept my shoes on feet gone soft from too many years of being shod.

Now there is a house on the location of grandmother's asparagus bed, a driveway where the rhubarb plants pushed their furled leaves through the cover of salt marsh mulch, but turning my back on all this, there were still the field and the dandelions, and unchanged the view of the wooded island, the marshes beaten and shaved by winter's ice, and the sand dunes, the salt river with the ocean sparkling in the spring sun.

A mess of greens to feed one solitary person doesn't take long to gather, and before returning, I sat for a little while where I used to sit beside my grandmother and found I could conjure her back to life after all these years.

Perhaps I was dozing and dreaming in the sun, but suddenly, there she was, her fine white hair pulled severely back and knotted in a bun, her eyes faded to a smoky blue in a face that was brown and seamed with laugh lines. I could see her hands twisted from years of hard work and the broad old-fashioned wedding band of reddish gold. Grandma was very old, almost seventy, and she wore a dress of heavy black stuff with a full skirt down to her boot tops, but in spite of this, she could move as briskly in the garden as she could in the chicken house.

Even then, she was as different from other children's grandmas as they would be from today's with their short skirts and blue-rinsed hair. The women of my grandma's generation down in Maine were country folk who might have travelled west with their men in the covered wagons. It just happened that Grandpa Fred stayed on and was a country doctor, driving among the farms and the logging camps in his buggy with my father, a little boy riding beside him, holding the ends of the reins, pretending to drive, even as I myself did as a child.

The other children's grandmas, whom I knew in the city, were delicate creatures, sitting in chairs by windows full of plants. I was sorry for my friends for not having a real grandma in Ipswich, one like mine, and a farm to go to on weekends and vacations in the long, long lovely summer.

After my little visit with grandmother, I gathered up my basket of greens and started home across the field, not looking at interloping houses, keeping my eyes on the unchanged and unchanging marshes. Grandma would not like to see the houses there, I thought. She was old and would have resented change.

Suddenly, I had the oddest thought: Grandma was no older than I am now, or not much older, anyway.

I wondered if she too felt surprised when she looked in the mirror and saw an old face looking out. If she did, she probably combed her hair in a hurry, splashed cold water on her face out of the pitcher and the bowl on the commode and hurried out to the chicken house to gather the eggs for breakfast, thinking, "If I am feeling like this, it must be time to cut a mess of dandelion greens for my spring tonic."

Dandelions

The Field of the Cloth of Gold, the French meadow where Henry VIII of England and François I of France met with all panoply and splendor was no more beautiful than our green Ipswich fields covered with golden dandelions in the emerald green. As I pass by them these days, I wish I could turn time back to those slowly moving hours of childhood, the spring hours drifting by like the clouds overhead as I lay flat on my back in the hayfield among the dandelions.

Grandma told me about the Field of the Cloth of Gold and the kings and the horses as we sat by the fire in her upstairs chamber on a chilly evening. And when armed with knives and baskets, we sallied forth to cut a nice mess of greens, she told me how, like all of us, the dandelion was an immigrant to this country, the seeds arriving by ship in a bit of earth tucked perhaps around the roots of some treasured plant brought from a dooryard in the old country, a touch of home in the new world.

Many plants, familiar now as roadside or meadow weeds, came this way, seeds clinging to the stockings of the early settlers or in the earth around bricks brought for ballast.

The purple loosestrife blazing in swampy places in August is an English garden flower gone wild here. No foreign planter has made itself so much at home or has set its long root so deep into the alien soil as the dandelion. The tiny seeds, parachuting on their puff of down, have travelled west, north, and south from the seaboard. The plants established well in early New England and provided the bitter greens so refreshing after a long winter of yellowing cabbage and withering carrots kept in sandboxes in the cellar.

No wonder that we, the men and women of today, are inches taller and live years longer than our ancestors whose only fresh foods all winter long were apples from the barrel and rooted vegetables. Once, in one of my varied jobs, this one cataloguing papers of a shipping firm, I was amazed to find from crew lists that the sailors of 200 years ago were really relatively tiny little men, five foot two or three. When one was six feet tall or more, it was notable that he was a "blackamoor," not too long from Africa, probably.

As for the knights of the Field of the Cloth of Gold, only a child of today could fit into their suits of chain mail and armor, but their great horses, ancestors of the Shires and Percherons, had to be strong enough to carry the weight of all that metal encasing the little human bodies.

It was before the dandelions flowered, when the buds were still tight little balls deep down in the crown, that Grandma and I went in search of our spring tonic and I danced ahead like a colt on skinny legs. In the mat of last year's grass, the green plants were spreading their saw-toothed leaves, *dents-de-lion*: dandelion. One's left hand gathered the leaves together, and the right hand with its sharp knife slashed off the root about an inch below the ground. A wasteful way, grandmother said. In Europe, everything is saved, and the root, cleaned and dried, is made into an infusion like coffee, chicory, to which it is cousin. Herb doctors of long ago boiled the roots and the toughest leaves to make a nasty bitter medicine, a tonic to purify the blood. Effective it must have been, for everybody knows that to be good for you, medicine must taste really nasty!

Some people, Grandma told me, gather bushels of the flowers and make them into wine with water and sugar and raisins. Ah, I thought, that is something I must try.

I spent about a week collecting equipment from that source of all treasures, our dump down behind the barn in the sumac jungle. A large old jelly kettle thrown away by wasteful adults, because the enamel was chipped and the metal underneath rusty, was just the thing because it didn't leak. Bottles of all shapes and sizes were everywhere in the dump and were washed out more or less in the horse trough at the barn. Sugar and raisins could vanish unnoticed from the abundance of the kitchen closet. The next thing was the flowers: "bushels," my grandmother said.

From some places well manured by many cows and horses, as on Argilla Farm pastures in some years, it wood be easy to gather bushels of flowers, but here, several miles away, they were never so plentiful, and it took lots of walking to get enough blossoms to cover the bottom of a bushel basket. Some flowers had gone by and turned to fluff; others were not out far enough. For this wine, only the best would do. The first bottle would be a surprise for my father, and he could drink it on the porch some night when he was hot and tired. No doubt I would be invited to have a sip, but if not, there would be plenty left for me and my friends.

I toiled back and forth across the hayfield, with frequent stops to rest and think of the wine I would make, and to watch the cloud shadows scurrying across the marsh, or to peer at a file of ants threading their way through the grass stems on some mysterious journey. Finally, I had enough flowers, a half bushel, maybe, and enough stems to make rings for a length of chain to wear around my neck.

The whole business, sugar, raisins, and flowers, was mixed with water in the old kettle in an unused room in the barn and then stirred with a stick, then left to turn into wine. I got involved in other things, and it was a week or ten days before I visited my vat; it was not an attractive sight: the rotting flowers were floating on the surface mixed with the bloated raisins and a few flies, but underneath, there was a brownish liquid, strong smelling . . . wine!

Selecting the best and the cleanest of my stock of bottles, I pushed the floating scummy mass to one side and dipped up a bottle full of reasonably clear liquid, stoppered it with a rag and carried it carefully up to my room.

I listened for my father coming from the thin and waited until he got established on the porch, and then I came out proudly with a little tray, the bottle, and a wine glass.

"Wine," I said, "I made it. Have a drink."

He poured out a little, sniffed it, and said, "It's pretty strong stuff. I think I'll take only a little. What's in it?"

When I told him dandelion flowers and stuff, he tossed it off and said he didn't care for any more, thank you. As I carried my tray and bottle away, I heard him telling something to my mother and laughing.

I thought when I tried it that grownups would drink anything, but I found I did not care for wine — nor did my friends. The wine sat mouldering in the barn for several weeks, and finally, it stunk so that I threw it out. Anyway, I needed the kettle and bottles for something else.

Tears Among the Spring Peach Blossoms

Walking through the sodden grass after the snow had melted, I saw what I thought was the castoff antler of a deer. But when I reached to pick it up it crumbled between my fingers. This bit of rotten wood with its fragment of bark is all that remains of the peach orchard.

The rows of fragile trees, running east and west along the borders of the marsh, even in youth carried the promise of early death. They were so frail, so delicate, that I lavished on them hours of time that I could ill afford, the kind of attention one gives to an invalid child not long for this world.

The peach orchard was my father's idea, and on a long ago April weekend, he and I set in the ground the little whips, carefully separating the tangled roots and rolling back the burlap wrappings, wheeling them in the wheelbarrow to the waiting holes, dug in the fall and only recently emptied of snow.

The apple trees that we had planted years before were sturdy things, already bearing fruit when the peach orchard was planted. They would go on blossoming and bearing for a hundred years, taking care of us all in our old age, or so my father dreamed, but the peaches would only flower and fruit for perhaps twenty years, no more.

Even so, my father lived to see only a few crops, a few springs when the south slope was a rosy mist of flowers, a few summers when the delicate branches bent and were braced to carry their burden of ripening fruit.

The peaches were all white-meated, rosy-cheeked, and juicy sweet, allowed to ripen on the tree, picked at the peak of perfection when they were so delicate that a finger touch would bruise them.

They were picked lovingly, one by one into baskets lined with shredded purple paper, carried to the barn as if they were crown jewels, and sold to epicures who came from far and near to buy a dozen or so of Crockett peaches.

"You see," my father said, triumphantly emptying his pocket of dollar bills and change, and even my mother, always a doubting Thomasina where the farm was concerned, had to admit that the peaches did quite well and certainly they were delicious.

We lived high off the windfalls, sliced with cream or churned to an ambrosial ice cream in the old wooden bucket with salt and ice on the back porch.

My father died in the darkest days of the Great Depression, and for seven years I struggled to prove correct his dream that the orchard of apples and peaches would take care of us all. No one else in the family had ever believed it, and, unfortunately, they were right.

But the absolute faith, the undying optimism that brushed aside calamities and looked always to a next and better year, had been acquired by me first from my grandmother when I trotted after her to feed the chickens, and later when I was older to point out to her failing eyes the green asparagus spears pricking through the black earth and the mulch, and still later milking the cows, fetching them in from pasture, or driving the hay rake and the cultivator.

And then there were the apples and the peaches that I helped plant. There were the winter days when we pruned the trees, noting the fat flower buds or the triple buds of the peaches, the messengers of next year's fruit.

Then there was the awful day when my father staggered, his face flushed almost purple, and he sat down on the frozen ground and put his head down between his knees. "Just tired, just a little dizzy," he said, and coming back to the house, he leaned on me, my father who had carried me on his shoulder so many times.

This was the warning, as sure as the rumble of distant thunder in the north. When the peaches blossomed in the spring he was not there to see them.

Alone and sad, that spring of '32, the peach orchard had never been so beautiful.

Every branch, every twig bore clusters of flowers of softest pink. I remember them on a day when the wind breathed in from the east and veils of fog floated by the island softening the rough outlines of the oaks. There was a chill in the wind, the sound of surf on the bar, and warmth and perfection of those lovely flowers. And that day I determined not to mourn, but to throw in my lot with the trees, certain that somehow they and we would survive.

When finally the farm came to an end and was no longer possible, it was the peaches that perished first, unloved and neglected. I came back in the spring to see them and they were broken from the ice of a hard winter, their trunks rent and bleeding amber-colored tears. It was when I saw one last cluster of flowers on a dying tree that finally, after all the years of disappointment and grief, I cried.

Thunder

Reading about the Tagasay people found living in a state of Stone Age innocence in the rain forests of the Philippines, I noted that the only thing they feared was thunder, rumbling and crashing far above the tops of the trees that screened them from the sun and moon, as well as from the doings of other men called civilized. To the Tagasy, thunder was the voice of an angry god; they had never heard the other noises with which men kill each other.

I have wondered often if it is an altogether good thing for the children of the West to learn in kindergartens and even before, that there is a scientific explanation for everything. The fears and superstitions that surrounded the children of my generation, when they were in the same stage of development as the Tagasay have been removed, I expect, by all this knowledge. I wonder if people so matter-of-fact and fearless are not missing something.

The first rumblings of thunder on a sultry afternoon would bring a shivering excitement and near terror. Seeing the hair standing up along the spine of my foolish timid boxer, Christy, the other day, I recalled the prickling of my scalp and weak little hairs on my back as they all rose and stirred with the muttering of thunder in the west. I was not alone in my fear. All the children with whom I played would climb on their bikes and leave the game when it thundered, no matter how fascinating and absorbing the play.

I thought myself less lucky than most in one way: my grandmother loved to sit on the porch under the linden tree during thunderstorms.

When I would come home, panting and breathless as the sky darkened, she always called to me to come sit with her and watch the approaching storm. I never dared to say that I would much rather crawl under the bed, that unfailing refuge in time of trouble, and, curled up in a ball against the wall, safe among the dust kittens, wait out the storm with my eyes squeezed tight.

But in another way I was luckier than my friends because I had a talisman against the lighting. So long as I clutched it, or, better still, sat on it, I was safe and could enjoy the crashing and flashing — unless, of course, it was too close. I cannot remember where I acquired the huge glass marble with its mysterious twist of blue and red deep in its crystal heart, nor how I knew that it was a protector against lightning. But no one, most especially no grownup, must ever see or touch it, or it would lose its magic power.

And so when I came rushing into the house, just as the first breaths of the thundersquall were rustling the topmost leaves of the linden tree, I ran first up the twisting staircase to my room, and groping in the bottom of my toy box, I felt and clutched the smooth cool glass of the magic marble. With it concealed in my hand, and the hand in the pocket of my bloomers, I came bravely out onto the porch where Grandma sat rocking her fine white hair parted in the middle and her blue eyes behind the steel rimmed spectacles fixed in fascination on the darkening sky.

"It's going to be a very bad storm," Grandma said with satisfaction. She was too absorbed to watch my maneuverings with the marble as I sneaked it out concealed in my hand and squatted on it like a hen on an egg. There we sat, the woman and the child, as the clouds rushed down almost in the top branches of the big tree. The lightning snapped and crackled while the thunder shook the house to its foundations. I thought I smelt brimstone, the Devil's smell. There was even a quick salvo of hail on the porch roof, and crystals of ice danced among the raindrops on the grass. The storm then went roaring off to the south. The lightning's forked tongue struck and struck again on the barc slope of Hog Island, and the marshes turned a sick and angry green.

Suddenly, it was deliciously cool. The air filled with the strong salty smell of the marsh and all the birds began to sing as the sun came out. I managed to get the marble back in my pocket and back again into the toy box unobserved before I went out to build dams and sail boats in the puddles in the yard.

Once there came the day when I was caught out in the yellow dory as the storm approached. The wind died as the sky grew black; the midges came out in biting multitudes, and I was still a long way from home, out in the middle of Essex Bay. I was much older then, too old for childish things, but still I longed for my magic marble as I rowed frantically for the beach, frightened to death and even crying a little.

The little boat grated on the sand as the storm wind came, icy cold from the northeast. Tossing out the anchor, I dropped the sail and crawled under it, alone and frightened, but excited too. The sail was old and porous, the rain poured through it. I was soaked and shivering when finally, half rowing half sailing, I made my way back to the cove in the fog that followed the storm.

For a long time I had been too old to play with the things in the toy box: too old forage one-eyed teddy bear, all his plush worn off, where I had beaten him, poor thing, in fits of temper or frustration; too old, too, for the spinning top, for the cloth books, the tin horse, and the delivery wagon. Someday soon, I suddenly realized, the box with all its things would join my father's toys in the attic, the moth-eaten Union soldier's hat and the tin sword. The magic marble should be taken out and put in a safer place, if indeed its mysterious powers remained undiminished.

Kneeling beside the box, I groped for the marble, yearning to feel its coolness in my hand . . . it had been such a long time; it had been so neglected . . . where was it? I felt in every corner, and finally in desperation I tipped the toy box contents onto the floor.

The marble was gone. It wasn't anywhere. It had vanished. As mysteriously as it had entered my life, it disappeared forever.

. . . Was it ever really there?

Hayfields

The hayfields of Ipswich yesterday are vanishing before the advancing forest of Ipswich tomorrow. Early explorers sailing along our coast observed the bare and rounded hills with fields of Indian corn. The fishermen from Europe who brought trade goods, and smallpox, to pacify the aborigines set up wooden stages or flakes for drying the codfish on the treeless slopes of Stage Hill and Little Neck and Great Neck.

A cool wet spring was perfect for the hay that early Ipswich farms grew in such abundance after the Indians and fishermen vanished. First is the June grass, timothy and redtop, to cure in the open fields under the summer sun, then to store in the haymows, piled to the rafters of the barns, enough to feed the stock all winter. On a good year there would be a surplus to sell to the stables of Boston for a bit of cash, that scarce commodity on the self-sufficient seacoast farms. Hereabouts, as on the high marshes of Rowley and Newbury to the north, there was black grass and salt hay to be harvested, filled with the life-giving salts of the sea.

On our island farm, curled like a sleeping dog on the green rug of salt marsh, there is now only one open grassy field left of all those acres. The pasture is a beginning forest of hickories and red oak descendants of the giant tree, a pasture oak so ancient that Indians could have rested in its shade, or farmhands enjoying a brief nooning drank what my grandmother called "switchel," as they leaned their sweaty backs against the huge rough trunk.

Haying was hot work and involved everyone, even children, and I can just remember the taste of "switchel," diluted by West Indian molasses in cool water with a dash of cinnamon, delicious and an invigorating potion. By contrast, iced tea seems a poor weak thing but then cutting grass is not what it used to be either, with power mowers and all.

The end of June is the time of year when farmers would watch their growing grasses ripen in the sun; the grasses' heads heavy with pollen and the stems rich with juice. The triangular knives of the mowing bar were sharpened to a razor edge on the grindstone. I remember turning the handle that revolved the big stone wheel, slow and steady and keeping it drenched with water from the rusty dipper; I was too skinny and light to work the foot paddle.

The mowing machine with its iron seat and cleated iron wheels waited alongside the horse-drawn rake with its curved comb of iron teeth, the hay wagon painted blue with huge iron tired wheels, the hubs oozing grease, and the shiny pitchforks and the wooden hand rakes all in a row. The nets for the horses to protect them against the fierce, biting, greenhead flies, hung beside the harness. We always hoped that the hay would be ripe before the greenheads came. This seldom happened in those days: the greenheads came earlier, but they did not stay so long. If they were really bad, we cut the hay at night by moonlight when the greenheads were sleeping in the marshes.

I thought it was wonderful to drive the hay rake at night. This was my job when I got older, raking the cut grass into long windrows, hopefully straight, lowering the comb of the teeth so that it skittered over the shorn stubble, lifting it when we reached the windrow, using a gearshift beside the driver's hand. The moonlight, with all the shadows black, the high tide, silver over the marshes, the field, mysteriously seeming larger than life, my hands on the reins, I too seemed larger than life, and all around was the smell of hay and the glitter of fireflies.

It was really old Billy, that wise bay horse, that knew how to rake the hay. All I had to do was raise and lower the rake, and the reins hung slack around my neck. He turned at the end of the field and came back just a rake's width from where we had gone before.

In the morning, early, early, we came with the wooden rakes to pick up the wisps that had been skipped in the dark, and then when the sun dried the grass, we stacked the hay with pitchforks into cocks that looked like pointed hats set down all over the field: giant hats, I used to think, and the giant bodies and the big feet were down there somewhere under the earth.

It was when the hay was in cocks that the farmers worried and etched the sky to the north for the approach of the black thunderclouds, heavy with wind and rain — or they looked to the east for a "sea turn," the shift of the wind to the northeast and the accompanying rain and fog that might last for days, while the hay blackened with mildew and spoiled.

I can remember once, or was it many times, when all hands were working frantically, that we pitched the hay from the cocks to the wagon, higher and higher. A strong man could take a whole cock in one forkful, and then we on top stomped it down. All the while the sky to the north grew black; a strange greenish light lay over everything; the river was leaden colored, and all the sailboats swung nervously at their moorings as the first breath of the thunder squall boxed the compass.

The lightning stitched the bellies of the clouds. The thunder rumbled and growled, louder and louder. Treading and stomping frantically on top of the load, I wondered when we were ever going to head for the barn, one more cock, and one more, and one more.

Finally, everyone swung aboard, the eager horses headed to the barn, galloping; the wagon lurched, and every minute it seemed as though the load would shift and dump us all in the field. As we passed the horse trough in the barnyard, there was a tremendous flash and crash right together, a gust of wind that turned all the leaves pale sides up and then came the first big bold drops of rain.

We were safe in the barn, the horses panting and blowing when the rain began pounding on the shingles overhead, overflowing the gutters, splattering in the barnyard dust, harder and harder, until there was a muddy lake spinning with leaves, twigs, and yellow foam.

Now in this season, our last remaining field of grass is ripe for cutting, chin height to the child that is gone. Long ago, gone too are the cows and the horses and the people who shouted and laughed in that careening ride to the barn. There is just that one field of waving grass that is kept to remind us. Someday, maybe, there will be again a bobolink there, black and gold, singing once more the song of summer.

Decoration Day

Then, as now, the ways of grownups were mysterious to children.

Decoration Day was a time of sad faces and the ritual of gathering flowers for the cemetery to decorate the graves . . . of Grandpa Fred, whom I knew only from the daguerreotype in Grandma's bedroom, of Aunt Lucy and Uncle Hosea, whom I vaguely remembered as very old sad sort of Maine folks transplanted to Somerville. Other unknown Crocketts were in the cemetery in Norway, Maine, and so the flowers had to be put aboard the train at Ipswich Depot.

To me, this was a festive affair, culminating with Grandma driving the democrat wagon between the stone walls of the Argilla Road to the Depot with the flowers after an all night soaking in carefully wrapped wet newspapers in the bathtub. The cows were out to pasture in the green fields, the birds were singing, everything was coming into new leaf; red of the oaks and maples, greeny gold of the poplars and hickories, and then the great linden with its heavily muscled branches, brilliant emerald green with leaves clear to the very top.

How could anyone be sad on Decoration Day when all the world was decorated for spring? And so, kicking my heels against the wagon seat, I sang louder and louder, in time to the squeaking of General's harness, my song of spring, of freedom, of welcome to Ipswich and the long summer days ahead. Only when we came to town did Grandma tell me to hush: so much noise was not seemly.

Decoration Day marked the end of my Boston school. Only the day before, I had come home over the uneven bricks of Marlborough Street to find the car being loaded, everyone cross and hectic, the furniture in the sitting room covered with cloths, the smell of mothballs everywhere, and in the front hall were the goldfish bowl and Fritz Kreisler, the canary, in his cage covered with a towel. Everyone had been waiting for me to station what was then a two hour ride, but even on such a day, I had to linger for one final scuffle in the schoolyard, and to climb the tree after I played David with his slingshot attacking the giant, Goliath.

There was the car, its brass shining even to the tank of the acetylene on the running board, for lights in case we were benighted on the way. My little nest was among the suitcases and baskets on the back seat just room for me and the bird cage and the fish bowl which was already spilling.

With bulb horn blowing, *beep beep*, we threaded our way among the teams and drays on Rutherford Avenue, Charleston, over the floating bridge and then the Lynn and Saugus marshes, so reminiscent of home, past the red brick factories of Lynn and the stately houses of Washington Square, Salem, and then over the Beverly Harbor Bridge. Each year, we paused at the fish market, still there now, which my father thought had the freshest haddock right off the boats to bring home to Grandma for our supper. Then on again to the open country, the sweet-smelling spring of lilacs and apple blossoms and green, green fields. I hang and wriggled out of my shoes and stockings, ready to feel the grass of home under my bare feet.

All through my childhood and youth and maturity, I have come home so many times to the old square house under the linden tree, but never with such joy as on those Decoration Days when I was a very little girl. It was not as though I had not seen Grandma and Ipswich. I had, all winter on weekends and vacations, but this was permanent — or so I thought every spring, forgetting that fall and winter must inevitably follow.

Black Nixie, frolicking and barking greeted us, and after setting down the goldfish and the bird and giving Grandma a quick hug and kiss, I was off to visit the barn, the chicken house, the pasture — so eager that I hardly felt the pain in my newly liberated feet, which would toughen up come summer so that I would be able to run across the hayfield stubble without wincing.

The first weeks were for exploring. On the wooded island, only a few dogtooth violets still blossomed, the great mass on the southern bank overlooking the broad marshes having gone by. One year, I picked a huge bunch, but they wilted in my hot hand before I could get them home. "Wild flowers, not vase flowers," my grandmother said, when I was disappointed.

Dandelions too were not house flowers, but the hollow stems could be made into links for chains around the neck, the white sap looked like milk, but tasted bitter and stained the fingers — no matter! The north slope, the summer pasture, was blue with violets, set close to the ground with stems too short for picking but beautiful to see, as if a bit of sky had fallen. In the wet land along the borders of the marsh, the white violets grew, just a few, semiprecious because they were so rare. I was close to disappointed when I found a mass of them on the edges of a cranberry bog in the dunes: they were not supposed to be common.

The ancient lilac in front of the house with stems thicker than a child's leg was a mass of dark purple blossoms, and the sweet smell floated in my window at night, so delicious that first night in my bed in the little room facing east and the sunrise. All night while I slept, the stars moved through the elm branches, and in the morning I woke to the sound of singing birds and the smell of lilacs.

My explorings every year took me out in concentric circles with the house at the center. First circle to the apple orchard, deep pink buds and pale pink flowers humming with bees: I lay on my back under the Russet tree and looked up at the sky through the flowers, listened to the bees and felt as though I would burst with happiness.

Then, further and wider circles to the cove and the salt marsh, still sallow after a long winter, but beginning to flush with green as the sharp spears of thatch pushed upward through the mud. At half tide, the paired horseshoe crabs crept up the streams; the shore birds whistled their sad and lonely cries, and as the tides receded, the clams spouted little fountains.

I left my line of tracks in the mud alongside those of the plover and the snipe. The tides have long since washed away those child's tracks, the blowing sands wiped them from dune to grove, but nothing perhaps not even death itself, can banish the memory of a world seen fresh and sweet by child eyes in the spring of the year.

Crockett house, approx. 1920

SUMMER

... It was more than a half century ago, how much more-never mind, that I clattered down the stairs of the city elementary schooling joined the under-the-breath chant, "Goodbye teacher, Goodbye school . . . ." It was not until we were out on the sidewalk that we finished the rhyme at the tops of our voices: "Goodbye . . . (here, add the name of an unpopular member of the administration) . . . danged old fool."...

Welcome, Summer . . . More Than Ever

Welcome, summer! The trees are rich with leaves, the grasses heavy with pollen, the marshes emerald green. The little red sailboat swings at her mooring eager to go once again flying along the creeks and rivers of her small and lovely world.

I, too, am eager. Not for me anymore are the wider waters, the urge to sail away to Rockport or along the Plum Island beach, or to brave the treacheries of the Essex Entrance, the tiderips, the running breakers, the bars and the rocks of the Wingaersheek shore.

When I was a child, I was happy sailing my yellow dory in this small watery world. To me, nourished all winter on sea stories and tales of high adventure, this was my Amazon, my Congo, my Nile. I was Crusoe, leaving a line of barefoot tracks on a deserted beach.

I built my fires on the shore and steamed in seaweed my take of clams and mussels. Eaten half raw out of the shell they were delicious. Crouching over my fire, crying in the smoke, I felt no need of people. So long as I had my dory with her leg o' mutton sail, thole pins and oars, my cooking pot and tin cull stashed in the piney woods near the fresh water pool in the dunes, I was a happy escapee from the world of chores, shod feet, soap and water, and grown-up demands.

There were adventures.

One day when I was having a cooling swim, naked in shoulder deep water, a seal surfaced right beside me. We were both startled: he by the hairless body without tail and flippers, and I by the round whiskered face so close to my own. He peered at me from nearsighted clouded eyes, then with a great splash, he turned, sounded, and headed for deep water. At a safe distance, he rose again, pounded the water with his flippers, and when I did not move, he floated away with the tide, his round head like a ball on the water.

Like me, he was an escapee from family life, a seal colony established on a patch of marsh across the river on the Hog Island shore. I had seen them many times as I sailed by, a group of about twenty, lying in the sun, dozing, scratching, barking. They did not fear the passage of the sailboat, which was to them just another bird moving quietly on a single wing.

There were days when the fog moved in from sea, smoking along the water, blotting out the familiar landmarks, the round pudding shape of the island, and the great linden, and two giant elms that marked the site of home. Although I was happy to be away, I was reassured to see them there, and when they disappeared, I was uneasy. So much for the solitary spirit that must still keep some connection with the known and the familiar.

As the fog closed in, I marked the direction of the wind, raised the anchor, hoisted the sail, and groped my way home, happy to see at last the anchored boats, the float, and the safe and familiar things.

More terrifying was the thunderstorm. I was exploring in the dunes that day, observing the heron rookery in the pine grove. There were hundreds of long-necked birds guarding their untidy nests of twigs in the trees, feeding their naked young. The ground was a litter of broken eggshells and fish bones. The stench was horrific, the scolding hoarse voices of the parents, constant and exciting.

The racket drowned out the ominous rumbling in the north. It was the change in the light to a greenish darkness that first attracted my attention. It was windless and sultry in the woods, but overhead the clouds were boiling in turmoil.

I jumped up and ran up dune and down dune for the safety of my boat, arriving with the first blasts of the thundersquall, the first cold pelting raindrops.

Hauling the dory to shallow water, fixing the anchor firmly in the sand, I crawled in underlie sail and lay there trembling. Around me all Hell broke loose. The squalls came screeching down the river, the rain beat on the canvas and poured through in chilling drops, the thunder followed hard on the heels of the lightning, deafening and incessant.

As quickly as it came, the storm was gone, growling away over Cape Ann and out to sea. In its wake came a light breeze out of the east, a fair wind home, and as I sailed along the shore, I heard the birds singing in the woods.

Arrived home, it was surprising to find everything just as usual, my grandmother shelling peas on the porch under the dripping linden tree. No one knew I had been out in the boat. I had started the day reading my book in the hayloft by the light of the cobwebbed window of the barn.

All very far away and long ago. The yellow dory has been many times reincarnated, finally into my pretty little red sloop that lies waiting at her mooring. I cannot move as briskly as once I could, but I can still sail away on a gentle breeze, enjoying the lovely familiar places, the islands, the malt marshes, the threading silver creeks, the shoal emerald wafers of Essex Bay.

In the seventh decade, who could ask for more: happy memories, a responsive little boat, the interwoven joy and sadness of a long life.

Welcome, summer, more than ever welcome because there may not be too many more left.

Summer Begins

It was more than a half century ago, how much more-never mind, that I clattered down the stairs of the city elementary schooling joined the under-the-breath chant, "Goodbye teacher, Goodbye school . . . ." It was not until we were out on the sidewalk that we finished the rhyme at the tops of our voices: "Goodbye . . . (here, add the name of an unpopular member of the administration) . . . danged old fool."

And so we were free, heading off our separate ways to home and summer, most of us not to meet again until autumn. I can still remember that feeling of heart bursting with joy, remember leaping and skipping swinging my books on their strap, *blam*, against the trees and mailboxes. By afternoon, I would be home in Ipswich.

In front of the house I could see the car, that great battleship of a thing as necessary to a doctor of the day as the bag of instruments and the head mirror with the hole in the middle. The "tonneau," as it was Frenchily called, was piled with boxes and my suitcase with room in the seat for me and Lassie, the Airedale, and the birdcage draped with a towel so that Fritz, the canary, would not take a chill. There was the usual crisis over the goldfish bowl, spilling already, but it had to go so that the goldfish could be released to freedom in Goodales' pond, where the descendants live there to this day.

And then without a backward look, we wheeled away, my father at the helm, everyone but me cross and tired already with a long, long ride ahead, through Charleston where the police were said to travel in threes, things were so rough, out Rutherford Avenue with its clots of horse-drawn drays and shouting drivers, and then finally to the Turnpike, dusty and unpaved, but running straight as a die, uphill and down dale to Ipswich.

As the car hummed along through open country, I sang along with it, strings of words or wordless notes all run together, a chant of joy unrolling out behind on the warm breeze, sweet with the breath of new leaves and June grass. The car labored up the steep grades of Witch Hill and River Hill and raced down the other side. Cattle grazed along Topsfield Road as we approached the town. There were the familiar steeples and roofs sheltering under Town Hill; and then we were rolling along Argilla Road to our old square house shaded under the elms and the giant linden, . . . home.

Grandmother came out onto the stone porch to greet us, her blue eyes smiling behind steel-rimmed glasses, fine white hair puffed out over a "rat," a wire and horsehair roll that I had seen sometimes on her bureau. Time only a quick kiss and a hug: there were things to do and see.

First, off with the shoes and socks, the grass cool and soft between the toes and the gravel on soles still tender from too many months in shoes. Lassie ran barking and leaping and chased Flyer, the cat, up the Porter apple tree by the kitchen door; this was ritual: they were best of friends. Then a quick visit to the pasture where the cows were already congregating around the barn door — I should be milking presently. Then to the barn where Sugar and old Billy, their day's work done, were in their stalls; they turned and stared and snorted — next time, I would bring them sugar lumps.

And, finally, to the linden tree, the great trunk rough and gray as I imagined an elephant's hide, the immense wide spreading branches muscled like giant arms. A myriad of leaves of freshest green, each one with its corresponding rootlet under the ground, Grandma said. I leaned against the rough bark of the trunk and thought of the other trunk, deep down there in the dark; I thought this must be how it was far down somewhere, almost to China: surely, the thread of root matched the highest twig and leaf.

It was a dizzying thought, like staring at the stars at night, trying to imagine that there were worlds with suns and moons, the book said, perhaps even with children such as myself on them. I preferred to think as I always had, that the sky was an immense blue curtain pricked all through with little holes that let through points of light from some immense fire, blazing and flickering away out there somewhere. Hell, perhaps, where naughty children were sure to go. But if that was Hell, where, then, was Heaven with all the tiresome good children…? Best not think about it, and surely no place could be as wonderful as right here under the linden tree in Ipswich.

And so, city-soft still, I reached for the remembered toehold and hand hold on the trunk and heaved myself onto the first spreading branch. From here, just as I remembered, it was almost like a ladder, branch following branch, a child's breadth apart, round and round like a circular staircase. I never liked to look down, so I went on up and up pausing only for breath and for holding on tight, then up again until the branches grew smaller, no thicker than my leg and closer together.

Suddenly, I burst through into the sunlight above the sea of leaves, and there was a whole circle of the summer world, the ocean, and on its horizon, a schooner, all sails set, beating around Cape Ann, heading to Gloucester or Boston.

I could see Hog Island, round as a pudding, bare of trees then, with the cattle looking no bigger than fleas. And there were all the veins and arteries of water between the new green of the marsh grass, along which I would be sailing in my yellow dory. I could see the sand dunes and the woods and, inland, the bare low hills and the wooded islands of the marsh.

How nice it would be to fly from treetop to treetop with the birds, or to wing from branch to branch by the tail, like a monkey, or to race up and down the trunk, like a squirrel, instead of having to climb foot by foot, hand by hand, like a child.

Asparagus on toast for supper, the southwester blowing softly from the marshes all night . . ., everything told me it was the beginning of summer, and nothing could be better.

Idle Hands

Another school year has ended, and the last day now, as when I was a child, is greeted with the traditional enthusiasm: ahead lie ten whole weeks with nothing to do. How great in prospect, but for most, how boring it will become.

"Satan finds work for idle hands to do," my grandmother used to say, looking at me severely through steel-rimmed glasses as I swung in the hammock, dreamily looking up at the knotholes in the porch ceiling while I pushed against the house wall with one leg to keep the hammock moving.

There was work to do for a child on a summer morning, cows to milk and turn out to pasture, eggs to gather in the henhouse, vegetables to pick, strawberries, currants, gooseberries, and blackberries ripening on the vine, each in its season. There was corn to hoe, the garden to weed, all sorts of tasks for a small child. And for an older child, there was driving the one-horse cultivator or the hay rake, or helping fork the hay up onto the wagon or higher up into the dusty loft of the barn.

Only when the day's tasks were done was there time to sail my boat, or if the tide was out, dig some clams, or row down to the spindle buoy at the Essex River mouth to catch a mess of cunners. These pleasures were earned when the chores were well done: sloppy work in the morning meant "do it over in the afternoon," and no amount of whining or fussing could change that. My grandmother worked, my father worked, and I was expected to work as well: on the farm, there was always plenty to do, and each child was to perform to the limit of his capacity.

Even though I was paid, my chores were not performed with enthusiasm. Other children received allowances, sometimes even a quarter a week without having to earn it. They could sail their boats when the tide was high in the morning. They could gather on the Townsends' porch and play 21, and they were asked, not ordered, to pick wild strawberries, so that their mother could make jam. They even could ride their bikes to the beach, stopping on the way to watch me work in the vegetable garden before continuing on their way.

I did not think it was fair and said so to my father. I remember well the occasion. I had skinned off, leaving my hoe in the furrow, and sailed my yellow dory into Essex Bay for a stolen day. I did not enjoy it all so much as it turned out. I quarreled with Charley Townsend, sailing in his *Peep*, the white sister to my dory. We whacked each other with oars, swore, and called names, until he finally sailed off and left me. At last, I came home, walking slowly up the driveway to where my father was sitting on the stone porch, lemonade in hand. He had heard of my defection when he returned from a hot hard day in Boston.

He began by telling me that I could not use my boat for a week, and when I began to argue, he warned that if I was fresh, it would be two weeks.

Trying not to cry, I said in a trembling voice that I did not think it was fair, none of the other kids had to work in the summer.

"Eddie Goodale's father doesn't make him work They have a man to do the chores. Charlesy's grandmother doesn't work. Ellen Sprague's mother gives each of the children a piece of candy after lunch. She gave me two pieces because she said I had to work so hard," I said.

I added that doctors made money enough so that their children should not have to work all summer.

My father was silent for so long that l began to be nervous. Finally, in quite a different voice, he said that what I said was true, and that unlike when he was a poor boy in Maine, my work was not a family necessity. He said, talking half to himself, that he supposed that my work was an artificial kind of thing.

"Then I don't have to do it anymore unless I want to?" I asked.

"Of course you have to do it. I won't have you growing up idle and useless. Now go right out, right now, and finish that row before supper; the hoe is right where you left it," he said, and I did, knowing that any further complaint was in vain.

Years later when we were pruning the apple orchard, we both remembered the conversation and laughed about it. He said that making me work was one of the hardest things he had to do, and I replied that I hated him for it at the time, but that I was glad that he had stuck to his guns, so that when life dealt me a few bad hands, I was able to cope.

I have never been sorry, and many times, all these years, the things I learned as a child have paid off, even to the extent of producing a peculiar sort of pride.

Unfortunately for today's kids, lawn mowers and boats are propelled by engines. Milk comes delivered in a bottle and vegetables are packed in cellophane. TV has supplanted books, and no one has to wash a kerosene lamp chimney, or trim the wick of a candle, or pump water from the well.

Labor has been saved, but what to do for the ten whole weeks when there is nothing to do but enjoy yourself? Even for children who want to work, there is little work to be done: machines do it all.

"Well, I suppose," Grandma said, "Satan finds work for idle hands to do."

In the Long, Lovely Days of Summer

When school was out, and there was no longer any common meeting ground for the young the kids of my generation had to seek their own fun or mischief. By today's standards, we were deprived, I guess, no TV, no radio, no planned amusements, playgrounds, Little League, no elaborate toys, trail bikes, or gasoline-powered Karts.

And sometimes I feel like a living archeological specimen, when I am asked, "What did you do in the summertime when you were a little girl? And did your family let you watch TV whenever you wanted to?" No TV? Incredible!

I was asked this question recently by an unknown child in the post office, that meeting place of Ipswich old and young, and really I hardly knew how to answer in any way that was comprehensible. So, casting about, I said, "Oh, I rode my bike a lot," and this seemed understood. Later, I saw the same child flying down Market Street on a ten-speed shiny wonder and recalled how my legs ached on the long hot ride from town on the heavy bike without gears. Well, it did have a coaster brake, 'though many did not. But it was hard pushing along the four miles of dusty road, even though there was only one little hill in the entire distance.

But later, I tried to think what I should have said and how I could have bridged the gap of a half century between a childhood before the first war and today with its fantastic abundance of "things."

I was not a deprived child. Money was hardly ever discussed, and I remember how awed I was when my father's secretary let slip the information that he was a very successful man with an income of $10,000 a year. I looked at him with a new respect, and the thought crossed my mind that it was very mean, that I had to earn my bike, hoeing corn and picking berries when my father was so rich.

My grandmother assured me that I would appreciate the bike more for having earned the money myself, that I would understand its value, and would be less likely to leave it lying outdoors in the rain to get all rusty. There was no truth to the theory, because I treasured my wagon with its wooden spokes and EXPRESS written in flowing gold letters on the side that I got for my birthday, and my sled with its fixed runners, painted green and gold that I was given for Christmas. And my yellow dory with its single sail, the greatest treasure of all. I could never have earned all the money it cost, $30.

The bike cost only $10, secondhand.

"You are a very lucky little girl," my grandmother reminded me, and when she said that when she was my age down in Maine, that all she had was a sewing box and a rag doll with a painted face, I thought I was at that.

The first weeks after leaving the city and school were spent in ritual observances, a sort of establishing continuity with all those other summers. There was the visit to the fallen hickory in the pasture on the edge of the marsh, carpeted all around with white violets, so much more rare and delicate than the purple ones. I lay in the soft mass beside the log and sniffed the unearthly fragrance of the tiny flowers.

Then there were hours spent in the barn and the henhouse and the brooder house, where my grandmother's chicks shrilled and shrilled till my ears rang with their crying even after I had gone outside into the sunshine.

The hay in the hayloft had shrunken down far below the cobwebbed window, and it was dry and dusty. It was not nice to lie and read there till the new crop was in, but there was a new calf in the box stall. He sucked my fingers and the hem of my dress before turning away to his mother. And the big workhorses, Billy and Sugar, the sweat of plowing was drying on their coats still shedding the long hairs of winter.

And finally, there was the first dizzy climb to the top of the linden tree, and, braced between the branches of the last fork, I looked out at the sea and saw far out beyond the Cape the sails of a Gloucesterman beating home.

It was only when all these things were done that I sought out my summer friends on the hill, Townsends' Hill, going first in my dory, tacking up the narrow reach against the summer southwester. I tied the dory between the Townsends' white *Peep* and the Taylors' black *Crow*. We would be racing later, and *Peep* too often won.

Then my bare feet found the remembered grassy path up the hill to the house, past the rows of sticks that Dr. Townsend called his "forest." They are big trees now. I could hear the voices of my friends on the porch and stopped, suddenly shy. Perhaps they would have forgotten me since last summer, perhaps they would not want to play with me anymore. There they all were, sitting around the table, playing 21. Bob Goodale and David Richardson, the older boys, were taller and longer-legged than I remembered, and when they spoke, their voices sounded funny. But all the others looked just the same. I lingered, hoping that they remembered that it was I who ferried all the flagstones for the roofs of our city, built in the shadow of the water tank, the previous summer, and that it was I who was allowed to sail to the gravelly island all by myself.

I hung silently at the foot of the steps while they played out their hand, and then Mrs. Townsend, her faded blonde hair in neat braids around her head, came out with a pitcher of lemonade and a plate of cookies, and said, "Why, here's Kitty Crockett back again, come up, child, come up and have some lemonade." And from Dr. Townsend sitting behind his beard and his book, there was a sound almost like a groan.

He did not like me very much, thought I was too fresh and wild. It was all a part of summer, the long lovely days that surely would never end.

A Native Knows About Greenheads

We were standing on a North Carolina beach — miles of white sand, curls of surf, and over the shoals, the water was emerald under the spring sun. Behind up there were salt marshes, acres and acres.

"It's a good thing you came now," the game warden said. "Later, there are these flies. They take a chunk right out of you when they bite. They have green heads."

"Yes," I said, "I know.

A native of Ipswich, born and raised on the fringes of the salt marshes, knows about greenheads.

When I was a child, there was nothing you could put on yourself for protection. In the early thirties, Union Carbide came out with some stuff called StaWay, God's gift to clammers, haymakers, corn hoers, vegetable pickers. But StaWay went to war and never came back. I do not know whether its basic ingredient found its way into any of the several sprays and lotions that work pretty well nowadays, but every inch has to be covered from hair to toe. A hungry greenhead on a muggy day can thrust his dagger through all but the heaviest clothing.

In the unprotected days of childhood, we suffered, man and beast alike. The horses and the cows stayed in their stalls, let out to graze only at night or on foggy days when the greenheads sulk among the salt grasses. The bathing suit hung dry on the line. The sails stayed furled, and the oar blades cracked in the sun. But the chores still had to be done, berries picked, the garden weeded, and in so far as was possible, these were carried out at dawn and dusk. To spare the horses and ourselves, we did the haying sometimes by the light of the full moon, that magic time of black and silver, black trees and shadows, silver fields, and flooded marshes at the time of the neap tide.

It was wonderful to be out so late when all the children were asleep in their beds, to go jolting up and down the field, riding the hayrack, gathering the new mown hay into long windrows. It smelt delicious, the driving grass, the spice of wild roses, the salt breeze from the marshes. The moonlight silvered the dappled coat of Sugar, the big gray horse, until he looked a ghost horse out of some old fairy tale. I loved it, haying at night. It almost made greenhead season worthwhile.

Greenheads were part of Ipswich summer. They came with the rain, went with the rain, we were told. A heavy thunderstorm or a high tide flooding the marshes brought them out in their millions. After ten days or two weeks of satisfying their blood hunger, they gradually tapered off, and if we were lucky enough to have a three-day northeaster, they vanished, leaving only a few stragglers to nip the unwary.

Creatures of salt water, they love salty skin, sweaty or wet from swimming. Sadistically, I used to try to punish them by drowning stunning them with a smart slap and holding them underwater for minutes at a time. No good. They were only strengthened and savaged by the experience, like Antaeus when he touched the earth.

It was not until after the war, when increasing numbers of "summer people" settled the former cow pasture of Great Neck, that it occurred to anyone that something might be done to rid the Ipswich world of greenheads. The magic potion DDT had been discovered, but Rachel Carson had not yet warned of its danger. Influential voices cried aloud to the legislature, and the State Reclamation Board sent scientists to make a study, which was always a first and sometimes a last step. The students did not get their feet wet or muddy. They patrolled the high marsh area along the edges of the upland, and discovering quantities of greenheads there, concluded that this was where they bred.

No problem, simply send a low-flying crop-duster plane with tanks of DDT to spread death to the flies.

Voices were raised in alarm: what about the clams, the fish, the birds? But we were assured that the spray would be just in this narrow belt and would be applied only at high tide when the flats were covered. However, the planes came when convenient, and the wind carried the spray, and the spray ran in the ditches, and it soon became apparent that all was not well with the clams. The clams lay sick on the surface of the mud, their necks lolling out of the shell, their bellies soft and watery. An immediate clamor from the clam towns along the coast brought an abrupt end to the spraying. Some people thought the greenheads had diminished, others felt that they had reached the end of their seasonal cycle; but, one thing was learned: no more spraying of the marshes, not now, not ever.

It was a young high school science teacher, Lawrence Ulrich, who about fifteen years ago made a serious study of greenheads and developed a safe and sane method of control. He discovered that they bred everywhere in the salt marshes, the larvae emerging from the mud, developing their wings and blood hunger in the grasses, and at the end of the season, laying their eggs to winter over for another crop.

He noted the greenheads' predilection for hot places, for instance a car parked in the sun, and desired a trap based on the same principle; these are those legged boxes that you see along the edges of the marsh in strategic places. Working with the mosquito control district with ever more and better traps, Ulrich has been responsible for the death of millions, billions of greenheads over the years. There may be trillions left but the optimists among us feel that there are really fewer than there used to be, and someday with patience, they may be gone.

I used to think it would be nice to live in a place where the tide never went out, and there were no greenheads. But no greenheads, more people? Perhaps they do us a favor after all.

Haying was a High Point

The moon was full, a summer moon red-gold above the flooded marshes and the fields. The air was sweet with the smell of new-mown hay: no perfume of Araby was ever sweeter, more nostalgic.

Haying was the high point of the farm summer of my childhood. With an expert eye my grandmother watched the ripening grasses, timothy, June grass, redtop. She watched the sky, hoping for a dry spell. She oversaw the preparations of the machinery, the mower with its steel wheels, the long cutter bar with razor sharp triangular teeth, the rake with its curved tines.

We never did have a tedder. I wished we did. I found it fascinating the kicking motion of this machine like a row of crickets, long legs tossing the drying grass. We did that work by hand with a three-tined pitchfork. And then there was the hay wagon, painted the traditional sky blue of course, the big wheels, freshly greased at the hubs, oozing waiting to smear the careless child.

I used to think the horses knew that haying time was approaching. Surely, General did, the wise old horse, a veteran like my father of the Spanish War. It must have been demeaning to him to haul a jolting clattering hay rake back and forth across the field.

I used to perch on the edge of his iron water trough in his stall, stoking his soft nose, and wishing he could tell of his adventurous days when the bugles blew and the flags fluttered in the wind. Although he never heard a shot fire in anger, to me he was a true war horse, related to the Civil War chargers, the cavalry steeds of the Indian Wars. Perhaps his remote ancestors had carried knights in armor, "pricking across the plain" with even a touch of Pegasus thrown in.

He was an old horse, yellow of tooth, sunken of eye, but he had spirit, and there was never a year when General did not run away with the hayrack as I clung to the reins and the jolting iron seat.

He stopped when he got ready, gasping and blowing, then meekly retraced his steps to complete the raked windrows, which in turn were cocked up into orderly rows of stacks when they were completely dry.

The final step in the hay making process was the gathering of the stacked hay into the wagon, hauling it to the barn, and forking it up into the haymow, clear up to the eaves where sweet and dry it would bring something of summer into winter.

Two stout horses, Billy and Sugar, hauled the wagon between the rows of cocks. I was not tall enough or strong enough to fork the hay up into the wagon; this was left to "hired men," Nova Scotians who told stories of life in the Maritimes, where, they said, the farms stretched away to the horizon and bordered on the sea. They taught me how to dance the Highland fling and sometimes said things I didn't understand but which made me uneasy.

My favorite job was to fork the hay evenly in the wagon, to trample it down, and spread it into the corners, higher and higher. To me, knee deep in the soft hay, the field, the men, the haycocks, all were dwarfed far down below. I was King of the Castle up there, never mind the blazing sun, the itchy hay seeds, and the sneezy pollen.

Then there was the sweaty ride back to the barn, and if the heat was blasting in the field, it was nothing compared to the suffocation of the hayloft where once again the hay was spread and trampled, on good years filling every inch clear up to the hand-hewn roof timbers.

This was how it was when all went well; however, it didn't always. There was the disaster of a three-day northeast rainstorm, when the hay was down but not cured. When finally the sun returned, the hay was black, rotten, useless. Or it showered on the cocks in the night, and in the morning they had to be spread once again to dry in the sun. Damp hay in a hot barn brought fire: "spontaneous combustion," my father said, and I rolled the words on my tongue.

Then there were the sultry days with thunder in the air. We hurried the wagon up and down the rows of cocks, while in the north, the thunderheads mounted: peaks, coils, turrets of cloud towards the zenith. In the windless quiet, no birds sang, but our voices sounded loud. "Giddap, horses, hurry, hurry, one more row and one more."

Then with the first breath of the thundersquall, we raced for the barn; some of the load spilled as we swung around, but no time for that. Lightning stitched the clouds, the thunder roared, the wagon rattled, the horses snorted, we shouted. The first cold drops fell as we reached the barn, but in time. As we forked up the hay, the rain splashed on the roof, lashed the puddles of the barnyard.

I watch the hay-making in today's shrunken fields, all very efficient, those cubes of packed hay, machine tied. But there is no haymow for a child to play, to tunnel out a cave, to fashion a sweet smelling couch under the window to read.

And vanished too, along with so many other childhood games: the forking down of a big pile from the haymow onto the barn floor, and then a breathtaking jump from a high rafter. The closest thing to flying, that free falling moment in the air.

"You'll break your neck" my grandmother said, but I didn't — and neither did she, when she was a little girl on the farm in Maine.

After a Bang-up Fourth, Quiet Summer Stars

"The Glorious Fourth" of my childhood was gunpowder, picnics on the grass, family gatherings, and home-churned strawberry ice cream after fresh salmon and peas from the garden. And for days afterward, there were black headlines in the papers detailing the holiday accidents, kids losing eyes, hands, and fingers from premature explosions of firecrackers, or rockets gone wild and snaking among the screaming crowds of spectators.

I am sorry to say that my family was among the "do gooders" who supported the banning of these lethal things, and I was allowed only a few sparklers to run around with on the night before, and a cap pistol, and some small torpedoes wrapped in bright paper and about the size of cherries that exploded on the stone porch with a little bang and a shower of pebbles.

But for weeks before, I had been saving my pennies, and by the time the Fourth arrived, I had quite a store, including several "cannon crackers," big fellers that could blow a child's hand off, strings of medium-sized firecrackers, devil red, and you lighted the fuse and to impress the observers, you held it as long as you dared before hurling the whole string snapping and banging its life away.

For weeks before the Fourth, the kids uptown had been celebrating and, lying in my bed four miles away, I could hear the explosions and thought how rich they must be to be able to afford so many cannon crackers and explosives of first magnitude.

My Airedale, "Lassie," did not share my enthusiasm and spent a miserable ten days cowering under my bed or under the car in the automobile house. Although she had a fierce bearded face and a bold and aggressive air, Lassie was afraid of thunder and firecrackers and was a very different dog from the proud creature who brought home the mangled remnants of a woodchuck almost as big as she was, and left it on the stone porch for our interest.

And so, after I had put on my little show on the stone porch and my mother and grandmother had obligingly squealed and covered their ears, I drifted away casually toward the barn, mounted my bike, and rode away.

The night before I had slipped out of the house with my box of treasures, the cherry bombs, cannon crackers, and firecrackers, and stashed them behind the stone wall under the pear tree. Now was the time to gather them up and pedal away to meet the other children down near Townsends' boathouse.

Fortunately, no grown-ups were attracted by the tremendous racket, and we younger children were delirious with delight at all the noise and the intoxicating smell of gunpowder smoke. All the while we were doing our thing, the older boys were preparing for the climax, the really big *bang*. First, a length of pipe was securely stoppered, then gunpowder was poured in and tamped down, and, finally, a long snake of fuse was unrolled in the grass. We all withdrew to a safe distance, as the fuse, sputtering burned its way toward the bomb. Sometimes, it went out midway and had to be relighted, a dangerous maneuver, or it kept burning but ever so slowly. It seemed an eternity of waiting.

Then, at last, the explosion, the pipe blown high in the air and such a bang as caused our ears to ring for hours afterward.

Surrounded by bits of uttered red paper, stunned by the sudden silence, we sat and looked at each other: it was over.

But, there was one more thing to come: the fireworks. The neighborhood families had been canvassed for contributions and enough was raised for a $100 set. The wooden box arrived by express from Boston, and wooden troughs for the rockets and stands for the "set pieces", pinwheels and flower pots, were constructed in the Robbins' field.

Neighborhood families and swarms of mosquitoes assembled simultaneously, and we waited and waited for it to grow dark.

The ladies sat sedately in a row enveloped in a cloud of citronella, the men fussed around the open wooden box, arguing about the order of the display, laying out the rockets, setting up the pinwheels, planting the Roman candles carefully pointed away from the crowd, and the children, wild with excitement and impatience, chased each other, waving sparklers, or fought and wrestled in the mass.

The sunset faded, the evening star popped out above the marsh, and the kids chorused "Star Light, Star Bright, first star seen tonight," and before we finished, *whoosh*, the first rocket. It roared skyward from its trough and exploded high overhead into showers of balls, blue, red, and green, and there was a tremendous bang followed by "aaaahhh" from the crowd. Then, there were the Roman candles, the balls popping out and floating away, and the pinwheels turning, turning, or spluttering motionless, and the flares set in the grass casting an unearthly light over all the eager faces. And finally, the last, the biggest rocket of all with successive explosions of balls and a tremendous series of *bang*s. The echoes rolled away across the marsh, and there in the suddenly quiet sky were all the stars of summer.

There was ice cream on the porch, and everyone said, "This year's were the best fireworks." Home in my bed, I dreamed of skies filled with colored lights.

Time has faded the brilliance of the fireworks, and the whole generation of parents has vanished from the scene. But to me, they live still in memory, and I see us all together for one moment in the light of the flares, before the darkness, and the stars.

Summer Birthday — An August Event

I was sorry for my friends who had their birthdays in the wintertime. A few of the most unfortunate were on a collision course with Christmas and felt sure they were gypped of presents. Even though some bore cards saying "Happy Birthday," and others said "Merry Christmas," the recipients knew they were being shortchanged. There was one unhappy boy born on Christmas morning whose parents named him. "Noel": what a name. He was a sullen type, and no wonder.

But my birthday came in high summer, this week, in fact, after the greenheads and before frost. A perfect time to have been born, to catch a first squalling breath upstairs in the old house, in the room with the yellow roses on the wallpaper.

People were not born in hospitals in those days. Dr. Townsend came with his black beard and worn bag of instruments, when he was called from down the road and did the honors. In spite of this intimate association, he did not have a sentimental attachment for me as I was growing up along with his children and others.

He told me once that he had found me under a cabbage leaf in the garden and that perhaps he should have looked further till he found a good little girl among the flowers.

I thought about this quite a bit and wondered if I had been left among the cabbages to be found by someone else, who I would have been. I disliked the thought of someone else, a flower child, probably with curly hair, sleeping in my bed, playing with my toys, or maybe cooing over a family of dolls, as nice lithe girls were supposed to do.

It made my head ache to think about such things, especially when I considered that if the doctor had looked around a bit, he might have found a baby boy there, and that would have been splendid, a different and more desirable me.

As a matter of fact, the following summer Dr. Townsend did find a baby boy, but it was not till years later that I knew the baby brother had died after only a few months of uncertain life. My parents were devastated by this tragedy and went away on a trip leaving me in grandma's care, but of course, I did not know about this either.

In all the years, this short-lived baby was never mentioned, and when I did finally learn of his brief existence, I indulged in the kind of fantasies that children use to explain things half understood. I imagined that this brother of mine had not really died, but had gone away somewhere to other parents and another home. I thought that he was looking for me to play with, that he was trying to find his way back to the old square house under the big elm trees. I fancied he would look enough like me so that I would recognize him, and I found myself watching for him in places where children gathered, at the park or at the circus.

Of course, he would not know anything being a year younger and all, but I would teach him how to row the yellow dory and we would go fishing for flounders or cunners down at the spindle buoy. It would be fine to have someone to talk to on these solitary excursions, someone to row the boat when I got tired. I tried a few times to ask my mother about this missing brother of mine, but she only looked very sad and changed the subject.

There was no connection between this spirit companion and my real brother born when I was six. It seems strange that I was taken unaware by such an unusual event, that I had no inkling particularly when I was familiar with the births of calves, pigs, puppies, kittens, and the emergence of chickens from eggs.

I can remember that I was playing with my express wagon on the grass on a hot July day with thunderheads in the west, when my father looking strangely excited, came out to tell me of the birth of a baby brother. Dr. Townsend sat down for a glass of iced tea before going home, and he told my father and grandmother that everything was just fine.

From upstairs came a hoarse squalling sound of protest, and when I was taken up to see the new arrival, he was unattractive, red-faced, toothless, with tiny knotted fists too small ever to row a boat or handle a fishing line.

By the time my second brother was born two years later, I was blasé about babies. What good are people six and four years old when one is already twelve?

The two little boys were close enough in age to have their own world of companionship, while I continued to be the same child that I had always been.

Gradually, the memory of my dream brother faded; but until he vanished, he used to return on my birthday, and I felt his silent presence on the birthday hayrides to the beach among all the crew of shouting children, and he sat with me on the bow of our motorboat, a place of honor for the birthday girl on the fishing trips to Grape Island and the Bluffs.

It is years since I have thought of him, and if I do so now, is it because he plans to return again this year? Why, he would be an old man, how strange.

Once on a Perfect Day in August

  Only a few times this summer has there been just the right combination of tide and wind and free hours that encouraged me to sail my little boat out through the Essex entrance to come ashore among the bars at the point of the beach. The tide runs strongly through the narrow gut between our beach and Wingaersheek, draining all the expanse of Essex Bay and the tidal rivers. Six hours out, six hours in, with a breather of slack water at tile high and the low.

  When there is any roll to the sea, it is an ugly place of running breakers, showing their fangs first as they meet the shoal water a half mile offshore, then racing in a smother of foam along both sides of the narrow channel to shatter on the beach and withdraw with a sigh and a swirl of sand.

  I was constantly warned as a child against the dangers of the Essex Entrance and forbidden to venture into the sea in my yellow dory, but once around the bend in the river and out of sight, who but the birds and the seals were to know where I went and what I did.

  Carrying my lunch pail, I set off in the early morning, tacking along the inner beach, helped by the outgoing tide. I used often to stop at the spindle buoy off Wingaersheek to fish for cunners, those bony, spiny little fish that lurked among the weed-grown chunks of granite.

  My lunch pail contained, besides the sandwiches of thick slices of homemade bread with meat from Sunday's roast, a thermos of sweet lemonade, a banana from the stem ripening in the cellar, or a handful of peaches from the orchard. There were a few kitchen matches in a watertight bottle; if it was a long day I might need them to make a fire and roast the cunners after the sandwiches were gone. Charred or half raw, they still tasted pretty good.

After the fishing, when the greedy cunners had consumed the last of my bait, I hauled anchor, hoisted the mildewed mainsail, and winging along on the last of the tide, I left the stone houses and the point of the beach behind me and headed out for open sea.

I did not venture very far offshore, but was content to thread my way among the channels between the drying bars. Leaving the dory high and dry, I gathered a few sea clams with my hands feeling for them just below the surface of my bare feet. Sea clams were greeted with enthusiasm at home and should have been an indication of where I had spent the day, but there were no questions asked or explanations given.

I never had a watch and only knew the time by the sun: noon — when I cast no shadow on the sand; afternoon — when the shadow pointed easterly. The red can buoy showed the change of the tide.

I watched it shift from the beach where I had gone to make my fire from dried poverty grass and pitch pine twigs, and as the green water came sliding over the bar to float the dory, I waded out, climbed aboard, and set sail for home.

The southwester had freshened in the afternoon, and the dory bowled briskly along, and even though I had to tack through the entrance and among the tiderips, the incoming tide pushed me along until I could ease the sheet, haul up the centerboard and start the long run home.

I have become more cautious in my old age, sad to say, and all those old warnings keep coming back to haunt me. Several times I have ventured around the bay side of the entrance, only to turn back, and continue my sail in the safer sheltered waters.

But there was this one day, this perfect August day, with tide and wind just right, the sun blazing down, the sea calm, with only a ripple along the fringes of the bars. This was the day, and so I headed out and ran for awhile along the beach.

It was midweek. There were few boats abroad and only a couple of people in the far distance walking on the sand. Almost the way it used to be for a little while.

I eased the boat ashore and sat still for awhile, the sail flapping idly while I ate my lunch, listened, and remembered.

The shorebirds, the plover and snipe and dainty sandpipers, had paused on their long migration and were running and crying and feeding along the edges of the tide. The last time I had seen and heard so many was on the black volcanic hand of an Iceland beach and the sound of their voices carried me back to Ipswich.

My husband used to say what all sailors know, that men of the sea when they die become seagulls and follow the big ship far onshore.

I should like to think that someday I too can become a bird of the beaches, a golden plover, perhaps, running daintily with wet feet along the edges of the waves, leaving a lacy fringe of tracks to wash away when the tide comes in, and crying with a sad little voice for all the good times gone, but still remembered.

Kitty, about 1938

BOATS

... It was Antaeus of old who gained strength from contact with the earth. But for me, it is a little boat, moving sweetly through the familiar waters, a white sail against a sky of puffy clouds and a brisk breeze from the east. ...

Sailboats

My little red sailboat, my treasure, is still in winter quarters upside down in the barn. Her scarlet topsides are dusty, and on her bottom, there are desiccated beards of weed and a skeletal barnacle or two left from last summer. But she is made of fiberglass, a marvelous material undreamed of in my childhood, and it will take only a minimum of elbow grease and no paint to ready her for another happy season on the creeks and rivers.

Everything about this little modern craft is so easy: the oval mast seems light as a feather, the nylon sheets and halyards show no sign of water, the dacron sail and jib — no sign of mildew; indeed, they never get really wet even in capsizes.

As I looked at her the other day, anticipating how soon we would be sailing, I thought of all my other boats and all the other summers of sailing, dating way back to when I used to go out with my father in a cranky overhauled catboat we had when I was a little girl. My father, a reckless enthusiast when it came to a sailboat, found me a most satisfactory companion because I had not sense enough to be frightened.

My grandmother annoyed him by keeping a death grip on the cockpit coaming till her knuckles were white and by clenching her teeth every time a cat's-paw laid the boat rail under. My mother had a habit of emitting muffled screams at tense moments and becoming totally paralyzed with fear. She had a terror of the water dating back to her childhood when the sinister Mississippi River, uneasily contained between levees of earth, flowed past the family plantation house at the level of the rooftop. One night the levee burst, and the rampaging yellow water scoured across the fields of rice and sugar cane, while the family sat on the roof waiting for rescue. This was the final ruin for the family, so no wonder she was frightened and did not want to venture even on the peaceful ripples of Essex Bay, except on those rare occasions when it could not be avoided.

But as for me, I had a passion for boats as far back as I can remember, back to when I was so small that I put my small brown paw on the tiller beside my father's hand and thought I was sailing.

We had the usual misadventures in the catboat: becalmed in an outgoing tide, stuck on mud banks, chewed by midges and greenheads, rained on in thundershowers, . . . but nothing dampened my enthusiasm or yearning for a boat of my own. Finally, the day came when I was about seven, when I was skipper of the yellow half dory, fourteen feet long with a centerboard and a leg o' mutton sail.

At first, I was allowed to sail only in Sprague's Cove by myself, which was a tiny body of water ankle-deep in mud at low tide. Then I was allowed out into the river, but always upstream, never down, until finally I could go downstream as far as Rocky Island. Once this far, who was to say that I didn't go further? — and so I did, at last around the corner of Hog Island, down onto the broad waters of Essex Bay. Thinking about it now, so many years later, I feel the lively ghost of the old thrill stirring within me, that marvelous sense of being as free as the wind, and I can hear in my inner ear the sound of the bow wave of that little boat.

My next vessel was a remarkable craft designed and built by the late Ed Norman, a house builder with a flair for the sea. Somewhere Ed had seen what used to be called a "punkinseed," a flat low freeboard sort of box, shaped like a flatiron and just about as handy. He made some adaptations of his own and sold the boat to my trusting father "as just the thing for Kitty, so safe."

I thought the boat was great; it even had a jib, and it leaked only a little bit, but safe, it was not, being a wild heavy thing not capsizable, but very sinkable. Running before the wind with all sail set, this crazy boat became a submarine, diving into the waves and seemingly never coming up. Still, she was mine. I was used to her cranky ways, and she was a lot more boat than the other children had, cursed as they were with nervous parents.

The other children, almost all of them older than I, were bitterly envious of my freedom to come and go on the water, and the parents complained to my father that their children were discontented with the safe life and wished to share the hazards with me. My father only laughed as I went my merry way on the long summer days, alone in my flatiron, pausing to eat my lunch on the beach, to take a swim, naked as a jaybird, all alone under the summer sky, not a soul in sight anywhere.

I was never lonely that I recall, blessed as I was with a rich imagination that peopled my world with pirates, sea captains, treasure seekers. The best days were those when I sailed out with the tide to spend the long day digging clams on the beach, cooking some over the fire and eating them half raw, bringing the rest home for the family. In the evening on a dying southwester, I floated home with the tide, reaching my mooring just as the first swarms of midges began their evening flight.

Best of all, as I came up the driveway, muddy, sunburned, and holding my basket of clams, was to see the family gathered on the stone porch and to find that no one, not even my mother, had been worried: after all, I could swim and I could walk — but fortunately, I had to do neither to get home.

Later, when I was about fourteen, I received a "real boat" for my birthday, a Manchester 15. After the flatiron, she seemed like a winged thing, fast as lightning her varnished mast so tall, her Marconi sail like a wing with a racing number on it. For years and years, I had that lovely boat, until finally, she collapsed and died of old age.

There were then long years when I had no time or money to sail. Imagine how happy I was to receive a lovely little sailboat as a present from my daughter on my 65th birthday.

Her name? *Medicare*, of course!

River Bottom

The little red sailboat moves delicately over the shoal water with hardly a ripple cranking from her bow. The water over the sandy bottom is emerald green clear, and four feet down below, the drowsy helmsman can see the undisturbed small creatures going about their business as the tide brings in a fresh supply of invisible plants and animals, plankton from the rich harvest of the sea.

The clams, which drew in their siphons and toed themselves down to the cool bottoms of their holes as the hot sun baked their flats, have opened their star-shaped mouths and are sucking in the clean water with its life-giving food. A hermit crab, fitting his soft body into a borrowed cockle shell, scurries across the flat, his tiny legs sending up spurts of sand like smoke. He is not afraid of the huge shadow of the sailboat looming like fate overhead, . . . a cloud shadow, a boat shadow, what difference in his watery world where the pursuit of food sends him racing this way and that, and where he can squat in his rented home, pulling in his claws, a motionless shell when an enemy approaches. He is safe at high tide. At low tide, when the hungry sea gulls gather on the flats, he can scoop out a little depression in the sand and sit there motionless, until the water again comes lapping over the sand, and the gulls move on.

A breath of breeze, like a cool hand, pushes the little red boat. The bow ripple spreads and whispers; the bottom moves by faster — a dark patch of mussels, a bit of green sea lettuce from which tiny and almost transparent shrimps dart out and bury themselves in the sand, a few waving stands of eelgrass. Once, there were forests of this stuff everywhere, as feed for the ducks, as a hiding place for eels, and as a spawning ground for fish. It was gathered and dried for insulating material, but this did not cause its disappearance. All the way down the coast, from Nova Scotia to Long Island, the eelgrass began to thin out and finally to vanish about thirty years ago. It has never returned. Why? Who knows. The creatures of the estuaries have now found other forage, and I watch them as I glide by.

There are three ways of seeing the world around us, of seeing the world of the sea where it meets the upland meadows and beginning forests and the sky overhead with its wheeling stars at night. There is the camera's eye, and there is the painter's eye, and there is the child's eye. The camera in the hand of an artist can catch so marvelously the color and can so freeze and pattern the perfection of detail that the painter has had to surrender his traditional arrangement of nature in favor of juxtaposition of line and color. What he used to say in one way, the camera can say better and so he has had to develop other languages.

But there are those of us fortunate enough to have been able to keep some memory of the world seen through the child's eye: the summer world observed so carefully by day and relived all over again just before dropping off to sleep on a warm night, when the southwest wind blew in the windows that overlooked the old lilac bush, the rough trunk of the great elm outside, the salt river where the sailing dory tugged at her moorings and the wide marsh beyond.

Under the sheets, the muscles of the child's legs relaxed, tired from the day of running barefoot through the hay stubble or over the thatch grass. It took weeks to harden feet that had been in school shoes all winter so that they could resist the marsh grasses sharp as swords. Arm and shoulder muscles ached from pulling the oars of the dory when the wind died and the tide ran out, and there were various twinges from clamshell cuts, blackberry vine scratches, and a poison ivy itch between fingers and toes.

The red sailboat, many removes from the yellow dory with her leg o'mutton sail, still carries me to the same places not too much changed in more than half a century, and I can, thank God, still see the familiar things with something of that long ago child's wonder and joy.

The multiple dusty rose flowers of the milkweed still tumble with honeybees; the blue chicory is lovely by the roadside, but it withers and fades in a vase in the house; the wild roses are charming as any garden flowers but, like the chicory, they belong by the stone wall or in an abandoned pasture.

I stopped the other day to scoop up a handful of wild strawberries and remembered how there used to be so many open fields that it was possible to pick enough wild strawberries for jam. It was the desire to please a beloved parent that led me every year to pick enough wild strawberries, a quart or two, for a shortcake. This was an all day job, considering that all of the smallest berries had to be eaten on the spot. On the porch under the linden tree, my father, tired from a day in the city, ate the rich concoction with an enjoyment that was my reward, and every year, he said, "This is the best wild strawberry shortcake I ever tasted, better than last year, even."

To hear this made it all worthwhile to have been bitten by mosquitoes and greenheads and midges during a long day, which of course included time out to watch an army of ants breaking camp among the grass stems, a safari which included a train of workers, each carrying a tiny white egg, flanked by warriors and ladies-in-waiting, and somewhere, perhaps, a queen — although I was never sure which one she was, or if she was there at all.

On berry picking days, the yellow dory strained at her mooring line like a dog anxious to go for a walk. When I knew how to swim and row and handle the single sheet, there were all the near and distant places to go. Essex Bay at high tide seemed like a vast ocean ringed by the hills of Essex and West Gloucester. The shoreline of the inside beach was deserted then, and children could anchor their boats, three identical dories — the yellow one, the black one, and the white one — and then swim or dig clams.

Venturing even further, a child could venture in the fast-running tide at the spindle in the Essex River mouth and catch a few cunners or flounders, or once, even a small tautog. We never heard of striped bass in my childhood — there must not have been any, or I am sure we would have known. On berry picking days, the yellow dory stayed at home in the cove, I hoped content with my promise for tomorrow.

The vast distances have shrunk. Motorboats line the inner beach shore, and hundreds of children play on the sand where a half dozen of us, at most, used to leave our footprints and our sand castles. Still, peering over the side of tile red sailboat, I can see the unchanged world of the river bottom — but it is startling to see reflected back an old face instead of the child's face that smiled back at me: jaundiced-colored in the mirror image of my dory.

Quietly, the Little Boat Slips Along . . .

If my little red sailboat were to be dignified with a port of call, it would have to be Essex.

At least when the wind blows from the north, and she swings to her mooring she rides in Essex waters. The meandering shallow channel of the Castle Neck River is the dividing line between the two towns that once were one. The clam flats across the channel, the broad marsh, Hog Island, Dean Island, and wide sound in between, all are in Essex. A cosmopolitan traveler, little *Medicare*, in one two-hour sail on Sunday afternoon, tacked and ran through the waters of three towns: Ipswich, Essex and along the southerly edge of Essex Bay in Gloucester.

How very little the lovely Essex shoreline has changed in the sixty years since I first sailed here with my father in our old catboat. The once grassy fields, kept open by grazing cattle, are now grown-up to woods, hickories and oaks and the planted evergreens of Hog Island, but so it was in Indian times, patches of Indian corn and woods. Thus, Champlain described it as he sailed along the coast.

I thought of the old catboat as I sailed along the familiar route on Sunday, the huge mainsail of canvas that had to be hoisted and dried after every rain to avoid mildew, the heavy gaff, the mast hoops that caught and bound as you raised the sail. She was an old boat when my father bought her, one of the bargains that he so eagerly pursued when it came to boats and horses; for an extravagantly generous man, it was such an odd remnant of a penurious childhood.

Nobody but me enjoyed going on those wild sails, too much wind, too much sail, the tide going out, or the flat calms with their swarms of greenheads and midges. First, my grandmother and then my mother were described disgustedly as "totally useless," and so as I grew big enough, I was the willing crew member, and they were happily left behind.

The catboat spent the winters upside down on the shore of the cove, and in the hot spring sun, the seams opened, the caulking spewed out, and my father and I spent hours with putty knife and paintbrush. We were a messy pair of painters with more on ourselves and our clothes than on the boat. There were brush marks and "holidays" in the white painted sides and the green bottom; but to us she looked fine.

Then there was the launching on the May flood tide, the shouts and cussing the pushing and hauling, till finally, she floated with the water gushing up through the open seams in spite of all our efforts with the putty knife.

Every year I was in despair, every year my father said, "She'll swell, you'll see," and so she did, until she hardly leaked at all, just enough to keep me busy with the bailing scoop. Friends and neighbors, lured by the promise of a sail, were enlisted to help step the heavy wooden mast. It and the boom and gaff and the sail, already mildewed, had spent the winter in the barn, where they lead been befouled by the droppings of bats and squirrels.

My father, too nearsighted to notice, did not observe this desecration till I pointed it out to him, and then he said, "The rain will wash it away," and so it did.

I used to sit on the wharf between sails, admiring the catboat riding at her mooring. To me, she was the most beautiful thing, a swan on the water; I saw her as kin to the Santa Maria, and like Columbus, we would rail in search of the Indies, or as kin to the Mayflower, in which we would find a new world.

Until I was old enough to have a boat of my own, I spent many hours on the wharf, lying flat on my stomach with my eye to a crack, watching the green water down below and the creatures of the deep going about their business. Schools of minnows darted in and out of eye range; cockles spread their skirts and traveled overdue mud. Horseshoe crabs lumbered past, and the clams opened their star-shaped siphons and fed undisturbed.

There is reassurance in these familiar things, so little changed in a changing world. In day-to-day life, change is invigorating but the still waters restore the soul. How quietly the little boat slips along, while the marsh birds, recognizing her as another winged thing, watch from along the borders of the cracks. The great blue heron, carrying his spear and striding on his stilts, gives only a glance from a yellow eye before continuing his search for minnows.

I miss the seals that used to be here in such numbers. Killed off by that stupid bounty, they have never returned. They had a roosting place on the rocky shore of the island, where, before anyone can remember now, someone built a little house of squared stones with a red-tiled roof. I have sheltered there in rain and thunder. I must land there again before summer turns to fall, I thought on Sunday, but the wind was too good, and so I kept sailing past the leaning piles of the old hay wharf on Hog Island, battered by so many winters of moving ice. There was more of it standing when we sailed by it in the catboat, and sometimes we tied up to it and fished for flounders.

Schooners sailed up to stand loaded up with Hog Island hay for the horses of Boston, my father said. I do not know whether he saw them or only that he heard. But he did see, and I also dimly remember, the gundalows, long barges that loaded up with salt hay and were poled through Fox Creek Canal and up to Ipswich town.

And finally, out into the broad wafers of Essex Bay, green over the shallows. To me, once it seemed vast as the ocean, and it was almost with disappointment that when I tipped over in my yellow dory I found myself standing on the sandy bottom, hardly waist-deep.

It was Antaeus of old who gained strength from contact with the earth. But for me, it is a little boat, moving sweetly through the familiar waters, a white sail against a sky of puffy clouds and a brisk breeze from the east.

Kelpie

From the beach the other day, I saw a fishing boat, a dragger, moving along the horizon like a bead on a string. She was too far away for me to recognize, but there was a time when the outlines of the vessels of the Gloucester inshore fleet were as familiar as the faces of old friends. That was when we fished in our *Kelpie*. Designed and built by my husband, she was started before the war and finished after. The sight of the dragger brought back to me a flood tide of memories of those happy days.

We shared the long hours, the often rough seas, the successes and the disappointments in a close companionship with the captains and crews of the Italian boats and also with the little clique of fishermen whose small draggers were moored cheek by jowl with us in Annisquam Harbor. It was a unique experience for me to be accepted at mug-ups on stormy days or at barroom tables on weigh-out and pay-off days, to be respected and kidded because I could do my share of work on the *Kelpie*. In my turn, I learned to respect and admire the men of the sea, particularly the Italians, descended from a long line of Mediterranean fishermen whose ancestors had worked the rough waters of that shallow sea back to Roman times.

Exhausted from long hours of backbreaking toil on the rolling deck of the *Kelpie*, in my uniform or smeared oilskins and scaly rubber boots, cutting fish in the keeler box while the sea gulls screamed incessantly, I used to pause to think how lucky I was and how for once my sex had not prevented me from doing something that I had always wanted to do: work, really work on the sea, to be part, really part of the life of the sea.

Those four years on the *Kelpie,* the bitter winters and the broiling hot summers, were the high point of a long working life, and I thought my heart would break when I saw the *Kelpie* sailing away, sold, with another hand on the wheel. My husband, used to the wide oceans and foreign harbors, did not share my enthusiasm for day after day going round and round in circles, dragging a net with chains and floats along the muddy bottom. The merchantman has traditionally held the fisherman in contempt, and the *Kelpie*'s narrow deck, slippery with gurry, was far different from the steel deck of the freighter, throbbing to the beat of a powerful engine.

Once the war was over, and the *Kelpie* completed and then launched at the Robinson Shipyard in Ipswich, we began fishing in the spring.

We were the greenest of greenhorns ever to sail out of Gloucester into the teeth of a spring nor'wester. No one else was so foolish as to put out that day, so we struggled alone to set the net and the wildly banging iron-shod doors that were supposed to ride alone the bottom and hold it open. The new winch stuck that first day, and we were able to get only about half the wire out with *Kelpie* rolling scuppers under by that time. We did not dare to try to haul it in again for fear that she would roll over altogether. So we dragged the whole tangled mess all the way from the tip of Cape Ann to a little bit of shelter just outside the breakers on Plum Island Beach, and there we hauled aboard the incredible snarl of new net, doors, wires, chains, and floats. It took hours of cussing and mashed fingers to get it all straight again.

Day after day, week after week, we struggled and caught nothing until finally we borrowed a set of doors from a sympathetic Italian. Immediately and magically, *Kelpie* began to fish, and from that time on, she caught her fair share.

The abundance of fish brought a whole new train of problems. Except for the flounders which we caught in the winter, the other fish — whiting, cod, and haddock — all required treatment before they were iced down in the hold. Here, again, we were clumsy: the only fish I had ever cleaned were the cunners and occasional mackerel I had caught as a child. There is a trick to it, and while we were never as skillful as the Italians, we learned. Everything, including setting the net, had to be learned from the ground up. Learn as you earn, and, at first, we did not earn very much for all the hours of work. But we had a wonderful little boat and a faithful diesel engine and good gear, so we managed.

The days were long, starting when we rolled out of bed just before dawn, and ending when we rolled in long after dark. The sky was growing bright as we headed out from Annisquam, and morning after morning we watched the sun rise from the sea, sometimes blood red and strangely distorted. The only rest we had was on the run out, about an hour, and during the first tow when there were no fish to cut.

Everything was in rhythm, the throb of the diesel, the trampling of the *Kelpie* through the waves, the setting of the net, the haul back, the cutting. Two days fishing and one day taking out, round and round, day after day, the only break in the pattern being when it was too rough to fish.

But it was never monotonous, to me at least. Every day, there was something different. A shark rubbing his blue back against the *Kelpie*'s blue side, and from my perch on the wire rail, I saw his cold eye looking up at me and his hungry mouth grinning, or a whale sounding, throwing his flukes in the air a quarter of a mile from where we fished — and then we saw the bubbles coming towards us. We wondered what would happen if he fouled the towing wires — he was longer than the *Kelpie* — but he slipped under us without touching and rose close aboard to blow . . . *whoosh*.

As we towed, we were watched by invisible gulls. When we stopped to haul back, there they were, converging upon us from all directions out of seeming nowhere: businesslike adults in their gray feathers and screaming, fighting youngsters in dirty brown. They perched on the keeler box, reaching down to grab a choice bit of liver. They brushed our faces with their wings and fought over the little fish that floated out through the meshes of the net. We learned that when exhausted by their screeching, we could obtain instant silence by hammering with a knife handle on the rail, and there would be a few welcome moments when we could hear once more the wash of the sea around the *Kelpie*'s bow and the whistle of the wind in the rigging.

And then there was the day when we saw a migration of porpoises, hundreds and hundreds of them, traveling from north to south on some mysterious errand, in groups of three's and six's, then ten's and thirty's, passing us all day long, moving swiftly and without effort through the oily calm sea.

There were stormy days, thundery sultry days, winter snow squalls, and, occasionally, the terrifying fog that left little *Kelpie* all alone in her little circle, her bit of world enclosed by the moving gray walls. Sometimes, it gives pleasure to remember even these things.

A Mad March Day off Gloucester

These are the "mad March days" that John Masefield wrote of describing the salt-caked little collier butting her way down the English channel. It was on a mad March day in 1946 that our *Kelpie*, the smallest commercial fishing boat in Gloucester, took to the sea for the first time. Before the oil smell of the new shipmate stove had blown away, *Kelpie* was pitching in the steep chop of the nor'wester sweeping down from the coast of Maine and dashing on the rocks of the Lanesville shore.

While the rest of the fleet were safe in harbor, the crews enjoying a mug-up or staggering from bar to bar along Gloucester's Main street, there was *Kelpie* all alone heading out toward a horizon sawtoothed with a running sea.

As we came abreast of Halibut Point, *Kelpie*'s captain, my husband, Bill, and his one woman crew looked at each other. Should we go on? Yes, we had waited long enough.

For the four years of the war, while Bill had sailed the wider and more dangerous oceans, *Kelpie*, framed of New Hampshire oak and half planked, waited in the barn. Then there were the months to finish her, watch her take her graceful shape, built like a little yacht, every fastening bored and plugged every narrow deck plank notched and fitted. Then there were the months when she lay at anchor in the Robinson Basin waiting for her gear — the gallows frame, the doors, the winch, the net with its chains and floats — and finally, at last, the engine, a navy generating diesel still in its crate when the war ended.

When finally she was ready to go, we could wait no longer, not even for the March nor'wester to give way to the soft airs of April.

During the years of war as Chief Mate in the merchant marine, Bill had lost his taste for boat building and never had thought much of fishing as a way of life. The enthusiasm was mine, and working on the assembly line in Sylvania, my mind was far away at sea, reliving the one day I had gone fishing with Bunt Davis out of 'Squam and picturing myself in oilskins and boots among the slithering fish on *Kelpie*'s heaving deck. Every day would be like the one of the *Ellen Jean*, smooth seas, plenty of fish, good company: what a wonderful way to earn a living. As for Bill, distracted and unsettled by the war, perhaps fishing would be as good a way of life as any other, although traditionally the merchant mariner and the fisherman have viewed each other, as I have said before, with distrust and contempt.

I could not foresee then that going fishing with one's wife would be a crowning humiliation, and Bill could not imagine how irritating it would be to him, hating every minute of the long days, to see me so much enjoying myself. He became ever more the dour Scot, grim and silent, while I disported myself in Gloucester, laughing and joking with the lumpers on the wharves, the men at the ice pier, and the kind Italians who called and waved to us and were always eager to help.

It's a wonder our marriage survived such a strain, but on the mad March day off Halibut Point, all this lay ahead. Also, I was miserable which helped.

I had emerged from the superheated factory only the week before with no time to become acclimated. The bitter wind penetrated oil-skins and sweaters. My feet froze in the new rubber boots, and my hands were numb in their soaking mittens. The spray blown from the wave tops burned my face as I fussed around on deck dreading the moment when I would set the net, my job, working the winch which I only understood in theory. I longed for the meager warmth of the Shipmate stove, but it was not to be. My place was on deck, said Captain Bligh.

Any people with any sense would not have tried to set a net on such a day, not for the first time anyway; but as the lights of Thatcher's lined up astern, and we knew we were where we wanted to be, neither of us would admit to the other our qualms, and so we went ahead anyway.

As Bill swung *Kelpie* broadside to the sea, and we paid out the new meshes of the net, the little boat rolled wildly, the doors slammed against the gallows frames, and balancing with difficulty on the wire rail, I released the winch as I had been taught and prepared to drop the iron-shod doors that hopefully would spread the wings of the net apart.

Unfortunately, the new winch did not run freely. The doors dropped unevenly, one over the other and instantly there was such a snarl of doors, wires, chains, meshes and floats as you can't imagine. It took an hour of cursing and heaving to get it all straightened out and back on board, during which I several times thought longingly of the warm factory and wondered what on earth I was doing.

During our struggles, the wind had picked up, but we had another go at it. This time things went better: the doors were launched properly, and the wires came ripping out off the drum, but halfway out, they would go no further.

By this time it was too rough to try to haul back so we fought our way all across the boiling bay to the lee of Plum Island Beach and there we hauled back without capsizing, although *Kelpie* rolled scuppers under at every wave. The net had never once touched bottom as it was supposed to do, but there among the twine was one lone codfish, a stray from some deep swimming school.

Our first fish! We took it home and ate it for supper.

Lying in bed warm and cozy as the March wind roared outside I remembered *Kelpie* and Bill and the years of fishing out of Gloucester. It was never an easy life, 'though never again as grim as that first day, but I knew, even bone-tired and covered with fish gurry, that the long days on the sea had become a part of me that would stay with me always, and so they have done.

Bill, do you remember, wherever you are?

...And Only We Who Were Lost

Dawn comes early these days, but often I am wakened at first light by the singing of the birds. They enjoy themselves in the twisted branches of the abandoned orchard or in the pines and firs planted long ago as a windbreak along the top of the hill to shelter the apple trees from the bitter north winds. There is nothing that makes you realize more the passing of time than to see a tree you planted as a child, now grown tall with a thick rough trunk and wide spreading branches.

The birds find forage and shelter here, and so they sing.

It was early the other morning that I opened a sleepy eye on a cloudless day; but an hour later when the alarm clock jangled me awake, it was to a different day, all blurred and softened by the fog that had moved in from the sea on a breath of east wind.

There have not been many foggy days this chill and rainy spring, and I welcomed this one, lying in my bed those few last precious moments, listening to the sound of little waves running on the distant bar and from far away, the voice of the fog horn at Thatcher's Island off the Cape Ann shore.

Once upon a time, we heard that horn blasting a warning to our little dragger, *Kelpie*, caught with her nets down when the fog bank that had been hanging all day onshore, suddenly moved in on all the Gloucester dragger fleet working the whiting grounds off the tip of the cape.

One by one, they disappeared, all those familiar outlines: the sober gray of the Yankee boats with their prosaic family names, and the Italian boats that ran to brighter colors and religious names. All that was left of them was their voices when the fog moved in a chorus of hoots and toots and wails and the thrumming of their diesels. As regular as the slow beating of a heart, the big diaphone horn of the rocky shore blasted out its raucous warning.

With a deathly chill, the fog enclosed *Kelpie* in a narrowing circle of gray sea. She added her voice to those of the others that sometimes sounded near, too near, and next time, faint and distant. The fog plays tricks on the ears and the eyes. Standing on the deck in already dripping oilskins, staring at the gray wall, I felt there to be shapes moving there, not the familiar outlines of the fishing boats, but something larger and more menacing: a big vessel moving down on us under sail.

Several times, I almost shouted a warning and tooted frantically on the horn until the vision dissolved like a dream, and there was only the soft moving wall of fog.

Or sometimes, I could swear I heard the sound of surf on rocks and even thought to see the smooth swells of deep water cresting as if to break. Before I could cry a warning it disappeared, and there was only the smooth sea lapping *Kelpie's* blue side, the spreading ripple from the bow, and the trawl wires cutting through the water as easily as a hot knife through butter.

It was only by watching the wires that I could be sure that we had not swung around and changed direction. Looking down from my accustomed perch on the deck leaning against the empty drums of the winch, I could see Bill's hand steady on the wheel, eyes fixed steadily ahead, and I was reassured.

There was a dour Scottish silence on the *Kelpie*. Bill's brother, Sandy, went out as crew once for about a week much to my dismay. At the end of the seven days, he came ashore for good.

"How do you stand it? He never said a word to me for fifteen hours!" Sandy said, as he walked up the Annisquam gangway with gear.

Looking at my husband's inscrutable face, I used to wonder what he was thinking. Remembering wider oceans and bigger ships perhaps, or the voices of old shipmates, or the bustle and clatter of exotic ports half the world away? Or perhaps, he was simply hating fishing, the long circling hours dragging the net over the bottom, *Kelpie* imprisoned by her own reason for being.

Sometimes as we floated, drifting as we cut the heads off thousands of silvery whiting I could hear with a touch of envy the voices from an Italian boat working nearby, the chattering and the laughter that continued dawn to dark and along the wharves and the ice pier in Gloucester. I made up for lost time then, joining in me fun, while Bill looked on sour and disapproving.

But in the long hours of silence, thoughts and perceptions were sharpened. Foggy days or fair days, there was an awareness: impressions and memories etched into my mind forever. Chattering I might have missed hearing the loon laughing wildly in the fog or seeing his black shape, larger than life, the snaky head and pointed beak. Or the cold green eye of the gull, keeping pace on long wings beside the slowly moving *Kelpie*, the greedy eye peering into the keeler box in the hopes of a bit of fish liver left over from the last tow.

Even when we completed our tow in the fog and swung broadside on, to haul back a net hopefully filled with fish, the gulls knew, and there they were in the hundreds, screaming and swooping, even before the meshes broke the surface. How did they know, how could they see the little blue boat all by herself in a forty-foot circle of gray sea, surrounded by the impenetrable and softly moving walls?

There were the porpoises, traveling in straight ranks on some mysterious journey, guided — how? — to their destination.

The birds of the air and the fish of the sea could find their ways. It was only we, the interlopers, who were lost.

Kelpie Proudly Continued on Course

In the spring of the year, the fish leave the sunless deeps of the ocean and move toward the shallows to spawn. Standing on the deck of the *Kelpie*, our little fishing dragger back in the forties, I used to picture the fish pouring up over the lip of the continental shelf like the spring flight of the birds overhead. There was plenty of time to ponder about these things, while sturdy *Kelpie* shuffled through the waves, dragging her load of gear along the bottom, iron-shod doors spreading the jaws of the cone-shaped net with all its paraphernalia of chains and floats. Leaning against the gallows frame during the hour-long tow, I used to watch the towing wires knifing through the clear water and the run of ripple along *Kelpie*'s blue side and picture in my mind all the swarming life of the sea bottom.

The fish in the ocean, the birds in the air, the mirror sea in the mornings, the running whitecaps as the breeze picked up in the afternoons . . . for a long time, it made me too sad to remember those things and those days.

But lately, now that it is spring again and I wake up early in the dawn as I used to do in those years when we went fishing out of Gloucester, I find myself remembering without too much pain. Not often do we appreciate at the moment that an experience is rare and special, it is only afterwards. But with fishing from our first voyage on that long ago March day, I realized that these days on the sea, the working-not-playing days, were something that I was beyond words lucky to be sharing even if for only a little while. It stretched out over four years, winter and summer as it happened, but for me, it never became monotonous.

I had to keep my joy to myself because my husband hated every minute, being used to the wide oceans and foreign harbors. He had the merchantman's contempt for the fisherman's sloppy ways, the rusty gear, the scales, and the dried bits of gut along the rail. *Kelpie* was all spit and polish, the winch and gallows frames red leaded. We never came into 'Squam Harbor at night without a good wash-down, followed by the reward of a can of beer that had been carried all day on the ice in the hold.

The fishermen used to laugh at our efforts to keep everything shipshape and Bristol fashion pointing out that the idea was to catch fish. But on take out days in Gloucester there was admiration in the friendly dark eyes of the Italian fishermen, and one captain of a big dragger confessed to me one day that he would happily dispose of his vessel with all her problems if he could have a little boat like *Kelpie*. He said that was how it was in Italy, all in the family, not usually the wives — they were too busy at home with the bambinos — but sons, brothers, uncles, two or three to a boat, setting out from Sicilian harbors into the stormy Mediterranean.

"In America it is different, all big Big boats, BIG money," he said. He walked slowly back along the wharf to his vessel, the Holy Family or Immaculate Conception or St. Joseph, it was one of those, and smiled and waved to me with my scrubbing brush and bucket, before he went aboard and below.

I was a sort of pet and a curiosity along the wharves of Gloucester, and I must say, I enjoyed it, not the tourists staring down from the wharves at this strange feature in scaly dungarees, but the fishermen, the lumpers on the wharves, the weigh-out men, the guys on the fuel oil boat, "Captain Dave," and on the ice pier.

"There you are, Captain," they said to Bill, and he didn't like it, although he would have been a captain himself if the war had lasted three months longer. He often thought of that three months for his captain's ticket and regretted that he had not remained to get it — war or no war. So, Bill had his reasons for disliking fishing, for him, fishing was demeaning. He was often grumpy while I was gay, and as you can imagine, this led to problems with two such different attitudes alone on the heaving deck of the *Kelpie* for all those hours and hours.

It was hard for Bill to unlearn the rules of the road and to realize that for the fisherman, the biggest boat always has the right of way.

There was the time off Provincetown when Bill challenged a big dragger and we had the right of way. We held our course, a collision course, and after one protest, I kept quiet, leaning on the gallows frame and watching as the two vessels, the big dragger and the little *Kelpie* came closer and closer together, each of us towing a net and moving slowly.

Seven or eight men lined the rail of the other boat. We could see the whites of their eyes. The captain in the pilothouse shouted something and gestured to us to give way. I can see Bill now at *Kelpie*'s wheel, eyes narrowed and jaw set grimly.

Suddenly, the captain of the big vessel spun the wheel and spat out the window, almost onto the deck of *Kelpie*, we were so close. A couple of crew members of the dragger laughed and one waved to me as Kelpie proudly continued on course, dragging her little net.

So Bill had his satisfactions, although they came less frequently than mine. That day off P-town was one he enjoyed and liked to remember, I am sure.

Can it be thirty years ago that *Kelpie* carried us out to the fishing grounds at dawn and back to port at night, day after day, around the clock of the seasons?

For me, *Kelpie* lives, and I remember.

Beware the Deep, Cooling Sea

Before I went fishing for a living aboard our little dragger, *Kelpie*, I used to think the place to be on a sultry August day was far out on the cool sea. That was before the tropical summer of 1946.

On the sweltering wharves of Gloucester, the crews of the draggers waiting for ice lounged in the bits of shade cast by the buildings and swapped tales of how the Gulf Stream must have shifted to bring close to shore schools of sharks, pilot fish, Portuguese men of war, and pogies, plus menhaden in countless thousands. Following them like the sea birds were the fishing boats from Virginia and the Carolina banks, and in the bars and along the wharves, the soft Southern drawl sounded strangely on the ear.

Even now after all the years, I dream sometimes of the sounds of Gloucester: the twang of Yankee speech, the Scottish burr of the Novies that they never lose, and the fluid Italian so softly spoken that it was hard to remember that the words and phrases learned there were not suitable for polite society. Then there was the squeal of the winches hoisting the scaly canvas buckets from the hold, loaded with the catch: cod, haddock, whiting, flatfish, and from the big vessels, the redfish caught far offshore on long voyages.

That warm day, the boats taking on ice lined up bow to stern at the ice pier. *Kelpie*, clean and tidy as a little yacht, was almost lost from view between two big Southern steel draggers, stinking with gurry in the hot sun. Twenty, thirty, forty tons of ice came roaring and rattling down the chute into their deep holds, and later, when it was our turn, the men on the ice pier laughed when "Captain Robertson of the *Kelpie*" held up two fingers, meaning two tons.

Bill hated to be called "Captain" Robertson, thinking of the remote gold-braided figures on the bridge of merchantmen. To him, it was a put-down, and it further soured him when I joked and laughed with the guys on the other boats or on the wharves. I was enjoying every minute: that was the difference.

Finally, the ice, steaming in the sultry air, was stowed aboard, the hatches battened down, and *Kelpie* headed along the familiar route to sea, under the lifted draw of the Blynman Bridge, while tourists peered down at the little blue boat with her neatly triced-up net; then under the railroad bridge with its surge of tide around the ice-scarred pilings, and along the meandering course past the granite monuments marking the channel. Big rich mussels grew on these, and sometimes we could stop at low tide, so that I could scrape off a few.

At length, the white dunes of Wingaersheek came into view, and beyond, the sea. Past the lighthouse, skirting the bar where even on the calmest days there was a ruffle or surf, along the Lanesville shore with its scores of lobster pot buoys; red and yellow, green and blue, each fisherman had his own distinctive color, and the land fell away astern. Ahead was the hazy sea, no sharp-ruled horizon line, the sea and sky were blended; behind us, the featureless land was only a darker blue.

And it was hot, the sun, like a brass plate slightly tarnished, blazed in the sky. The sea was oily smooth; the only air was the little breeze stirred by *Kelpie*'s passage. Unable to get a fix on the landmarks, Thatcher's twin lights, we ran by the clock and the compass.

When at last we stopped to set the net, the heat slapped us. *Kelpie* bowed to her reflection in the water, smooth as a looking glass. The beating heart of the diesel was the only sound, until the net with its chains and floats and the iron-shod doors splashed over side, and the winch began its squealing complaint as the trawl wires spun off the drums.

During the first tow, before there were any fish to cut, there was an hour of delicious idleness with only *Kelpie* working away, towing her heavy burden along the bottom where we hoped schools of fish were swimming. Peering down into the water where the sun's rays focused and got lost, I thought longingly of slipping over the side, towing slowly with a hand on the wires. Oh, to get out of scaly dungarees and crusty shirt, I thought, to feel the cool water on my skin. I kicked off my rubber boots and felt the smooth planks of the deck under my bare feet.

The water gurgling out of the wash-down hose was warm as soup. The Labrador current had gone down deep that day, and over it the water spread, warmed by the sun of that long ago hot summer. Bill dozed, hat over eyes, but hand still on the wheel. With any change in the rhythm of the engine, he would have been wide awake.

I hesitated, like a kid on a springboard, then climbed over the wire rail and was standing poised to dive, when I saw something moving deep down in the water. At first I thought it was *Kelpie*'s shadow or a trick of the light, but I drew back, my dive postponed.

Slowly in the green water, the long body, the pointed dorsal fin, the powerful tail took shape. A monster shark slid towards the surface, close enough to brush *Kelpie*'s side.

Paralyzed with fear, I stared down at it. I could see the cold green eye, and then in one smooth motion, he turned on his side, and the white-lipped mouth grinned up at me.

I scrambled back on deck, no swim that day. No, not ever, in the deep, cooling sea.

October Tides

The October full moon and the flooding high tide running deep over the golden marshes mark for us waterside folk the end of the boating season. This has always been the time to haul the floats and the boats, to raise and float ashore the moorings from their muddy beds.

For the months ahead, the river will be empty of man-made wings and open only to the rafts of black ducks resting and feeding in sheltered water, while breakers run and roar on the bars, or open only to the Canada geese pausing on their flight south.

Last year, I saw them in their thousands on the broad marsh and heard them gabbling and chuckling together. I wished I had my sailboat still in the water, so that I could sail up close to these noble birds. The wild things do not fear a sailboat, recognizing it as a child of the wind like themselves.

September is too soon, November is too late, and often by Thanksgiving time, there is a skim of ice on the river, sharp and clear as a sheet of glass. So, it must be October and the neap tide for the pull-out.

Before the days of trailers and such conveniences, the hauling out of the boats was a neighborhood undertaking, like a barn raising, and only the smallest boats were light enough to be taken to the shelter of the shed. The big boats were hauled up out of reach of the winter tides and turned over with much grunting and cussing.

Most of my boats were no longer young. If the yellow dory was ever new, I don't remember it. My father's racing catboat, that wild and crazy thing, had seams that opened as wide as a child's finger every spring. It took a week for her to swell tight as a bottle after the first agonizing moment when the water poured through the open seams in spite of all our efforts with stranded cotton and putty. When we had the catboat, I was so little and my interest span so short that I spent most of the time playing with the putty, rolling it into little balls or worms or snakes, trying to make a dog's head or a horse's.

Then there was my little "flatiron," cross planked. She always leaked, try as I would to make her tight. Seeing her half filled with water in midsummer, her creator, Ed Norman, remarked, "She does leak enough to keep her sweet, I guess."

My Manchester 15, well, come to think of it, she was new, a glorious present on a long ago birthday. I wonder if she really sailed as fast or as sensitively as I remember, her with her high mainsail and sharply cut jib. Since I was used to clumsy homemade jobs, I flipped her over in my first sail.

Even as I went down with her, I remember wondering, agonized, whether she would be taken away until I was more capable. When my horse, Hardy, threw me a half dozen times on our first ride, there was no one there to see; after climbing back over and over again in tears of frustration, the little horse tried no more tricks and I came riding home in triumph. I had the Manchester until she rotted and fell apart and Hardy until he went tragically lame.

The little horse was unable to bear even my light weight on his back, and so for days and weeks, we walked around and around the pasture, he limping and I leading, hoping that tomorrow he would be better, would lift his hanging head and show once more his old gay spirit. One day I came to the stall to find him gone, I never asked where, but still I can remember the tears running down to my ears as I lay in my bed at night.

I had grown up and gone away, leaving the fifteen-footer to lie in the hot sun all one summer; when I returned for a visit, the grass had grown up through the seams, the bright varnish had grayed. She would never sail again, and I knew at that moment that I would never be a carefree child again either.

It was years later that I saw in Essex an old Manchester 15, sadly neglected and forlorn, and knew that I must have her. I bought her for $25.00 (that I could ill afford) and set her mildewed sails and sailed her home. Old and leaky as she was, she had the same spirit as my former boat, and for two years, with bailing bucket always handy, we sailed in all the familiar places — Essex Bay, around Hog Island, through Conomo Gut, and up to Hardy's Landing in Essex.

I always think how lucky I am to have once more a sailboat, to be able to fly with the wind, or to drift with the light airs, looking down through the green clear water at the clam holes and the scurrying hermit crabs, or even when I am particularly lucky, to see a small flounder kicking up a puff of sand.

And so, each year when *Medicare*, my new boat, comes out of the water, it will be just till another spring, another full moon, and another floating tide.

Medicare, sailing on the Castle Neck River

AUTUMN

... In the autumn of life and the autumn of the year, I start remembering, particularly because I still live in the same place where so much, yet so little, is changed. The trees have taken over the once bare fields, cars speed over the road where I rode my horse or pedaled my bike, the tires leaving a wavering track in the soft dust. ...

Sailing Days Dwindle Down

The high tides of Autumn creep between the golden stems of the salt grass. Gone are the summer's gentle breezes. The red sailboat swings and dances at her mooring, bouncing on waves that running against the tide have fierce little crests of foam. The summer river, so gently blue, has turned harsh, glittering like polished steel under the wind.

There are only a few more sailing days left. The sun has lost its power. Twilight casts an early shadow across the marshes, and even under the Indian summer sun, there is a chill, a foreboding of the days when the first ice rims the creeks and all the little boats are snug in winter quarters.

Goodbye summer, goodbye sailing, till spring come back again, and *Medicare* fresh in new paint and varnish takes to the waters once more.

It is a sad time, this golden October, in spite of all its beauty of glowing leaves and brilliant skies and the bright cold circle of the hunter's moon.

I always felt it to be so, even when I was a child, and not only because it meant the prison brick walls of the city and the confinement of the school room. Every Friday night while my grandmother was alive, I came home to Ipswich on the train, but I came as a visitor, my feet already softening in city shoes. I felt that my friend the cow had forgotten me. Why else did she place her cloven hoof in the bucket when I went to milk her, as I had every night of the long summer?

My summer comrades were no longer to be found. They were not so lucky as to have a grandma and a home in Ipswich.

Even scuffing in the fallen leaves under the hickory tree and competing with the squirrels for the hard-shelled little nuts, I was sad.

The tomato vines were black and frosted, hanging limp on their wires with only a few green fruits that had come to nothing. There were left in Grandma's garden only the parsnips and carrots and a few bloated beets, and soon they too would join the cabbages in the boxes of sand in the cellar. Even while I did my summer chore of hoeing, I enjoyed the neat rows of beans and peas and spinach, the squashes golden and green, and the feathery rows of asparagus left to grow, and to strengthen those fat green spears that we would cut in spring.

Crunching on a windfall Baldwin that I had found in the rank grass under the tree, I wandered down to where the yellow dory lay upside down on the bank and sat on it, disconsolate.

I was, I suppose, in a sort of limbo, midway between the city and the country and part of neither.

It was only when the low sun signaled the evening chores, and the cows waited in the barnyard, and the hens had gone to roost, that I cheered up a little bit. I always found solace with the animals in the barn and ran to them for comfort when I had been naughty and punished. There they all were, those familiar friends, Billy and Sugar, the big farm horses, and the cows breathing in long sighs in their stanchions, and a silly calf or two, bucking and kicking in the box stall, showing off as I peered in.

And it was nice in the evening after supper, cracking the hickory nuts on the bricks of the hearth and handing the largest meats up to Grandma and eating the crumbs myself. The fire crackled, the wind roared in the chimney, and every now and then a spark caught the soot on the old bricks, and for an instant there was a march of glowing particles, "soldiers" my grandmother called them.

Saturday night was bath night, and so, before bedtime, the round tin tub was placed beside the kitchen stove, filled with hot water from the tank with a dipper, and I soaped and splashed.

When Flyer, the cat, came carelessly too close, I grabbed him and pulled him in to share my bath. He squalled and raked my legs with his claws and ran under the stove to sulk.

"There now," said Grandma, seeing me bleeding. "It serves you right. Cats hate the water."

"But they can swim," I said. "When I took Flyer out rowing, he jumped overboard and swam ashore."

I did not want to think of Flyer in the boat. It reminded me of summer.

Lying in my bed beside the window while the hunter's moon, lopsided now and past the full, silvered the last leaves of the hawthorn outside, I felt the October sadness, year's end, life's end. Soon would come the snow to cover it all, the stalks of summer flowers and the summer dreams.

But the red sailboat still lies at her mooring in the river. "Please, October, one more Indian summer day, one last sail."

Initials

Long ago, when I was a child in school, we used to memorize and recite what passed for poetry in those days: the rhyming verse of Tennyson and John Greenleaf Whittier were fine for little folks. Although our teachers occasionally tried to encourage us to do it — "Once again, with feeling" — too often we droned out our assignments, tapping a foot on the floor in time with the meter. We learned our lessons well, however, and still, after all these years, I can recite most of "Snowbound," and often on the sunny days after a winter blizzard, I find the words coming to mind as I look out the window on a new bright world.

A favorite of generations of old-time teachers was "October's Bright Blue Weather." It was a good one to begin with, easy to learn, and appropriate to the days soon after the start of school, or so we thought. But I, chained to my desk after a free summer outdoors, resented the poem and thought very silly the poetess, Helen Hunt Jackson, who was willing to trade June for October.

Sitting in my hard chair anchored to the floor, I thought it very sad to see the bright leaves falling through the windless air. Soon, it would be snowflakes sifting down, but even the excitement of a blizzard could not compensate for the lost summer, for my boat and the happy days running the marshes, and fields barefoot in the summer sun.

As a reminder, I used to carry my jackknife in the pocket of my school dress, along with an always grimy handkerchief. I found its rough handle comforting, and during bored or pensive moments in school, I used to get it out and furtively begin carving my initials, KG, in the wooden desk top along with those of generations of boys, grown up and gone.

I have always been grateful to my parents for not trying to force me into a feminine mold too soon, for not making me feel odd because I treasured my jackknife, my baseball bat and glove, and for allowing me my little stable of animals. The boys accepted me as I was, because I could run as fast and throw a ball as well as they. The girls with their doll buggies were aloof with me, but then so was I with them: I didn't need them!

A boy I knew on the next block in Boston, named Kinnicut (poor thing), was prevailed upon to keep a shirt and a pair of knickers for me, which I wore to play football or baseball or prisoner's base or stealing eggs in the afternoon: a strange sight, pigtails flying. I always changed back in the furnace room at Kinnicut's house before going home, dirty, hot, and disheveled — but at least properly dressed.

Even in Ipswich, I could only wear bloomers or blue cotton as a concession to the country, decently full and unrevealing from waist to knee; above was a middy blouse with a blue sailor collar. With bare feet, I managed quite well, but it was not like shorts or sawed-off dungarees, no indeed. Dungarees were unheard of; the nearest thing was overalls with a bib: blue for farmers, white for painters and carpenters — not the same as jeans at all.

When the boys outgrew me, I spent some solitary years and often felt I didn't fit in anywhere, but I learned to get along quite happily, a lesson that has since stood me in good stead.

As a little child, I had none of these anxieties and went about with my jackknife carving K.C. on the rails of the Canal Bridge, the side of the barn, the telephone poles, the blades of my oars, but never, I am happy to say, in the bark of trees and never in writing with paint on rocks. It gave me quite a sad feeling of the passage of time, a few years back, when I was rummaging for something in the barn loft and came upon K.C. still readable on one of the old beams, though covered with dust.

It must be the feeling of time passing that makes October a sad month: the rapidly shortening days, the weakening sun as the earth tips to the north. There is a sense of urgency, like tide or life running out: so many things to do before winter, before death.

Even in my childhood, there was something left of the pioneer's effort to prepare for the long cold months ahead when the ground was iron hard and no longer produced food for the family. There were the apples to pick and sort over into barrels and to be stored in the cellar. The Rhode Island Greenings came from the tree with the short thick trunk and the low branches almost sweeping the ground; these were the pie apples with rich granular juicy flesh — good through Thanksgiving. There were the Baldwins, red and firm, and the crimson-streaked Northern Spies which lasted into January. Last were the Russets, wrinkled but still quite tasty into April. There were potatoes to dig and trundle down to the cellar. The last of the tomatoes were brought into the house to ripen in a sunny window, and the grapes were stripped from the old vine whose trunk was as thick as a child's leg.

Then came the morning of the black frost. All Grandma's flowers hung their heads, their frozen leaves felt stiff and metallic to the touch; but when the sun touched them, suddenly they were rotten and without life. It did not console me to be reminded that they would all come up again in the spring, as good as new. Spring seemed a long way off. . ., and what if some year they did not.

They might be dead like Mr. Brown from Castle Hill Farm, who always drove by our house every afternoon in his shiny carriage with the two matched chestnut horses, and who never failed to wave to me.

One day he didn't appear.

"Where is he?"

"Dead," said my grandmother.

Dead like old Nixie, the dog, who one morning did not get out of his basket, and when I touched him, he was stiff and cold. Dead like the pigs, who were frolicking in their pen under the oak tree when we went off for a picnic, and when we came back, they were hanging in the barn, all pink with their bellies slit and propped open with sticks of wood.

It did no good for my grandmother to tell me that Mr. Brown was not dead like that: instead, he had gone to heaven. I did not argue, but I knew that Mr. Brown was somewhere in the ground, like Nixie, and I cried and cried in the hayloft and wondered who was feeding his horses.

But I got out my jackknife and, still sniffling, began carefully carving KG on a beam until I felt better.

"October's Bright Blue Weather...." Indeed, the woman who wrote that poem knew nothing of life and death, not even as much as children know.

Another October coming? Now, where's my jackknife?

A Time for Apple Picking

The October breeze that filters through the window where I sleep is spicy with the smell of fallen Baldwin apples from the tree outside. Warm in my bed in the early dark before the jangling alarm clock signals another day, I sniff the fragrance carried on the salty east wind, and I remember.

There is nothing like a smell to trigger memory. Roses, long stemmed and overbred in the winter greenhouse, recall the wild roses that fringed the Argilla Road of my childhood, where my bike tracks left a wavering furrow in the dust. Wild roses signalled June, the beginning of the long Ipswich summer. The apples speak to me of other autumns and the fun and laughter of the family harvest from the row of ancient trees beside the ban.

The trees are long gone now, fallen one by one in winter gales or summer thundersqualls, the branches brittle with age, the trunks hollow and channeled with the burrows of carpenter ants. But for more than a century, these trees, planted when the house and barn were built almost 200 years ago, were harvested.

The trees were so high that it took an extension ladder to reach the topmost branches. It was my father's job, assisted sometimes by neighborhood men and boys, to climb the ladder with a bushel basket that hung from an S-hook from the highest rungs and to pick the reddest apples from branches bathed in sunlight all summer long. With a smaller basket, hanging from a cord around my neck, I scrambled among the high branches, gathering the apples that the ladder would not reach, running along the branches like a squirrel I knew every hand and foothold from a summer of climbing.

The trees were my refuge. I hid among the leaves after I had been punished for some childish sin or other. People came calling for me at dinnertime, but motionless upon my high perch, I did not answer, enjoying the sound of desperation in my mother's voice, or thinking how funny my grandmother's sunbonnet looked when seen from high above. It pleased me to think how worried they must be, sitting around the dining room table where my chair was empty and the napkin still in its silver ring. I was quite disappointed when finally driven down by the pangs of hunger, I found that they had eaten up everything with good appetite. If they had been really worried about me, I thought angrily, they would have left me more than a small saucer of peas and a half dozen strawberries from the garden.

I knew my way around the trees, which branches would bear my weight and which would bend and crack, and the comfortable crotches where I could curl up with my book and read and dream away the long summer afternoons.

The knowledge stood me in good stead come harvest time, when I ran up and down with my little basket, adding the contents to the growing pile on the grass.

My mother and my grandmother, seated on a blanket, sorted the fruit: the sound, firm apples for the barrels in the cellar, and the flawed ones for applesauce or jelly or cider. It was a ritual, like picking the currants and the gooseberries, the strawberries and the raspberries, or trailing after my grandmother through the asparagus bed to spot with sharp eyes the first green spears pushing up through the black earth.

The Baldwin tree outside my window is second generation planted by my father. A chill 19th of April holiday was tree planting time, and there was still a trace of snow in the holes dug the previous autumn. It seemed hard to imagine that the little whips, their roots swathed in burlap, would ever grow to a size that would hide a child in the high branches. Trundled out to the orchard in the wheelbarrow, set in the holes, the earth filled in with chilled fingers and stamped down around the tiny trunks. I felt a twinge of sadness when my father said that the trees would be here long after we had gone.

Who would be climbing in the high branches? Who would harvest the crops, the red Baldwins, the smooth-skinned Greenings, the striped Northern Spies, the golden Russets so crisp and tasty from the barrel in February? It made me dizzy to think of all this, like looking up at the night sky and trying to understand other worlds and suns and perhaps even people way out there.

As I lay in my bed in the dark of the early morning, I heard an apple fall from the tree, already past its prime, but still able to produce its crop of bright fruit, still able to fling garlands of pink flowers into the soft spring sky.

Rooted in the past and the future, the tree still bears its harvest of memories, sharing with me so long as we both shall live.

Autumn

The earth turns its northern cheek away from the sun. The nights grow short and cold. The owl cries on the hill. The fox barks at night, and the song of the cricket slows and slows to eventual silence. No amount of bright days and nights of brilliant stars can mask the season of approaching death.

Even when I was a child I thought of autumn as a sad time. I had to crowd my toes into shoes after a summer of freedom, my lanky frame into a school dress of Anderson gingham or some dull brown or blue stuff, smocked in the hopes of giving me a "figure" — a horrid, embarrassing thought. Even in my ignorance, I sensed that having what was also called a "shape" would lead to all sorts of complications and eventually to that undesirable condition known as being grown up.

These dismal thoughts always seemed to occur in the autumn before the first snow shrouded the corpse of another summer. The ghosts of these old apprehensions still rise to haunt me when the leaves blaze and fall, and the gray clouds come smoking in from the north.

Not all the childhood autumn days were sad. I could forget my troubles here at the farm when we picked apples from the old trees, and I could go searching for the hickory nuts that had burst from their green leathery cases. I wondered how the squirrels managed to crack open those golden shells, so hard that it took all my effort with a hammer on a brick hearth to expose the tiny little meats which had to be picked out with a pin.

My grandmother sat in her rocking chair beside the kerosene lamp, engaged in that endless needlework — centerpieces, doilies, little mats — some of which I have to this day. She tried to teach me how, but I was too restless and clumsy-fingered. Finally, she gave up, 'though she never called me "unladylike" or "tomboy" because I preferred to run through the fields barefoot, or fool around with my boat, or play with the animals in the barn.

I would pick the fox grapes, the barberries in the pasture, the yellow Porter apples from the tree by the kitchen, and would help make the jelly: green mint, yellow apple, golden quince, scarlet barberry or purple grape. The kitchen then would smell so delicious, and the jars glowing like jewels on the windowsill were so pretty. We had jelly on our breakfast toast all the years round. When the seven o'clock factory whistle blew in Boston while we sat at the table in winter, I tasted Ipswich with every bite.

After more than sixty years now, I can remember how Grandma looked in her chair under the lamp, but I can't remember what we talked about. Probably I babbled on and on about what I had been doing or would do. I remember her as being "down Maine silent," smiling, listening, occasionally telling stories, the ever fascinating "When I was a little girl . . . ." When I was naughty and had been punished, I rushed up the front stairs to Grandma's room, the room with the yellow roses on the wallpaper, and flung myself down and cried, or hammered my heels on the straw matting in frustration and rage.

Grandma never said anything, but after I had cried myself out, she would take me in her lap in the rocking chair and hold me tight as she rocked. The rocking chair squeaked, a log in the fireplace fell into the ashes, the elm branches tapped against the window. I don't remember that we ever talked. She did not ask me what I had done to be punished, and I did not tell her how I hated my father or my mother or my teacher or whomever it was who had punished me "for my own good."

In the autumn of life and the autumn of the year, I start remembering, particularly because I still live in the same place where so much, yet so little, is changed. The trees have taken over the once bare fields, cars speed over the road where I rode my horse or pedaled my bike, the tires leaving a wavering track in the soft dust.

If all the miles I have traveled on the Argilla Road, leaving foot tracks, bike tracks, horse tracks, and tire tracks were laid end to end, they would reach around the world, I imagine, to Hong Kong and the

Spice Islands of the mysterious East, to Siberia and Lapland, and even to the countries blazing under the equatorial sun.

I traveled to many countries as a child. My yellow dory took me across wide oceans. A chip boat with a leaf sail in a March puddle was a pirate ship off the Barbary Coast, or sometimes a clipper ship running southerly down in the trade winds. Snowshoe tracks in the winter pasture led to the North Pole, and a scooped-out snowdrift was an Eskimo house.

But the autumn nights were always the time to stay close to home, the time for ghosts and goblins, unfriendly threatening things that could devour a child or carry her away. I used to wonder, and at times still do, whether I should be afraid if I met a ghost of one of those dear people on an autumn night under the trees of the old orchard. I have gone out looking but all in vain. The only ghosts are in my mind and memory: very welcome they are too, even when their presence deepens the sadness of an early autumn.

The Devil Walked Abroad on Halloween

The Devil was a very real person in my young life, and why not? I had been told often enough that the Devil must have got into me to make me do this and that, and my misdeeds were referred to often as "devilment." No one that I can recall ever called me an angel. If they had, the whole course of my life might have been different — you know "give a dog a bad name . . . ."

My supernatural hierarchy was blended in my imagination from occasional and unsatisfactory attendance at Sunday school plus religious picture books with a stern and bearded God, looking cross among clouds and surrounded by bland-faced angels with nice looking wings.

The Devil, referred to as His Satanic Majesty, had a full page in the book: a splendid figure in scarlet cape, carrying that familiar tool, a pitchfork. Horns showed among his grizzled curls, and his feet were cloven hoofs like those of our cows. But there was nothing else cowlike about him. His slanted eyes gleamed fiercely from the page. They haunted me, those eyes, and standing in front of the mirror, I narrowed mine and curled my lip, looking so savage that I frightened even myself. And there was a kinship too in his entourage. Instead of the repulsive fat cherubs with their saintly expressions, the Devil was surrounded by imps, peering from behind his legs, peeking from the shrubbery, laughing and having fun: a congenial crew.

Seated in the creaking wicker chair on the owl cushion with green glass eyes, I pored over the picture, studying every detail, fixing it in my mind so firmly that the colors remain unfaded to this day.

A sort of devil worship was one of the rites carried out secretly in my bedroom with the door shut and the school books flung unopened on the bed.

On Halloween, the Devil walked abroad. He was the king of the witches, the ghosts, and the goblins. The smell of pumpkin meat frying in the flame of my jack-o'-lantern candle might have been brimstone.

I did not really expect to meet the Devil on the streets of Boston, where I celebrated with howling bands of masked and sheeted figures when Halloween fell on a school night. We ran shrieking across the grass plots in front of staid and lighted houses, and we rang doorbells.

Old Mr. Binney from across the street threw a bucket of water on me from the upstairs bay window, putting out the candle of my jack-0'-lantern. He could not know it was I, masked and shrouded, but he would have been happy if he had. We had been feuding, and he even called the police from Station 16 when my baseball broke his basement window. I spent quite a bit of time in Station 16, feeding the horses and waiting for my father to come and get me.

We ran through the back alleys, tearing our ghost robes on the fences, and finally when the candles guttered out in the jack-o'-lanterns, we smashed our pumpkins on the sidewalk and went indoors to parties.

There was no time or place for the Devil here, only for devilment. But when Halloween fell on a Friday or a Saturday night, in Ipswich it was different.

There were no neighborhood children in the wintertime, and the Townsend house, where I had played blackjack on the porch in the summer, was shuttered and dark.

First, there was a ritual of carving the pumpkin, cutting out rhomboids for eyes and snaggle teeth. On Grandma's orders, each bit of pulp was carefully saved to make a-pumpkin pie.

After supper, it would have been tempting to stay with Grandma by the fire, but it was Halloween and there was ritual to be observed. And so, all alone, dressed in my sheet, carrying my lighted pumpkin, I went out the back door into the yard.

When the door closed behind me, it was inky dark and frosty. Overhead the stars glittered, and low over the marsh to the southeast rose the moon, angry red and lopsided. There was not a breath of wind, not a sound, till far away an owl hooted. It was a night for witches, a night for the Devil to walk abroad.

With thumping heart, I made my way across the frosty grass towards the barn, leaving a line of black tracks distinct in the faint moonlight. The candle in the pumpkin cast hardly any light at all. There were stirrings and whisperings in the bushes as I passed. The familiar barn looked enormous and strange inside, the animals were quiet. I was greatly tempted to go in, wait awhile, and then go back to the house to tell Grandma that I had a fine walk and settle down again beside the fire. But pride drove me on, out into the pasture where the short cropped grass, silvery with frost, was broken by inky pools of shadow from bushes and scrubby trees. I shivered with chill, striking through the sheet, or was it fear? Finally, thinking I had gone far enough, I stopped near a clump of bayberries and paused to listen. The sweet spicy smell mixed with the roasting pumpkin was reassuring.

Suddenly, there was a loud snort, half whistly, a stamping of feet, and something moved in the bushes: the Devil himself.

I flung away the pumpkin and took to my heels. The Devil, it must have been the Devil, was running after me, I was sure of it as I headed for the back door. Suddenly, something caught me by the throat and flung me to the ground. Not waiting to see that it was only the clothesline in the back yard, I picked myself up and slammed into the house, breathless, terrified.

Grandma took me in her arms and hugged me, warmed me a glass of milk and asked me nothing.

The next morning, bold in the daylight, I went back to the pasture.

There was the broken pumpkin, and there beside it, distinct in the dust, the print of a cloven hoof.

Making Allowances for the Devil

It was to teach me the value of money, a vain effort as it turned out, that my father gave me from an early age what I referred to as my "lowance."

As surely as there were baked beans and brown bread for Saturday night supper, there beside my plate was a shiny dime. You could buy things with a dime in those day: ten pieces of candy, for instance, or five cedar pencils with soft lead, or from another child, a goodly number of cigarette pictures of baseball players, or vaudeville queens to add to my collection. I was amazed at the hourglass figures of these ladies, and standing naked before the mirror on my bureau, I wondered and decided that it would not be possible for such a slab-sided figure with every rib showing ever to develop into anything so lush.

Since I was not sure that this would be desirable anyway, I hoped instead for a mustache. I had discovered by holding the candle just right, so that my upper lip was shadowed, that a mustache would indeed be becoming.

But in the meantime, there was the dime, warm and sweaty from being fondled. Sitting in my bedroom on the owl cushion with its green eyes, I rubbed the dime and muttered over it, hoping I could magically make it grow into a quarter. A half dollar would be too much to expect.

Magical things were done in fairy tales, but no amount of abracadabras would change my dime into something more opulent, so finally I dropped it into the bank where it jingled with three or four others: truly an accumulating hoard.

Was it King Midas or King Croesus who enjoyed rolling naked among gold pieces? For awhile, I toyed with the idea of gathering enough dimes to fill the bathtub so that that I could roll in them, but finally I saw that it was hopeless. It would take a year to even cover the bottom of the tub.

The bank, a cast iron cottage with a slot in the chimney, was designed for storage rather than forced savings. The roof could be lifted to make available the coins within. There were rarely more than four or five dimes in the bank.

On winters when it snowed, I earned a few extras, shoveling off the sidewalk and the front steps, and then there was the year when the iron cottage suddenly grew heavy along about Easter time.

Attendance at Sunday School was not forced, and so it was sporadic, depending on whether I liked the teacher or if there was to be a worthwhile prize for good attendance.

My mother, who was a good church person, encouraged me. My father, who said that in his youth he was forced to attend enough church to last him for the rest of his life, did not. But when I came back on Ash Wednesday with a little cardboard container that could be folded into something called a "mite box," he was willing to contribute a weekly nickel.

This came about following what was known as "a scene" at the dinner table. With some difficulty, I had succeeded in assembling the box, folding and tucking in the edges. After congratulating me, my mother explained that since the money collected was going to make life happier for heathen children in foreign lands, I should be willing to make some small sacrifice and contribute my allowance in the weeks to come. I said I thought heathen children had a lot more fun. They did not have to go to school or wear shoes or anything. They lived in grass houses and went fishing and swimming all day. I had seen pictures. And when they were hungry, they climbed trees and picked coconuts, so why did they need my dimes? Besides, I needed them myself. My mother said I was selfish. I threw the mite box on the floor.

"Oh for God's sake," said my mother. I began to cry, tears not of remorse, but of rage. And at the same time, I sort of enjoyed the scene. Finally, the storm clouds passed and the sun came out when my father said he would give me an extra nickel for every week in Lent, and

I could put it in my mite box. I finished up my dessert, listened outside the door for awhile to my mother and father arguing about it, and then I went out to play.

By the time Easter rolled around, the mite box was quite heavy, and I thought I would open it and see how much was there. I carefully opened up one end and poured the nickels onto the bed. They made an impressive little pile.

I closed the box and was about to drop the first nickel in when Satan whispered. I knew that voice and how much trouble it always brought, but I listened.

And so when I advanced to put my mite box in the plate at Sunday school, who was to know that it was filled with buttons from the sewing room?

Grown-ups are so sneaky. The boxes were numbered, and there was to be a prize for the kid who contributed the most. Everybody knew that it was Kitty Crockett who cheated the Lord with buttons. Everybody, including my parents.

Satan, who had tempted me, failed to stand by in my hour of need. Both parents this time were united and so angry that I was quite frightened. I was a cheat and, worse, a thief who had stolen from the little heathen children. The only way that I could come out clean was to give back not only all the nickels, but also the equivalent in dimes.

Unfortunately, it being the season, I had invested my entire fortune in a bag of marbles, including an unprecedented number of rare agates, and I had lost them all in a game only the day before.

"You see?" said my mother. "That's what happens to ill-gotten gains." It took me till midsummer to pay my debt, and I didn't go to Sunday school anymore. I couldn't afford it.

Visit to a Haunted House on Halloween

When, as this year, Halloween in my childhood occurred in midweek, I had to celebrate it in Boston, and for once I did not mind not being here on the farm. Really, it was more fun to join the screaming mobs of children running through the back yards overturning trash barrels and knocking tacktacks on kitchen windows than to go out all alone dressed in a sheet with no one to scare but Grandma.

I had selected from the garden a choice pumpkin, round and fat and had carried it carefully on the train in a paper bag. No store-bought jack-o'-lanterns for me. No artificial pumpkin with paper eyes could take the place of one whittled out sitting on the front steps after school, leaning against the iron railing and stepped over by my father's patients coming to see the doctor during office hours.

I had sharpened my jackknife to a razor edge, honing it first on the grindstone in the barn and rubbing it lovingly with an oilstone for hours when I should have been doing my homework. It took a very sharp blade to cut off the stem end to make a cap and to pierce it with holes so that the candle could breathe. And then there were the eyes to cut out, triangular and slanted, one always higher than the other which gave a sinister appearance. The mouth had to be carefully done allowing for several snaggle teeth. The pulp was hollowed out with a sharpened kitchen spoon, leaving a hollow for the candle to be set in a bed of warm wax.

The seeds and bits of skin were swept up on doctor's orders, and the finished work of art was stored on the fire escape outside my bedroom window to await the day.

The yellow moon was rising above the rooftops as we assembled on the corner of the block; afraid already, we huddled together in the pool of light cast by the old gas street lamp. Dressed in sheets, some of us wore masks, a few had awful faces or were witches and goblins.

I had no mask, but I had taken the pillowcase from my bed and slashed eye holes in it with my jackknife: there would be trouble over this later. The candles flickered in the jack-o'-lanterns, and already there was the fine rich smell of roasting pumpkin meat.

In conspiratorial whispers, we planned our course of action: first stop — the home of old Mr. Binney who hated children. We would ring his doorbell and run. Then to the alley and through the back yards of Commonwealth Avenue where Irish cooks and maids could be counted on to scream in terror as they did every year. And finally, there was the closed and shuttered house on Hereford Street, which every child in the neighborhood knew was haunted.

It was a fine big corner house with steep slate roofs and towers, the upstairs windows blank and dark, the lower ones shuttered. Several times we had seen families moving in, loads of furniture arriving, and always a week or two later, the van came again, the furniture moved out, and the house was once again empty and dark.

There had been a murder there, we heard, there was a stain of blood on the stairs that no amount of scrubbing could wash away, and no family would stay for long in a house where a ghost walked wailing through the halls, carrying his head under his arm and leaving a trail of blood on the carpet.

What more exciting place to be on Halloween night than the back yard of the haunted house where there was a half dead pear tree and a neglected garden of rank grass and frostbitten flowers.

So we went on our rounds. Mr. Binney came roaring out at us before we even had a chance to ring his doorbell, and we scattered shrieking with delight and fear. A cook chased us, waving a broom. We crouched silently behind the ash barrels as the mounted officer from Station 16 rode by on his horse.

So finally, breathless, with sheets torn by the nails on the fences and candles guttering in the pumpkins, we reached the back gate of the haunted house. For a long time, we hesitated, daring each other in whispers. Finally, I put my hand on the gate, gave it a little push, and it swung open with a complaint of rusty hinges. I thought the others were right behind me, so I moved step by careful step across the frosty grass, clutching my jack-o'-lantern and peering nervously through the eye holes of the pillowcase. The moon was under a cloud, and it was very dark.

Suddenly the moon came out, and by its light I saw, sprawled on the ground, the ragged figure of a man, a bottle in his hand, his eyes wide open and staring. On his chest, a black cat was sitting, and it turned and snarled soundlessly at me. I was too terrified to move, but in that awful moment, I realized that I was all alone. No one had followed me into the yard.

As I stood there rooted to the spot, trembling and shivering, the man suddenly sat up, knocking away the cat and grinning horribly at me, and started to climb unsteadily to his feet. In a thick voice, he told me to wait, that he would not hurt me.

But I didn't wait to see. I flung down the pumpkin and tore the pillowcase off my head, and with pigtails flying, I took off for home as fast as I could run. There was no sign of the other children; they had all taken to their heels.

I dashed up the familiar front steps, burst open the front door and up the two flights of stairs to my room, where I dived under the bed and huddled against the wall. I crawled out when I heard my mother coming. I was sitting in my chair when she came in bringing a cup of cocoa and a cookie.

"Did you have a good time?" she asked.

"Yes," I said and began to cry.

A Raffle Ticket to Thanksgiving

A piece of paper, pristine white, is in the typewriter, and on it I have written a single word THANKSGIVING.

And then, chin on hand, I stare dreamily out the window, watching the north wind stripping the last withered leaves from the maple tree. They froze this year before they turned to gold, feeling perhaps that it would be always summer.

Like the maple tree, I was caught in a sudden freeze, after thinking that Thanksgiving, as Christmas and the Fourth of July, was eternal. There would always be, I thought, the damask tablecloth spread over the table extended to its fullest with all its leaves. The silver napkin rings were abandoned for the day, and every child had a huge folded napkin, big enough almost to cover the little ones from top to toe. There was an extra napkin at the head of the table where my father, a messy carver, would preside. There were dinner party silver dishes filled with nuts and curls of celery. Places were set for all of us and all the cousins, and maybe a stray medical student or two far from home, and as the magic moment neared and the whole house was rich with the smell of turkey and hot minced pie, everyone arrived laughing.

I did not want to think, in those happy prosperous days, that anywhere there were children who might not have a turkey, maybe not even a chicken on the table, and if indeed the thought like a dark cloud crossed my mind, I put it quickly away and applied myself to my heaping plate and laughed with full mouth, unreprimanded.

Thanksgiving was forever, as certain as the changing seasons, or so I thought, until one year my grandmother was no longer in her place beside me, to slip me a little special goody from her plate onto mine.

After that, things were never quite the same again.

Still, with fewer leaves in the table and fewer cousins at the door, we still managed a gay occasion, and even as we grew older, independent and impatient the rest of the year, we turned the clock back at Thanksgiving and laughed at the old jokes and pretended nothing had really changed.

More than forty years ago, in the spring, in the black year of the Great Depression, my father died, and like so many others, all our fortunes came crashing down. All that was left was the old house, groaning under its mortgage, the barn, and the apple orchard — and these things I determined would not be lost.

And so, with a cellar full of unsold apples and the family scattered to the four winds, I made up my mind that we would have Thanksgiving together, even though it might be for the last time. For there were occasions that year, when dead tired and despairing, that I wondered whether apples alone could be enough to keep our sinking ship afloat.

Going about my autumn chores in the orchard, I planned for the Thanksgiving dinner: first, a clam stew — I would dig the clams; then from the garden, potatoes, onions, carrots, and cabbage; and for dessert, pie — apple naturally, no mince this year.

When Thanksgiving week arrived, I had just one two-dollar bill after paying for a tankful of oil for the kitchen stove. There was firewood for one day's fire in the dining room fireplace. The rest of the house was empty and cold, and there was no way to rekindle life and warmth in the old square rooms overlooking the marshes.

The question came as to what to do about the turkey. I agonized over that: whether or not to blow the last of the money, even supposing I could get a bird for two dollars. It did not occur to me to try to borrow the money; I was deep enough in debt already.

I had long since moved out of my room with the yellow roses on the wallpaper, my grandmother's room where she told me stories and soothed my anguished spirit and protected me from the consequences of childish misdeeds. Lying in my narrow iron cot in the little cell above the kitchen, I thought about the turkey. I even dreamed about stealing one from the flock at Appleton Farms, imagining myself sneaking up through the woods, cornering a squawking bird, and wringing its wattled neck.

I had never stolen anything in my life except some sardines from the store in Essex, when becalmed in my sailboat, I was starving. I wouldn't have minded stealing the turkey, but I just couldn't face wringing its neck.

Then, going by the fire station, there was the sign for a raffle: "Three Thanksgiving Turkeys to be Given Away to Three Lucky Winners." Never, I thought, would I be a lucky winner at anything; but after walking by a few times, I ventured in and squandered a whole dollar on a book of tickets.

Three days before Thanksgiving, I was notified that my turkey was ready and waiting.

I cried over that naked bird, I really did, I was so happy.

We had a wonderful Thanksgiving that year; perhaps because we tried so hard to be gay, we were gay. We laughed and joked and told stories of our Depression jobs, and whatever we may have felt in our hearts, we never pined for the old days.

It was only when everyone had gone and the house was once more dark and quiet, that I squeezed out a few self-pitying tears, but they were the last ones.

That Thanksgiving was a turning point, although the end of our troubles was a long time coming. But here we are still, older and grayer, in Ipswich where we belong.

Melancholy Walk in Gray November

Sometimes when there is not time enough for a proper walk on the beach or in the sand dunes, I whistle for my dog, Christie, and we take a stroll along the north slope of this glacial moraine, coiled like a sleeping animal among the golden grasses of the salt marsh.

The gray clay lies close to the surface, and the thin soil was never productive. Apple trees planted there never grew. Now I stumble over their bones: fallen trunks and little branches like deer horns in a tangle of blackberry vines and poison ivy.

This neglected bit of ground is now returning to forest. Red oaks have taken over from the short-lived gray birch and aspen, with here and there a shag-barked hickory, abode of squirrels, native trees for whom the raw clay holds no terrors.

It is melancholy to walk here on a gray November afternoon, reminded by the size of the trees how long ago it was that I tried to coax life and fruit from the alien apple trees.

How different the south slope with its rich black loam, sweetened with the disintegrating shells of an Indian midden. I used to find things here: broken arrowheads, bits of coarse pottery. The Indians lived beside their dumping ground. Ours was stashed away far from the house on the north slope.

For quite a few years Bill and I and Betsy lived in a cottage on the edge of this wasteland, behind the barn and the row of rotting chicken houses. The low sun of winter hardly reached over the shoulder of the hill to shine briefly through the small-paned windows. We were perpetually in the shadow of the barn and were swept and battered by the fierce wind that roared and wailed and whined around the thin shingled walls and rattling windows of the little house.

Yet we were happy here, I remembered, as my wanderings brought me to the half filled cellar hole where once the house had stood.

The sumacs, against which I waged a constant war when we lived there, had taken over and still flew a few red flags of triumph. A lilac that I had planted so long ago still survived, choking in the jungle.

And on the peninsula that reached out into the marsh where gravel overlaid the clay, the solitary white pine had grown and spread above its bed of fallen needles. Even when we lived there, it was large enough to sing in the wind like the great pines of the north country.

When I hear people starting to complain about how chilly they will be with thermostats turned down, I have to smile to myself, remembering those winter days in the cottage when the wind came through the north wall and blew the papers around on the table. There was no fireplace, but crouching in the cellar was the great granddaddy of all hot air furnaces with a single pipe that led to a register in the living room floor. The heat was supposed to find its way up the narrow staircase to heat the two rooms and the bathroom above, but instead it dissipated through the south wall, leaving the bedrooms arctic and the bathroom pipes frozen. There was a coal and oil range in the kitchen, and here sometimes there was an illusion of warmth.

I ministered to that furnace like a parent to a sick child, constantly running up and down the cellar stairs to feed it more coal from the bin in the corner, shoveling out the ashes and hauling them on a sled to the growing pile in the dump. All day while I was at work and Betsy at school, the furnace was dormant and the house about 40, too cold for house plants and even for the goldfish.

My first job on reaching home was to open up the drafts and watch the dead coal come to life, first a flicker of blue flame, then shimmering red hot, and the heat poured up from the register and out through the loose-paned windows to warm all outdoors. When it began to smell hot as though the house would burn, I reluctantly shut it down, and gradually in came the creeping chill until defeated, we went off to bed.

Betsy and I sustained life in the cottage all through the war years alone, the dark war years when everything was blacked out because of prowling submarines off the coast. Betsy was too small to realize that everyone was not as cold as we were. For my part, I was so busy surviving, shoveling the snow and the coal and the ashes, that I could keep loneliness and apprehension at their distance. Everyone was gone to war which seemed to go on and on forever.

When I needed reassurance, I went up to the barn and looked at *Kelpie*, our boat, our hope for the future, left all framed up and waiting when Bill went off to the war. Someday she would be finished, someday she would be launched, someday we would make our living on the sea. I never doubted it, and so it came to pass.

Looking into the empty cellar hole on a gray November afternoon, I remembered these things. Sadly, I thought if only those times could come again, I would settle for the discomfort and the misery of that wretched little house.

To avoid a crisis of melancholy repinings, I whistled for Christie, and at the sight of that absurd boxer face and wagging stump of tail, I felt better, and we made our way back to this house where if we are cold, it is by design and not inevitable and forever.

Bill and Kitty, about 1938

RUMINATING ON FAMILIAR THINGS

... Our steamer hooted from the landing by the river. It was time to go, and I walked slowly away carrying my apricots and flowers and turned to wave and be waved to at the bend of the road. It was like a dream, as so many summers of childhood have become dreamlike with the passing years. ...

The Times They Are A-Changin'

I remember waking up in my bed here in Ipswich one long ago June day with all the birds singing in the elm tree outside and realizing that all those years of school were behind me, and at last I was free. To be sure, college lay just over the horizon, but this I was sure would be different, a grown-up kind of experience. I should be free to study what I chose, to come and go as I liked, to go barefoot in the street if I felt like it, to smoke, to drink, and disport myself in the company of college men, not kids.

It was a thought exhilarating and a little frightening too.

In the light of today's youthful experience, it is unbelievable how poorly all that rigid discipline prepared us to handle ourselves when finally the chains were off. Even though I had more freedom at home than most and took even more than I was given, I knew very little about sex; even the word was somehow dirty. I read grown-up books and novels from an early age and so had vague ideas that if certain things were done, one got pregnant, and of course from life with the animals on the farm, I was able to put two and two together, but I found such thoughts embarrassing and well enough left alone.

Most of the books in our library were historical novels or autobiographies of Indian fighters and Arctic explorers, exciting enough, good clean stuff about killing "savages" that were painted as hardly human. Even though I was squeamish about killing a chicken and cried for weeks when my dog died, the exploits of the buffalo hunters on the plains were like fairy tales, not real blood or real suffering.

The love affairs in the novels were cleaned up for Victorian readers, and only in the more earthy novels of the great Russian writers did I get the feeling of flesh and blood, half understood and vaguely troubling.

It seems unbelievable that it was not till I had finished two years of college that I met a homosexual on a transatlantic liner when very sophisticated indeed, I was bound for a summer of archaeological work in France. There were lots of students on the ship, but I picked this man out as most romantic. He played the piano beautifully and always looked very sad, which I found most attractive. I was beginning to see him as the great love of my life until one night on the boat deck under the moon, he explained to me his situation, the tragedy and the frustration. He was not one to glory in membership in gay society, if indeed there had been such a thing then, but was lost and lonely belonging nowhere in the world of that day. He explained all this to me in French in which we were both fluent, a language more suited to the subtleties of the situation. For years afterward, we corresponded, always in French; his letters seemed to me infinitely tragic.

Most amazing was my father's reaction. We never discussed sexual matters, not even about the birds and the bees. I learned what I knew from older children who in turn had picked up things from overhearing adult conversations and peeking through keyholes. But being nineteen years old and returning from a summer of varied adventures, which included an unscheduled stopover of several days in a crummy hotel in a poor part of Paris where prostitutes plied their trade openly on the street, I felt I was a pretty sophisticated character and able to discuss such things as homosexuality in an adult manner with an adult.

My father, smoking his cigar comfortably after lunch, listened to my rambling account of my adventures. But when I came to the part about my unfortunate friend, he slammed his cigar into the ashtray, jumped out of his chair, and told me to stop it, he didn't want to hear any more of such filthy stuff. He said my friend must be the worst kind of degenerate, preying in some way upon my sympathetic nature. I had hoped to learn something about homosexuality from a medical point of view, but for the first time, I felt my father was not all knowing, and I considered that probably there were no homosexuals in Maine and perhaps not even in Boston.

The end of school to me meant the shucking of all those chains and a real freedom from the constraints of growing up in the dying days of the Victorian age. It took a war and what amounted to a social revolution to make us free. Ill equipped, ill informed, and ill prepared, we fumbled our way into maturity which was a long time coming.

How much better nowadays, I used to think, when there are not all those taboos, and kids can be themselves and see the world as it really is, not a very pretty place but improving as the old prejudices and cruelties break down.

I was cheered by the activism of the sixties—the peace marches, the second emancipation, deplorably accompanied by violence, as change always is.

But again, change is a long time coming, knowledge has not dispelled confusion, and today's kids seem to be still troubled by the same things that troubled us so long ago. Perhaps, the moralities that I found so constraining had their place after all. Or maybe in our ignorance, we did not see the feet of clay in the national heroes, presidents, and soldiers.

Good luck, my young friends, and I hope you find life with all its cruelties and injustice as challenging, as interesting, and as ever fascinating as I have done. We all think we can do something about it, and maybe in all our little ways, we can.

A Fleet of T-bones

Times of austerity and times of plenty seem to follow each other like the progression of the seasons.

The extravagances of the twenties were followed by the Great Depression when people had no money to buy food and had to exist on short rations and the handouts from the "Gimmee Store" which dispensed government surplus from a center on Elm Street. Proud people went shamefaced to the "Gimme Store" and came away with whatever was surplus that week; one week, it was prunes, another flour. Sometimes, even butter was surplus, and inventive cooks built meals for their families around whatever was at hand.

So in a way we were conditioned for the scarcities of World War 2, and with a minimum of cheating, most of us made do with the meat we could buy with our red stamps, the gasoline allotted under A stamps for pleasure driving, and the B and C stamps that gave us a little more so that we could get to our war work.

At the Robinson Shipyard here in Ipswich in 1943, there were forged sheets of stamps for sale, but the people who purchased them were frowned upon. Many of the workers had sons or brothers in the service and were well aware that our cheating here might be short-changing them wherever they were on the far away front lines.

This is not to say that no one cheated, but at Robinson's, it was not the popular thing to do.

Not only gasoline and meat but everything was in short supply. There were weeks when there were no cigarettes, or when we addicts stood in line for a pack of a brand never heard of before or since. The next week it might be soap powder or some such commodity, with people shoving and grabbing around the dwindling stacks of boxes in the stores.

But meat was in perennially short supply, not expensive, but simply nonexistent. Each family member had a sheet of stamps, and large families with young children could collect enough red meat stamps to ensure a real Sunday dinner once a month or so. But Betsy and I had only two red stamps between us, and our Sunday dinners consisted of half a pound of hamburger if we were lucky.

I was ashamed of myself salivating over the memory of roast beef with Yorkshire pudding, the red dish full of gravy washing against the shore of gold pudding, or a leg of lamb all crispy brown, or even spareribs. I spent a lot of spare time thinking of meat.

But I knew, we all knew, that the meat we did not have was going to feed the soldiers and the sailors, and it did not occur to me to wonder why they were eating so much more in the service than they would have consumed at home.

I found out one reason why, one noontime at the shipyard, and the experience was both shattering and rewarding.

I was sitting on the bulkhead in the sun, eating my spartan lunch out of a paper bag. Nearby was tied up one of the subchasers we had built. The crew and skipper were on board, and there was about a week's delay while last minute things were being done. Then, the little vessel would sail away on the high tide, never to be seen again by those who created her.

As I watched, the cook in his dungarees came out from the galley with a pan of what looked like steaks, advanced to the rail and dumped them over the side. Stunned, I watched this treasure drifting out with the tide. Then I leaped to my feet, ran to where the yard dory was tied up, jumped in, and started rowing frantically downstream.

The guys in the steel shop at the end of the bulkhead cheered and waved as I went rowing by, but I had no time for them.

Out by the pilings at the mouth of the creek, I came upon a fleet of beefsteaks-T-bones-all sailing along together. I scooped them up, there were at least a dozen, and stashed them away in my car till quitting time.

Betsy and I feasted for several meals, and never did anything taste so delicious; a touch of saltwater only enhanced the flavor.

Several days later, I sidled up to the cook where he was languidly watching a fishing line. He once caught a smelt in the basin. "How come you threw all that lovely meat away?" I asked. He lit a cigarette, then seeing my greedy eye on the package, offered me one.

He explained that the boys in the crew were all what he called "Johnny Rebs," kids from the deep South who had never seen a beefsteak in their lives.

"They growl and complain all the time," he said. "All they want is hominy grits and fatback and greens." Chicken, they would eat, pork sometimes, beefsteaks never.

So they were starving aboard ship, and I was starving on the shore, each of us deprived of our accustomed victuals.

"I would have given you the steaks, but it is against orders. Anything not eaten, I have to throw away," the cook remarked.

I learned afterwards that food was not the only thing wasted in the war. On every island where the Yanks had landed and later moved on, there were left piles of rusting jeeps, trucks, cases of ammo, even guns, and those that could not be put to some use by the natives are still disintegrating in the jungles, I expect.

But of course, steaks and matériel are not the only things wasted in a war.

Who will Feel Nostalgia for the Seventies?

Those of us who remember the Black Depression days of the thirties feel a chill run down our spines when we see on TV the lines of marching men who are thrown out of work by the closing of their places of employment. If we follow the party line these days, we must remember to call our present troubles a "recession" or an "inflation" or both.

There are certainly marked differences from the bleak days of 1921, largely because of lessons learned in the years that led up to World War 11. I remember the Crash as something that happened almost overnight. Probably there were widening cracks in the structure of the economy which I was too uninformed to notice.

I was working at the Baker Library of Harvard in 1929, happily receiving each week a small pay envelope containing three $10 bills. I was quite happy with it since it provided my rent, my food, gas for my model A Ford, and a trip on the ski train to the mountains during the winter season.

I listened to the fairy tales of my fellow workers about their investments in the stock market, the stocks they had bought on margin, and how General Motors would soar to 1,000, whatever that meant. Everyone was in the market, everyone was going to be rich, except of course me. I toyed with the idea of doing what everyone else was doing, borrowing money to gamble with, but the idea made me uncomfortable and so I continued to live on my pay, down to the last dollar every Friday noon.

When I came to work the morning of the crash, I felt that I had been transported to the wailing wall. All around me, the people who had been so happy and confident were crying or sitting in stunned silence. Not only were all those dreams shattered overnight, but everything was lost, the houses, the cars, the bank accounts, everything that had been put up as security, and worst of all, gone were all those dreams of riches, the easy life.

That day was just the beginning of the long slide into despair, the breadlines, the apple sellers shivering on the street corners, the runs on the banks, factories and businesses closing down, and in those days, there was no social security, no unemployment compensation: these were "socialistic notions" developed by President Roosevelt, along with surplus food programs and the federal work programs, WPA and CWA.

The fact that the loss of a job does not mean immediate poverty today is one major difference from the days of the Great Depression, but now, as then, the economic dislocation seems to be worldwide, and the warning flags are flying.

But what is lacking now, I feel, is leadership. There is no Roosevelt to call upon us in a strong clear voice with the ringing words, "The only thing we have to fear is fear itself."

I remember sitting in front of my radio set, all alone in the cold house, hungry and discouraged with a cellar full of unsold apples from the orchard that was to keep the wolf from the door, feeling a thrill of hope.

My job, too, was long gone by this time, the pay envelope was only a happy memory. I have never been able to eat apples or hot oatmeal porridge since — I had them three times a day for too many days.

It would be nice to think that we came through the Depression as a result of our own efforts and that it was not a war that first brought us to a return of prosperity. Prosperity built on the manufacture of the engines of death is a house built on quicksand.

A phenomenon of these days is the nostalgia, the concern with the things of the past. I have wondered whether it is a groping for a lost strength and vitality and the kind of morality that made it safe to venture into the city streets at night or to leave country doors unlocked.

We gained a kind of strength in the Depression days when we were all in the same boat, and there was a sharing and concern for each other. I don't remember people stealing from each other, or murdering each other, or continuing the violence learned in war into the times of peace.

But of course, there was only one great war followed by the frenzy and the mad gaiety of the twenties, and since the thirties, the wars have been incessant, the threat of a world conflagration a constant fear. You can live in the shadow of a nuclear cloud for only so long before your soul is poisoned by it.

But with all the hideous problems, I still think it is a most exciting time to be alive, and the only thing that is discouraging is the lack of spirit, the acceptance of corruption in high places as a fact of life, and violence and crime and war as something to accept without any real effort to bring about a change.

It is time for new voices, for the emergence of a Roosevelt or a Lincoln, a leader tempered in the fires to tap the vitality that still exists in this country.

It is a dark hour, and I doubt whether there will ever be a wave of nostalgia for the seventies. Even softened by the mist of memory, they can hardly be regarded as a happy time.

Energy Crisis: a Blessing in Disguise?

In those days, energy was what kept a child running from dawn to dark. What kept us warm was coal for the kitchen range and the parlor stove, wood for the fireplace, and it was coal oil (kerosene) that lighted the lamps. And it was the candle in its brass candlestick selected from the row on the shelf in the hall that lighted a child up to bed, casting a grotesque shadow on the wall.

A dawdling child could do a lot of things with a candle. Tilted, it poured a cascade of hot wax into the tray. Malleable before it cooled, it could be shaped into animals and faces, or chewed, it had a nice tallowy taste. The shadow of a hand could be a rabbit's or a horse's head on the wall. Leaning close to the candle, it was even possible to read by its feeble light, until finally, it guttered and the wick drowned in a pool of melted wax.

Grown-ups read or sewed by the light of the parlor lamp downstairs while children had to make do with a candle. But one of the hated chores was cleaning the glass lamp chimneys that always seemed blackened by a carelessly trimmed wick.

Electric light was slow to come to the Argilla Road, east of the bridge, and town water was even slower. In my grandmother's day, we managed very well without such modern improvements.

The oven in the Glenwood range, with its design of leaves on the door and its crooked legs that raised it a couple of feet above the floor, was a good baker. Beans simmered all day to a delicious brown with a crisp topping of pork. Grandma's pies and cookies were always perfect,
and at canning time, the whole house smelled deliciously of pickling spice and vinegar.

The dog and cats slept under the stove on winter nights. I used to envy them as I took my candle up to the chilly chamber and crawled between the icy sheets.

The stove too, with its damper checked between meals, kept the water hot in the "reservoy," a square tank with a tin dipper hanging beside it.

The water was nice and soft: rainwater was from the big brick cistern underneath the house, filled from an intricate network of gutters and downspouts that drained the main house roof and the ell roof. The water was faintly brown and tasted of cedar from the shingles, very nice. The water was drawn up by a hand pump from the cistern; the "reservoy" was filled from a bucket.

We washed our faces and brushed our teeth at the soapstone kitchen sink, and for other needs, there was the one-holer in the woodshed. It was often cold out there and smelled horrible, but at least it was an improvement over a detached outhouse in the yard.

Every bedroom had its covered chamber pot, with a design of blue or pink roses, under the bed, and a commode with a china basin and pitcher filled with icy water.

Twentieth century amenities were slow to come to this outskirt of Ipswich town, a good half hour from the center of town in horse and buggy days. Strangely, there is a hiatus in memory, and I don't recall when the first light bulb was lighted. There must have been no ceremony, no great thing, when the lamps and candlesticks were carried down to the cellar. Everything on its way to the dump back of the barn stopped at a way station either in the cellar or the attic.

But even before the arrival of electricity, we had a real bathroom with a tinned copper tub, and the water was pumped by hand from the cistern, through the old lead pipes to a tank in the attic, and thence fed down by gravity. Pumping, one of my chores, I remember thinking, was a great deal of trouble just to get rid of the outhouse, the "reservoy," and the round tin tub with its pouring lip in which I took my Saturday night bath in the kitchen and supervised by Grandma to be sure I washed behind my ears.

Somewhere along the way, there arrived the hot air coal burning furnace for the cellar and the constant running up and down the stairs to open the draft, shut the draft, shovel in the coal, and shovel out the ashes which later had to be wheeled in the wheelbarrow to the dump to cover all sorts of earlier treasures.

The next luxury was our own well, and we could squander the water without worrying when it would rain again to fill the cistern. There had never been a well on the farm, only the cistern and a farm pond, long since mysteriously dried up, for the animals.

But we, in the beginnings of a new luxury, had to have a well and a buried line of pipe all the way to two tanks on the highest part of the hill, and a windmill to pump the water to the tanks. It had to be turned off to face the wind, and turned away when the tanks were full to overflowing with the water hard as a rock and brackish with sea salt. You had to use saltwater soap to wash in it. It corroded the pipes, and my father toyed with the idea of bottling it, making it fizzy, and selling it for mineral water.

"People would pay a lot for water like this," he said. I thought it tasted very nice even if we did have to go to a lot of trouble, and when the town water finally arrived, it tasted very flat and uninteresting.

Looking back over more than fifty years of association with this beloved piece of Ipswich terrain, do I perceive a transition paralleled in the country as a whole? Things achieved, leading to more things needed, round and round in a hectic circle: more, bigger, faster, higher—an endless compulsion. Our stepping stones to what we hope is an easier happier life has been a series of crises. The byproducts have been ulcers, heart attacks, mental troubles, alcohol, and drugs.

Now we have the energy crisis. Wouldn't it be funny if this turned out to be a blessing in disguise?

Lights Out: a Sunday Storm

Whipping down the Argilla Road the other day, I found myself thinking how shrunken the world has become in the last half century even on this familiar stretch of highway. It took an hour to walk to town once upon a time, or a half hour to bicycle, both allowing for stops, the lookings and listenings that no one has time for any more. Or twenty minutes on my fast stepping little horse. Now, I thought, all I have to do is to wind up my Volks and I am in town in five minutes any time I want to be or have to be.

There were times, I recalled, when snowdrifts blocked the roads, and one could not go to town for days. We were marooned here on a white peninsula, not caring very much.

"I expect it won't be like that ever anymore," I thought, as I walked into the house, snapping on the light, and greeted by a flow of warm air from the furnace.

But that, as you may guess, was before the Sunday storm.

I had not thought to see again a triumph of nature over man and his contrivances, so smug had I become in my dependence on the flow of power through the wires and the engines that turned the wheels to push the plough blades contemptuously through the deepest drifts. To go to sleep under an electric blanket, ah, what luxury, while a silent alarm clock moved on a volt or two, gently buzzing along towards morning and the shrilling voice that marked another day.

But the blanket turned chill, the hands of the clock ceased to turn, the dog moved fretfully off the cooling grating of the furnace, and outside the storm roared, the trees cracked under the mounting weight of snow, and there was no other sound but the angry voices of the wind.

All in the space of a few hours, we were transported back into old Ipswich, the times when the isolated farm fronted on a road where nothing moved but snow devils whirling in the wind. The only tracks were ours going to and from the barn where the old timbers creaked in the wind like a ship at sea, and the cows lay in their stanchions sighing with content after they were milked.

A single row of small tracks, the sharply defined prints of my new black cloth arctics with their four snap buckles, led down to the edge of the road where the snow stretched unbroken between the stone walls, and then the line of pigeon-toed tracks led to the back door, to the kitchen with its glowing black iron stove and the living room where the apple logs burned in the fireplace, bright flame, white ash, and blue smoke curling above the snowy shingles of the roof.

It takes something like the Sunday storm to show how citified we have become and how dependent. When the lights went out, the light department, highway garage, and police station were deluged with phone calls from people who were suddenly cold and dark and even afraid in their silent houses, where there was no reassuring cackle from the TV or blare from the radio. Eyes accustomed to electric light found it hard to read by the wavering light of a candle. Backyard chefs who last summer put on white hats and funny aprons to prepare sumptuous meals over the charcoal barbecue found it something else to cook supper and breakfast on the rickety logs of the fireplace. Housewives, who prided themselves that the outsides of their fry pans and saucepans were as shiny as the insides, discovered that wood smoke and baked-on grease can change all that in a single meal.

These discomforts and inconveniences did not last so long, perhaps twenty-four hours at the most, compared to three days snowed in at the Easter Sunday blizzard of 1916, or a week or more in the Portland Gale of 1898 — a legend of my childhood — and the countless other blizzards and old-fashioned nor'easters without names that are only memories now. These days, no armies of young men and boys with shovels turn up at the town hall, happy to work the tremendous drifts of Argilla, Essex Road, and Jeffreys Neck for a dollar a day.

I well remember walking on snowshoes up beyond North Gate in the grim lonely days of the Depression and seeing close to fifty shovelers like an army of ants in the towering drifts that seemed to blow back as fast as they were shoveled out. But that was when families lived on less than $25 a week and a dollar earned digging snow meant a little something extra on a spartan table.

Although our period of pioneering this time was short, one dark night and one chilly day, thanks to the superhuman efforts of the town forces in the face of impossible conditions, just this short time brought out some of the old neighborliness that once was so characteristic of New England. Several old people were encouraged to leave their lonely cold houses and move in with neighbors. Those who had heat and stoves that were operative shared with those who had none. Many people showed new concern for each other and for the town men toiling so hard to restore the comforts that we have come to expect.

Of all the hundreds of calls received by the various town departments, there were only a handful of people who were disagreeable and insistent on being taken care of immediately. Most called apologetically or even humorously to report lack of service and asked, perhaps plaintively, when relief could be expected.

It would be a grim remedy, but perhaps what we need is another Depression, a time of leveling with all of us in more or less the same economic boat. Depression's children developed a sense of self-reliance — saving and making do and sharing — now almost forgotten since a whole generation has grown up that never knew these days.

It has been said that what young people lack today is challenge; a twenty-four hour snow emergency was hardly that, but it was a beginning, and many people rose to the occasion.

Memories While Cleaning out an Attic

I was shocked as a child by all the perfectly good stuff that used to be wheelbarrowed down to the family dump in back of the barn every spring and fall during the semiannual cleanup.

I spent much of the summer picking it over and salvaging much that was useable and stashing it away in a repository of my own.

Cups with no handles, chipped enamel utensils, bottles of interesting shapes and sizes, some even with a wine residue, tasty if slightly vinegary. I suppose that somewhere among the poison ivy and the tree roots along the edge of the marsh lie buried all those useful things that I had stashed away.

In spite of the cleanup, there were always plenty of things left in the attic of our old house, in the bow-topped trunks shoved far back along the edges where even a child had to crawl to reach. There were the costumes of an earlier time, some stained by squirrels and rats, lace and ruching yellowed, the stripes and flowers faded. My skinny body, all straight lines and angles, was not adapted to these fashions of a former day. There was always a six-inch gap at the hourglass waist, and I wondered if I ever would have a shape like that.

Fortunately for me, the styles had changed by the time I was in my teens and twenties, and I even had for awhile a job modeling flapper fashions; my shapeless figure was just right.

There were other fascinating things in the attic: a rusty flintlock musket, my grandfather's Civil War sword — I was sure the stain on the blade was dried Rebel blood — his uniform, moth eaten but still quite grand, and some of my father's toys, including a box of lead soldiers some uniformed in blue, some in gray. And there was a dusty box of shells collected by some seafaring ancestor on Pacific beaches. Even in my childhood, the colors had faded, but some of the shells held to the ear still murmured with the voices of distant seas.

I spent many rainy dreamy afternoons in the attic.

In today's new houses, with only a crawl space under the roof and no cellar at all, the rummage sale, the garage sale, and the flea market have taken the place of the attic. Papers, cans, and bottles are recycled and residue crushed and buried in a common grave. In any event, in this nomadic age, there is neither space nor interest for souvenirs of old wars, and all the toys are plastic, played with, broken, outgrown, and put out with the trash.

It is unlikely that many of today's houses will last 200 years. Like the cars, they are built to be recycled.

But to one who grew up with pack-rat tendencies, it is impossible to throw everything away. The things that may come in handy someday must be put somewhere. In the dark crawl space under the low-pitched roof of this little house, reached by a trapdoor and a ladder, once or twice a year I climbed up with a little box of treasures, shoved it as far back as I could reach and forgot it. Maybe there were fifty or sixty trips over the years. And then last week came the day of reckoning when it became necessary to insulate above the ceiling, something that was not done when the house was built. So what used to be Betsy's bedroom lair when she lived at home is now piled with what was lovingly treasured, saved, and which now by some alchemy up there in the dark has become junk.

"Some of this stuff is yours," I said hopefully to Betsy. She opened the door, gave a horrified look, and said, "Throw it all away, except," she added, "the books, save those." And then she went to Africa.

And so, on a rainy Sunday afternoon, a good day to play in the attic, if there is one, I began on the records of thirty years of a small family's living in a little house. I should have bundled it all up into the back of the station wagon without looking at it and trucked it off to the dump. But I didn't, and now I am hooked.

Some things were easy to toss: I felt very virtuous when I bundled up those hideous curtains that Grandma Robertson (another pack rat) gave me so long ago, and the moth-eaten liner of a sleeping bag, and even with some hesitation, some Adlai Stevenson campaign literature — what a man, I thought looking at his picture and feeling the beginnings of melancholy.

Betsy was a shutterbug from an early age, and there were boxes of negatives and prints she had made herself, and this is where nostalgia really set in. Why ever did I start to look at them? There were pictures of Bill carving. Bill building the *Kelpie*, building the house, in his World War II uniform. I couldn't throw any of those away, it would be a betrayal somehow, but I couldn't bear to look at them either. So back into the box, along with Betsy's high school pictures and a couple of me, one standing alongside an immense tuna fish that I caught, no one would believe it without the picture.

And another to remind me that I was young once — oh dear, into the box. And then there were boxes of letters: mine to Bill and his to me, and mine to Betsy and hers to me. Those must be saved.

And an old, old radio, not a crystal set but almost, a collector's item perhaps, and a box of *Kelpie* records — payments from Gorton Pew for fish caught back in the forties. I thought then we made a lot of money, and I was right, we did, but for how many hours of work.

More pictures of old friends, looking younger. A couple of short stories I wrote in the thirties: no wonder no magazine accepted them. Betsy's trunk from camp — that might be useful to put things in. A suitcase with a busted zipper-that could be fixed. More books: I should go through those someday, now it is getting too dark.

And in the end, there was one bag of trash, and a roomful left, and if I were betting, it will go back through the trapdoor for someone else to pick over in another thirty years!

Only the Memories Aren't for Sale

On Tuesday, I went to an auction and I was sad.

The possessions being sold in a tent on the lawn were cherished by old neighbors and friends, all that remained of a family, now ended, extinct as far as the neighborhood goes. There was no one who cared for the things, only people unrelated by blood who wanted the money the things would bring.

There were crowds of people at the auction: dealers and professional auctions-goers looking for antiques. Others, looking for bargains, carried away triumphantly the kind of junk that families squirrel away through the years. Others, like me I suppose, were curiosity seekers. And perhaps like me, after hanging for awhile on the fringes of the crowd, they went home feeling disquieted and wishing they had not come.

There was something indelicate about beds and bureaus dragged from the places they had occupied for so long and arranged on the grass. People lay down on them to see if they were comfortable. A mother changed her baby's diaper on one, and this I thought had been done before, perhaps when the children of the family were little.

The auctioneer, gravel voiced, held up the pieces for bidding: the andirons from the fireplace, the silver forks and spoons, the bowls and cups and saucers, and the big things-bureaus, tables, and chairs, kitchen appliances, even the familiar car. And then there was all the stuff from the garage: rusty garden tools, an ancient outboard motor, a pair of old wheelbarrows, one I am sure used by old Mr. Sprague years and years ago in his continuing struggle to keep the washouts and weeds out of the driveway.

My association with this house goes back a long, long way. I played here as a child, trying to mind my manners at lunch off some of these same dishes, my mind on the piece of hard candy from the locked cupboard that Mrs. Sprague gave to each child who did not speak till spoken to (very hard that was), and who did not spill on the table mats. I once pried open a window in the winter and with a screwdriver removed the hasp from the padlocked cupboard. Who would have guessed that Mrs. Sprague would take the jar of hard candy with her to Brookline?

The house, much smaller then, not much more than a camp really, was sold with all its contents more than thirty years ago. I thought I recognized some of the things that had become almost a part of the house through the passing years.

It was when the little grand piano came up for sale that I thought I had stayed long enough. Sad and sick and solitary, the last inhabitant of the house played her piano all alone on winter nights when the wind roared in the chimney and the ice of the river cracked with the rising tide.

As I walked away over the trampled grass of the field, I passed a man loading his treasures into a shiny and expensive car, and I had to laugh when he showed me with pride all the things he had bought for a dollar: a pair of cracked paddles for a nonexistent canoe, a leaky length of garden hose, a hoe with a broken handle, and a box of rusty garden tools. He was as pleased with these treasures as the purchasers of the expensive chests and chairs and the antique pewter porringer from which Charlie Sprague used to eat his breakfast oatmeal.

It is dangerous business to get attached to material things. I realized it when I could hardly be parted from an old Plymouth automobile, a real character of a car, painted green with a cracked windshield and a broken window on the passenger side that let in the snows of winter. I waited for the speedometer to pass the 100,000 mile mark, and when all the numbers stood at zero, I stopped beside the road and patted the green hood and praised it for being a faithful friend. When the car died quietly one winter night and never ran again, I could not bear to watch as it was towed away to the graveyard.

There were squirrel people in my family too, because in our attic under the eaves, there was my father's toy box with a few lead soldiers in Civil War blue and gray, and trunks containing dresses worn by my mother to parties, all yellow laced and froufrou. I tried them on one rainy afternoon and was discouraged when the waist hooks and eyes were divorced by a foot or more. I was a skinny child and could not imagine the shape that would have fitted those dresses. I watched through the keyhole as my mother took a bath, hoping to solve the mystery, but she looked almost normal, at least as normal as any adult with all those lumps and protuberances that maturity so embarrassingly brought.

Rats and mice nested in the trunks and shredded the boxes of old letters tied with faded ribbon: I could never read the writing. The lead soldiers were carried away to the dump in some excess of cleanup zeal and melted down in one of the periodic fires. I found and rescued from the poison ivy and woodbine some of the shell collection brought home by seafaring ancestors from tropic beaches. I have them still: the colors are faded, but they still sing a song of distant seas to a listening ear. Better to the dump and the fire, I thought, than to be pawed over by strangers.

But saddest of all is to have no family to cherish the old things. I don't think I shall go to any more auctions for awhile.

Meanwhile, the house is an empty shell — and a strange place without memories.

Ike Belonged to a Different Age

Only in America would the President and general of the armies be known by the homely title of "Ike."

Our tendency to nickname our national heroes is considered both disrespectful and confusing by the rest of the world. Only in death do we accord the conventional honor to Ike and Jack and Bobby as we know them in our hearts.

There is a strangely childlike quality in Americans now in their forties and fifties and even older than leads so many of them to cling to a father image and a constant need for reassurance. People loved Dwight Eisenhower, the general, the President, not with awe but warmly with a cozy kind of affection.

Ike provided an inspiration to generations who had not yet discovered the corniness in the old-fashioned virtues of honesty and morality.

I often find myself embarrassed to discover in myself a sort of half-baked youthful simplicity when talking with people thirty and forty years younger than I am who sometimes seem so infinitely old. Eisenhower and those of us who were within shouting distance in years were young with the country and grew up in a time when all the lines of conduct were very clear cut, when right was white, wrong was black, and there were no confusing shades of gray.

God was in Heaven, father knew best. If you told the truth, did your work, and said your prayers, everything was sure to turn out all right.

But for some of us who were teenagers between the great world wars, there were those who even then were blown about by the winds of rebellion and of doubt, and for us, it was a hard and lonely road. We were mavericks in a conforming generation, and when the first winds of change began to blow, we did not have the comfort of many friendly bodies to huddle with and give us security.

There were quite terrible feelings of guilt when I began to doubt whether God was really taking a personal interest in my affairs. First, I noticed that he did not bring me a bicycle no matter how hard I prayed for it. Even more shattering was the discovery that my father could be wrong, unreasonable, and unfair: human, in other words.

The heavens did not fall either when I stole a whole lot of stuff out of the store at Conomo Point one day when Eddie Goodale and I got stuck in my sailboat when the tide went out. It was a long wait for it to come in again, and we were starving hungry. At my suggestion, we visited the store, and while Eddie deliberated with the storekeeper over spending the nickel that he had found in his pants pocket, I was busily scooping up cans of sardines and devilled ham and other items that could be secreted on one's person.

When we got back to the boat, and Eddie produced five pieces of penny candy, I fished out my loot. Eddie was so shocked that he refused to touch any of it, at least at first, and when he could no longer resist, he swallowed every mouthful as though it would be his last and was certain that something terrible would befall us on the way home. Nothing did, and I have loved sardines and devilled ham to this day.

There was a sequel to the story though. My conscience gave one of its last flutters and impelled me to go back to the store before the end of summer and pay for the stuff I had stolen. I came in feeling very virtuous with a dollar that I had got for my birthday. The storekeeper, an old man with a beard, quite resembling God in pictures, took my dollar, called my a thief, and forbade me to come into his store ever again.

I found this very confusing and tried to see in it a reason why it did not pay to be honest. However, the old-fashioned virtues had been so deeply ingrained during my childhood that I could not reason away the guilt feeling s that followed inevitably when I was impelled to the more exciting temptations of wrong doing.

I was, I guess, at the beginning of self-determination, the trial and error method that flourished in the twenties when prohibition made everyone a lawbreaker and built up the philosophy that everything was all right till you got caught at it.

I thought it was very silly of my mother to make such a fuss when my father paid the bootlegger in the front hall and brought upstairs a quart of gin "right off the boat" and made in a bathtub in Chelsea. She and General Eisenhower were, I guess, among the last of the moralists, and in a way I envy them.

It would be a great deal easier, as I am sure many teenagers would agree, to have the hard and fast lines marking off the straight and narrow path. It is very difficult to make these decisions of right and wrong for oneself at a young age, or at any age for that matter. One does develop guidelines after a series of mistakes and painful experiences, and this is what today's kids are trying to do, I suppose.

Preaching and ranting and assuming a holier-than-thou attitude does no good in dealing with kids, I am convinced of that. The only security is in love, deeply felt and warmly expressed, unless, like General Eisenhower, you can set an example through the serenity that comes with old-fashioned morality.

But even he, in his last words, spoke of love for his wife, his children, his grandchildren, and his country. To this statement, I would only add love and understanding of our fellow human beings wherever they are and whatever color, race, or creed.

Adèle LeBourgeois, What's in a Name?

"What's in a name, a rose by any other name would smell as sweet?"

That's what Shakespeare thought, but it was scant consolation to a child like me who hated the name I was given. Learning to write the heavy down-strokes and the light up-strokes which few people have carried into adulthood, painfully copying the Spencerian letters in the copybook, the first freehand expression was to write one's name. Fortunate were those who could write "John Jones" or "Jane Smith," while I struggled to inscribe Adele LeBourgeois Crockett, starting out bravely with the capital A, slashing the French accent on the first E, but petering out and running off the paper on the final T.

And how much can be perverted with a name like that-even the teacher called it Adeel or Adeelie, while my classmates made hay with Addle or even Addle LeBughouse.

I tried to hide under the comfortable shelter of Kitty, a good plain name, faintly Irish which in Boston was a good thing, but the horrible truth came out when I learned to write. My parents did try to atone for their initial mistake by calling me by a pet name which stuck; when asked my name, I said, "Kitty Crockett," but there was always someone to contradict me with, "No, it isn't, it's Addle B. LeBughouse."

Did they care that it was French and sort of aristocratic? No, they didn't, and neither did I; to me, it was a horror. Only one other child had such a problem, Betty De Blois, and her father always called her John. She thought of herself as John, acted like John, and found it comforting.

I would have liked it if someone had called me "Joe" or "Paul." As I've mentioned before, I spent quite a bit of time dreaming over what I could do if I could someday grow a real mustache: pacing the quarter deck of a ship, riding herd on a ranch, panning for gold, or even carrying a gun and fighting. This was of course years and years before the Russian women did all those things and more, and people thought all the more of them for it.

In a museum in Odessa, I saw a photograph of a merchant ship's captain whose name was Anastasia something, and very smart she was in her gold braid, a heroine of the Soviet Union. Oh dear, born too soon, I thought, and Captain Anastasia needed no moustache, she was in fact very pretty.

Born too soon: ah, there may have been the root of all my troubles, I have often thought, contrasting enviously the free and easy dress of today, the carefully splotched and bleached dungarees, sawed off and ravelled, the bare or sandalled feet, the flying shirttail. Even in my fairly free family, there was an explosion when I was seen playing baseball on the next block and wearing corduroy knickers and a shirt borrowed from a friend. Who could pitch in a dress? I said resentfully.

It was not that I wanted to be a boy, I tried to explain, it was just that I wanted to do what boys did: they had all the fun. They never had to push a doll buggy or hold the teacher's hand at recess. Well, no teacher wanted to hold my rough and grimy paw, and the feeling was mutual.

There was a divided feeling in the family about it. My mother, who forgot she had told me about running wild on the Louisiana plantation and galloping her horse across the fields when she was a little girl, thought that clothes made the woman. Shopping trips were a nightmare, and very seldom did I get the reward of a soda at Bailey's for being only moderately resistant. More often, I came back sullen, resolved that I would never wear the black velvet hat with the white felt rabbit's ears, and mother retired to her room with a headache. I never did wear the hat, or the Kate Greenaway dress from Paris, or the white corduroy coat, but someone did. I watched the ashman fishing the hat from the rubbish, twirling it admiringly on a finger, and laying it away carefully on the front seat of his wagon. Looking out the window, I wondered if his little girl would be pleased, or whether she too would not have preferred a blue baseball cap with a visor.

My father felt it was all tiresome nonsense.

Well, it all began with that unsuitable name, I am convinced. A numerologist or an astrologer would have done much better by me and my English cousin, also named Adèle LeBourgeois and known by her own insistence as Babs.

We met very seldom in childhood, the ocean then being a barrier, but when I was twenty and had begun to see some charms in boys beyond their skill at baseball, I stayed at my aunt's house in London. She too was in a state of perpetual dismay because of the odd habits of her daughter. The clothes closet was filled with Paris dresses mostly unworn. Handsome English boys down from Oxford and Cambridge were decoyed to the house for tea or dinner. And Babs, with her lovely rose petal complexion and curly hair, always came in sullenly, wearing her blue girl guide uniform, black stockings and square-toed shoes, and if she consented to talk at all, she told cockney stories with much braying laughter.

Her mother, the original Louisiana Adèle LeBourgeois for whom we were both named, suffered without understanding, and yet, she herself was immensely fat, a compulsive eater.

Were all those bad vibes in a name for her too?

I like to think I made the best of it. I wore the Paris clothes and had a great time in London. But, parents, be careful what you do — and consult the stars before you name your child.

Or will Women's Lib, or Bread and Roses, provide the answer, and names will no longer matter?

So What's New about Nudity?

The silly season did not go out with the eras of goldfish swallowing, marathon dancing, or flagpole sitting, I thought, as I saw on television the latest from my favorite city, known as the "Hub of the Universe."

There were thousands of men, many I was happy to observe "straight Types" with short haircuts and briefcases, pushing and shouting, whistling and neck craning, hysterical with anticipation. The attraction was the announced visit of none other than Miss Nude Universe.

I had only time to speculate on who else had been in the beauty contest, little green ladies from Mars perhaps, and where the contest was held, on some distant space platform surrounded by the winking stars?

There was a crescendo of shouts and whistles, and there she was, a scrawny little chick and not even naked. Out of deference to the Boston censors and the television sensibilities, she was dressed in a teeny-weeny bikini of black fish net. Her name was Kitten something-or-other, and she said something unintelligible in a little kitten voice, and then she was gone, back to outer space, leaving the screen to the Boston cops, struggling and sweating to handle the crowd and get the noonday traffic moving again.

How strange, I thought, that in this day of topless and bottomless barmaids, X flicks and porno shops, that nudity even from the Universe, should prove to be such an attraction. Not to mention the sights seen every hot day on a thousand beaches. Miss Nude Universe did not even have a nice coat of tan.

I was diverted and also disappointed to see such a reaction. It blew all my theories that in this modern day, nakedness is no longer a matter of prurient interest and concern. When I was a kid, it was different, as a museum exhibit of the evolution of the bathing suit (or dress) would show.

Long skirts and bloomers for the ladies, droopy drawers with tops and little half sleeves for the men. There is no longer any need for children to crowd around the knothole in the bathhouse, which seemed the only way to learn about anatomy since everything was covered.

In our family, the usual roles were reversed. It was my father who was "modest." My mother, whose grandmother in New Orleans took a bath (rarely) dressed in a long canvas nightie, revolted. She used to swim "skinny" in Sprague's cove in broad daylight, leaving her bathing dress on the float. There was the time when Mr. Sprague came down to the float while she was swimming, and not noticing the folded bathing suit, sat down and engaged her in conversation "for hours," she reported, while she stood feet in the mud and water up to her neck. "All I could think of was what if the tide went out, and he was still there," my mother said laughing.

My father did not think it was funny. "It would have served you right," he said.

But the more times change, the more they remain the same. I must have been about twelve years old at the time of the great Edna Wallace Hopper riot in Boston. I was going to school that year out in Longwood, and usually I walked and put the nickel trolley fare in my bank for a rainy day. You could get the money out with a hairpin when needed, so there was never much in it. As I crossed the Massachusetts Avenue intersection, I saw an enormous crowd gathered. There were mounted police from Station 16 on their horses and more people, mostly women, joining the crowd from every direction. So I went running up to see what was happening.

All it was going to be was Edna Wallace Hopper, no spring chicken even then, going to take a bath on the stage of Loews State Theatre, right in front of everybody, well not everybody, "women only." I was "women," or almost, and so — why not? — I joined the crowd.

Packed in between the women, like a sausage in its skin, I could see nothing. We moved at a snail's pace, still a block from the theatre. A woman trod with a high heel on my instep. Others pushed me. I began to get mad, and I pushed and shoved as hard as I could.

One woman said "lay off" in a surprisingly deep voice, and as I looked around, I saw there was a whole group of strange looking people, some in need of a shave, and even cloth hats did not hide that fact that their hair was short.

Somebody shouted "Harvard Students," and then the riot started.

The women were mostly middle-aged. (Edna Wallace Hopper was going to reveal the secret of keeping young.) And they were strong, and they were angry, as they had begun to realize that there would not be room in the theatre for everybody.

The women, swinging handbags and umbrellas, charged the students who tried to get away but were surrounded by the mob. I, too, took out my resentment, kicking the shins of the woman who had stepped on my foot. And suddenly, everyone was fighting, and I swung my school books on their strap and got in some good licks. For me, it had become a battle in the war of kids against grown-ups: in other words, most gratifying.

Then came the police on their horses, moving in a phalanx, the horses trained not to step on people, but you couldn't be sure. And everyone then tried to get away, and some fell down, and everyone screamed and yelled. And the ambulances and the paddy wagons came clanging up, and I thought it was time to go.

So I went weaseling and slithering through the crowd and ran all the way home, arriving not much more disheveled than usual.

The riot with pictures was all in the paper the next day. And I learned that the crowd broke down the doors of the theatre, and Edna Wallace Hopper swathed in a bath towel had been spirited out the back. I was sorry to have missed that.

A Golden Signal of Summer's End

One of the most endearing things about the Russian people, and there are many endearing things about them I found when I visited their beautiful country, is their love of flowers. Even in the cities, the old women carrying heavy loads of fruits and vegetables home from the market in string bags, always have room for a little bouquet from the flower stall or a small plant to brighten the window sill of a dreary little apartment in one of those mausoleum piles of cement that replace the bombed out buildings of the past.

Along the dusty country roads, the barefooted children carry a handful of wilted field flowers home to grandma as once I used to do myself when I was a little girl in Ipswich.

Bouquets of flowers are given as welcome and farewell. Every city has its park and on the benches there are always people sitting, reading or playing chess, and they frequently look up from the page or the board to admire the beds of flowers. Someone must talk nicely to the Russian flowers, they always bloom so beautifully.

I sometimes felt myself to be an alien presence on my corner of the park bench, unable to speak or understand a word of the quiet chatter that went on about me. Occasionally, oh very occasionally, I found myself missing the familiar things of home, my sailboat waiting at her mooring for my return, my little house which seemed a palace to the Russian friends who asked about it. A house with four rooms and a fireplace for only one old woman and her dog is the very height of luxury to the young girl who lived in a tiny apartment with grandpa and grandma, father and mother, sister and brother and kitten, all in a space much smaller than my little house at home.

It was in one of those rare moments of homesickness in the park in Moscow that I found another alien presence far from home. In a little square bed but in the place of honor near the Lenin statue, there was a group of plants, carefully watered and tended, but still not looking very vigorous, the coarse leaves yellowing at the edges. Two or three plants had put out stems crowned with feathery golden flowers, goldenrod.

Involuntarily, I clapped my hands at the sight and a young Russian woman standing nearby turned to me and smiled with a questioning, "Yes?"

"These flowers," I said, "they grow wild in the fields of America, at home."

"Here, they are strangers," she said, and was too polite to add, "like you."

I thought of this the other day when I saw the goldenrod coming into bloom along the roadsides and fringing the edges of the marshes. And among the salt grasses, that other harbinger of summer's end, the marsh lavender with its mist of tiny purple flowers.

The seasons of my childhood were marked by the procession of flowers, the violets and trout lilies of spring, the dandelions of early summer, and then, come August, the blue chicory that so soon and disappointingly faded when picked and held in a child's hot hand; finally would come the goldenrod accompanied by the dusty pink of the milkweed. When the pods formed and split to release the seeds borne on their silken parachutes, it would be fall with the samphire blazing scarlet in the marshes, the asters, frost flowers, and the fox grapes purple and heavy with juice.

Remembering Russia in high summer, I recalled walking along the dusty lane of a tiny village on the banks of the Dnieper River. Each thatch-roofed cottage with its bright-painted shutters was surrounded by gardens of vegetables and orchards of fruit trees.

No one spoke English there, but an old woman nodded and smiled a toothless smile when I signalled with raised eyebrows and questing hand that I should like to pick a fuzzy apricot from a branch propped and bending under its set of fruit. Warmed by the sun, it was juicy and delicious. The old woman hobbled out to the tree and pressed upon me a handful of apricots followed up by a little bunch of flowers from her garden.

Then she pointed out to me the stork's nest high in a tree where the stork stood on one leg and stared down at us with cold eye. He would fly away to Africa come winter and the snows of the north would bury the houses of the village up to the eaves. But now it was summer, with sunflowers in bloom and corn in tassel; I should have liked to walk barefoot in the dust of the village street where the cows had left their cloven hoof prints in the morning on their way to pasture.

Our steamer hooted from the landing by the river. It was time to go, and I walked slowly away carrying my apricots and flowers and turned to wave and be waved to at the bend of the road. It was like a dream as so many summers of childhood have become dreamlike with the passing years.

The spinning wheel of the seasons turns ever faster. Already the shadows are long early on the marshes and the heavy dews and the crickets mark the fall that comes too soon, too soon.

Ruminating on Familiar Things

"Ruminating," . . . what a lovely word, suggestive of a cow lying in the shade of a pasture oak after a morning of cropping the grass with the dew still on it and then placidly chewing and rechewing, with half-closed eyes, . . . content.

Freed at last from a structured job, nine to five in an office, I find myself ruminating, chewing over a lifetime of experiences, recalling old conversations and arguments, remembering with the vividness of dreams the faces and voices of people loved or hated, now forever vanished from this earth.

It is not a sad exercise, at least it need not be if one maintains a certain discipline and control. If drifting thoughts begin to lead towards the shoals of self-pity, or of regret for the things past or towards fears of an inevitable end, tomorrow, next week, next year or the year after, the ruminant must swallow the last cud and move across the pasture in search of companionship.

There are always other creatures in the field, to frolic with, awkward and stiff-legged, to pretend-fight with, lowered horns and rolling eyes. And at the day's end, there is the comfort of the stall: when at last I climb into my bed with all its familiar bumps and hollows, I laugh to hear myself giving the same kind of half sigh, half groan that I remember hearing in the barn at night.

It is a comparison only amusing, not profound, between the small and simple brain of the true ruminant and the intricate human instrument capable of developing the theory of relativity, creating a symphony with all the interwoven harmonies and counterpoint, or distilling into the hieroglyphics of the printed page, the sum of human emotion, love, hate, fear, ambition, and frustration.

None of these great things develop from my ruminations which I sometimes think lie somewhere in the area of a child's day dreams, an awareness of a bird singing outside, the moving leaves of trees grown tall since I have lived here, and the familiar things: the books in the bookcase, the carved wooden animals on the mantelpiece.

The red cover of Tolstoy's *Resurrection* is still faded and stained. Long ago, I fell asleep reading it in the bathtub and it fell in. My legs, folded Turk-fashion in the tub, became redder than any fresh sunburn; I thought the new shade quite becoming and regretted when it faded. At the time, I found *Resurrection* puzzling but did not feel like asking what it meant. It is comforting to be among the familiar things when I return late at night from meetings that, after 20 years, I find unrolling in a repetitious sort of pattern that sometimes seems woven of a web of old politics and futility.

There is the nightly ritual, a ceremonial greeting of Christie-Boxer at the door, "such a pretty, pretty dog." She loves that and waits for me to find a dog biscuit which I must first pretend to eat myself while she pretends to be anxious and then relieved. Before settling down to the typewriter to start distilling what juice I could find in the evening, there are a few moments to ruminate among the familiar things.

It is not fair, I sometimes think, that I should be here, alive and breathing, in this house that my husband built as a refuge from a stormy and frustrated life. Angrily, as he did so many things, he built it all himself, from the lines that he drew on a piece of watercolor paper and which with a twinge I discovered in an attic cleanup last winter.

In those long ago days, the purchase of rough boards, the nails, the windows, the hard pine flooring, the joists and frames were bought with scarce and hard earned cash. All the rest was labor, his labor in the cold months when there was snow on the piles of lumber and a bitter cold wind whistling over the roof. And in the spring, when we moved in, he built three small sailboats in the new living room, from the sale of which we bought a stove, a refrigerator and the plumbing.

On the walls are still, as always, his paintings. On the mantelpiece is the small scale model of the steam barkentine, "Bear of Oakland," on which he shipped as a young sailor all the way to Antarctica and back. Landlocked at his home during the Depression, a sea bird with clipped wings in the narrow confines of Ipswich, he worked all night while the family slept, fashioning with only a pen knife, the tiny model to scale. The masts, the yards, the threads of running rigging, the infinitesimal blocks and cleats, even the sails are carved and painted. The corner posts of the glass case are hand-shaped and carved; the sculptured waves of the running polar sea are painted in cold and unfaded greens and white.

The model was completed before ever we met and afterwards, though there were many voyages, none were ever again under sail.

Not lonely, and not with the bitterness of regret, I ruminate about our life together, surrounded by the things he made. His dog, a strange and often spooky little creature, saw him, I am sure, often in the house at night. But I could not, and now that the dog has joined him, neither of them has come back again.

Ruminating, I wonder if he will come back someday to see if I have taken care of his things, the "Bear" model and the paintings. I think not: his strange green eyes were always fixed on wider horizons, more distant stars.

Orchards

Long ago, when I worked in Cambridge, I had a Russian friend, an old man who had escaped from the Revolution and, somehow, had blown like a leaf in a gale half way across the world until he came to rest in a university city. He subsisted on a variety of little jobs and lived an inner life where voices, long since stopped with earth, still spoke, birds sang, and it was forever spring.

He was a sort of janitor's helper at the university, carrying out barrels of rubbish or working underground in the tunnels where the steam pipes ran from the heating plant down stream on the bank of the Charles. The Irish janitor in our building pointed out Mr. Lvov and said, "He was a Prince back in the old country."

One day, the old man smiled at me and we shook hands, and from then on we were friends.

We shared many a sandwich on the grassy riverbank during our spring lunch hours, often without exchanging a word. He was always listening to things I could not hear; sometimes his lips moved and he nodded his head and smiled, and I, not wanting to interrupt, also sat quietly, busy with my own thoughts. It was a strange relationship and I was often kidded about my crazy old friend: "What on earth do you talk about?"

"Nothing." For many weeks, even months, we didn't say anything but "hello" and then drifted down to the river bank where we both indulged our homesickness for the country: I, for Ipswich in the spring, and he, for the fields and orchards of Russia that he would never again see.

It was not till after months of meeting that he told me how the peasants on the estate had hidden him in a haystack when the

Bolsheviks came and how, after they had passed like a swarm of destroying locusts, he, the sole survivor of his family, was spirited from village to village at night and finally across the border into Turkey. He seemed to have no memory of or interest in his subsequent wanderings across Europe and across the ocean to America. How he came or where one day he went I never knew. He just vanished and came no more to the riverbank; I hoped that somehow he had gone to the country he longed for, either in this world or the next.

Standing on snowshoes among the broken branches of the apple orchard on Sunday, I found myself remembering Mr. Lvov and how one day he cried, the tears pouring from his faded blue eyes and splashing on the grass. From his haystack hiding place, he said, he watched the orchards of almonds and peaches and apples fall before the axes of the invaders.

"Each tree," he told me, "each living thing in nature has a soul. The ancient Greeks knew this. And on that day, all the souls-of the trees cried aloud . . . . I heard them, I hear them still."

I wondered if in the voices of the storm I was hearing the cries of the trees — the apples, hawthornes, the birch tree and the pines, as they were crushed and crippled. The apple trees of the old orchard are so intensely interwoven with my youth, with my life, that when I saw their wounds from the storm, I felt as though I, too, were bleeding.

It was on a 19th of April holiday that my father and I planted those trees. It had snowed all night before dawning to a raw, gray, windy day. There was snow in the holes dug the fall before; our hands were freezing as we spread out the roots and trowelled in the muddy raw earth. We wheeled the burlap-wrapped whips out from the barn into the field that one day would be an orchard, sloping to the south, warmed by the sun, protected from the wind by the shoulder of the hill.

A perfect place for an apple orchard! Into the holes went the different varieties: the new type Macintosh and the old standbys, Baldwins, Northern Spies, Rhode Island Greenings, and Russets, the mainstays of every old New England orchard.

A great deal was expected from those trees by the two optimists who planted them. They would go on growing year after year, thrusting their roots down into the glacial origin soil of the hillside, their branches high and wide against the grassy slope. After blossoming gloriously, all pink and white in the spring, there would be barrels and boxes of perfect fruit in the fall.

"They will take care of me in my retirement," my father said with satisfaction, looking down at the neat rows of frail little sticks from which so much was hoped and promised.

I felt a chill when he said, "These trees will be still in their prime in a hundred years when you and I are long gone."

No child can visualize the passing of time or anything beyond last week and next week. There must always be the same loving people, the same warm world, and I did not want to think of those cruel trees still growing and flowering when we were gone.

As my father pushed the empty wheelbarrow up through the field, I held tight to the tail of his tweed jacket, and to this day I can remember the feel of the reassuring wool.

So I felt quite quite sad and lonely as I stood in the snow among the broken branches, remembering the long ago spring and so much that has happened since, the hopes and the disappointments. But under the new snow, the roots are still there, strong and living; even for Mr. Lvov something remained and the Russian orchards flowered in his memory.

Montreal Express: Voice of Times Past

The Montreal Express comes roaring out of the north, speaking with many voices of times past, remembered.

There was that terrible winter of 1933-34, that February when the thermometer hit 18 below zero and never once did the glass rise above 10 degrees. Huddled on the sofa in the little circle of warmth from the Glenwood range, Freya, the Great Dane, and I spent day after day hibernating, while, outside, the snow blew incessantly past the kitchen window.

What if, I remember thinking. this is the return of the ice age and the glaciers come sliding down from the north, burying first the fragile peach trees, then the apples and, finally, the house itself, till only the tall chimneys show above the ice.

Hungry and always cold, you think strange things.

This was my second winter in the orchard. The first was full of promise. Day after mild day made it happen so that by the end of the winter, the pruning done, the brush piled and burned, the trees fed, the burst of bloom in May, shell-pink blossoms against a sky of softest blue with drifts of puffy clouds, was splendid.

I had never lost hope or doubted that from the Depression wreck I would be able to save the beloved place, this family center, cherished by my grandmother, my father, now by me, and who knew what generations to come. Buoyed by this vision of the past and the future, I happily rose at dawn. Each day was a challenge as I struggled with worn and balky machinery, the tractor and the spray engine.

Covered with grease and lime-sulfur spray, I defiantly stood off the man from the bank, come to see about the mortgage payments and demanding something on the principal, too. The hatred hung between us like a cloud. To him, I was the dirty, spray and sunburned obstacle to acquiring what someday would be a valuable property. To me, he, in his business suit and Cadillac, was the enemy, dangerous and threatening.

Everything was on my side, I thought, watching the apples ripening on the trees, clean, bright, perfect fruit. In jubilant mood, I and other Depression children picked, sorted, packed hundreds of boxes which were sold to old and new customers. The money came rolling in. The bank was paid off, enough, anyway, to keep them quiet. The bills were paid as promised; money was put by for the spring purchases; and a little, a very little bit, was set aside for Freya and me to see us through the winter.

And suddenly, too soon, winter was upon us.

The leaves were still on the trees that late October night of sudden, biting cold. In the morning, they were frozen, tinkling and brittle as glass. By noon, they had fallen, every one, and the trees were bare.

There was no Indian summer that year, no hazy warm days, no time to get the fall chores done before the ground froze. The snow came early-sharp little flakes hissing down on the hard earth.

Something had happened high up where the weather is made. Night after night, the cold fires of the northern lights flamed across the sky, fingers of white and red and green stabbing up to the zenith. Freya was uneasy and I was filled with foreboding.

I busied myself selling the apples, driving to Boston in my little Model A Ford, green with torn side curtains and a rumble seat, calling on purchasing agents in school and college cafeterias. The boxes were addressed, stacked by the cellar door; early on Monday mornings, Jim Wile came with his truck and carted them away. Greenings, McIntosh, Northern Spies, all were sold before the real winter closed in by mid-December . All that was left were some Russets from the oldest trees and some less than perfect fruit, which I ate, raw, baked or as sauce, staple of a meager diet. Small wonder that even to this day I never can eat apples.

Somehow we survived, Freya and I. When the first southwester brought the warm spring rain, and downspouts and gutters drip, drip, dripped outside the window, I felt again the stirrings of hope and even a ghost of the old enthusiasm.

But, never again in the four years that followed was there that sense of certainty of power, of inevitable victory. Grimly, I struggled on, until in the end the Depression eased. My brother who had been carrying on his own battle towards success was able to step in and pluck the brands from the burning.

He was too wise and practical to bother with the apple trees, but it was they, after all, who saved the day, those days, just as my father said they would.

Seals

Not too long ago I stood on a beach of black volcanic sand in Iceland and heard a thin crying above the wind that carried me back in one flash to the white sands of another beach and a long ago childhood.

Wheeling out of the smother of storm clouds, fog and spray, came a flock of the same plover which we used to call beetlehead. Circling above the beach they gave the three-toned call that I used to be able to imitate as a child, whistling in the passing flocks skimming along the shore. I tried it on the northern beach but the sound of the surf and the wind were too much. The birds ran, heedless of my call, following the line of the foam so white against the black sand on tiny feet, pausing to thrust their beaks into the bits of seaweed and crying, crying.

It was a wild day on that northern beach. The surge of the North Atlantic, the graybeard rollers came marching in rank upon rank out of the smother, tripping as the water shoaled, then mounting, cresting, curling before crashing down. Constantly, day and night, summer and winter, the ocean swells beat on this savage coast of lava rock and black sand, surging into coves where the brave little boats ride to an uneasy anchor.

No bell buoys warn of sunken ledges offshore; there is never a lighted buoy and hardly a lighthouse along this coast to which a thousand years ago the Viking long boats came to land, perhaps on this very beach, where did also the Irish adventurers in boats sheathed in skins. Only the birds ride in safely on the wind, to run and cry and feed on the sand or to nest among the rocks.

As I stood on the beach leaning against the wind, lashed by the rain, I caught a glimpse of dark shapes in the curling breakers, the seals that we had come to see. Nearby a river roars down from a glacier and brings food that attracts the fish on which the seals feed: they were there playing in the waves like surfers on holiday, feeding, poking up their round heads to stare at these unfamiliar creatures of the sand.

Since it was considered a marvel to see 15 or 20 seals at once and so close and whole skeins of shorebirds, I restrained myself from saying in the best American manner, "Where I come from, we have these birds and more on our beaches and more seals."

Alas, it is no longer true, but once it was. Walking on the white sand of our shore when I was young, I heard the cry of the plover and the snipe and watched the flocks skimming in from a smoother sea, wheeling and turning all at once by some unimaginable signal, the sunlight flashing on their wings. And the tiny sandpipers in their thousands and their varieties and the larger birds with stilt-like legs and long or strangely curved beaks, all these I saw again in the mind's eye when I heard the beetlehead on the beach in Iceland.

Where have they gone? They are protected now and even in the days when shooting them was considered great sport, they were tame and very trusting. A blind scooped out of sand and thinly disguised with beach grass, a group of painted wooden birds in the sand and a plaintive whistle would bring them in almost to the barrel of the gun. They were mowed down by dust shot and fell in tattered heaps of feathers but their brothers and their cousins still came circling in, heedless of all the slaughter.

Surely, creatures so bold and careless could not be frightened by the hundreds of people who have now invaded their territory, or is it just that they prefer to be alone with their own kind on deserted beaches?

Ours was once a deserted beach which is hard to imagine now. I expect we shall never see again the herds of seals that lived here in my childhood. On a section of the bar not too far off the beach and which fell sharply into what we used to call the ship channel, the largest herd would gather on summer low tides, a hundred or more, to scratch, to roll and bark, or to sleep or to play fight in the deep water close to their resting place. At the approach of a motor boat, they would all roll clumsily across the sand and into the water where they would poke out their round faces and pop eyes to give another look.

A sailboat like mine was just another bird to them: they paid no heed at all, and on light winds I could creep in very close, floating, watching. There were the big bull seals and the sleek cows with the silly gamboling puppies, for all the world like baby dogs or foxes. Once, after considerable thought and planning, I made myself look like a seal, pulling a dark painted paper bag over my head with peepholes and encased my legs up to the waist in a burlap feed sack. Thus attired, I landed my boat on the bar and crawled towards the seal herd, quite successfully imitating their clumsy motion on land.

It was a hot day and many of the seals were sleeping, sprawled belly up on the sand, occasionally sluggishly scratching with a flipper. I was so close that when a big bull yawned, I saw rows of formidable teeth. He lifted his head and stared at me and I stared back as bravely as I could through the peepholes. Then he rolled over and lifted his head and half his great body. I panicked and jumped up; divesting myself of the sack and ripping off the paper bag, I ran for my boat. There was panic then in the seal herd, too. Young and old headed for the water, shouldering and pushing like a subway crowd. Their heads with the staring eyes were all around me as I sailed away.

There is No Escaping the Omens

Superstitions persist from childhood. To this day, I try to avoid stepping on the cracks of cement sidewalks or seeing the new moon over the left shoulder. Spilled salt, of course, should be tossed over the left shoulder to escape who knows what sinister happenings.

There was something reassuring about the grandfather clock in the hall, tick-tocking away, the beating heart of time. When for no apparent reason it fell silent, it was an omen. My grandmother died that day: my first encounter with human death.

Beloved dogs and cats, my canary bird, even the goldfish had died, and they were wept over and ritually buried. The clock did not stop for them.

The clock radio on the table is a far cry from the grandfather clock with its sun and moon and zodiac signs, its chimes sounding the hours. The electric clock is mysteriously silent, emitting only a faint click when new minutes and hours appear on the dial. So long as electricity courses through the wires, the clock runs, or at least it did. Suddenly, early on a May morning, it stopped, the numbers frozen at 6:41.

The light was still on in the kitchen, the plug still in the wall. I corrected the numbers by hand: no go. I shook it gently, tapped it smartly: no go. I swore at it, all methods that have worked for other mechanical, and for that matter human, failures.

The clock remained inert, even though the radio played loudly on demand, as if to justify its existence. Abandoning the thought of probing the guts inside the imitation wood case, I put the half dead creature back in its place and used the living half all summer.

It happened that the day the clock stopped was town election day.

People who live alone get in the habit of talking to themselves, sometimes aloud to the empty walls or more satisfyingly to a beloved animal. And so that morning, I said to my dog, "Well, Christie, we are going to lose today," and so indeed, we did. It came as no shock, no surprise. I had been forewarned.

Last week with sympathetic interest, I watched the reactions of losers and winners in a much larger and more important contest, the pain and the triumph of people who had staked everything on the outcome. As a so recent loser, I was especially concerned with the losers who had to play the good sport under the watchful eyes of millions, who had to stand smiling and dignified before the television cameras. For the most part, from the governor on down, especially the governor, they behaved gallantly. It is as hard, though not as painful, to be a graceful winner, to resist the temptation to gloat while surrounded by cavorting, shouting supporters.

They were at the beginning of their careers, while I was nearing the end of mine, hardened in the fires of years of successes and failures, none of them major, but important to me nonetheless.

And then of course, I had been forewarned by premonition and the stopped clock.

But there is no escaping the omens, whether interpreted by soothsayers from the guts of animals, whispered in riddles from the depths of caves, conjured up in smoke or from the steaming brew of witches.

It was on the first cool night of the changing season that there came from the table a familiar click. As suddenly as it had stopped in May, time began to run again in September. I adjusted the numbers to what my watch said was correct, and so far, day and night, they have kept pace.

If anyone has a logical explanation for this phenomenon, don't tell me. I don't want to hear about a grain of dust in a tube, dissolved or burned away, or a sudden surge of power that jolted something back to life.

I am reassured: the clock is running, and life goes on, picking up where limbo left off.

Failure: Only a Shift of the Wind

For three years while I have been a Selectman in Ipswich, the typewriter has squatted under its cover, untouched.

Occasionally, in recent weeks, I have whacked out a few things on it, surprised to find that after so long a layoff the fingers could still find their places among the letters. Like swimming, or milking a cow, some skills you never lose.

Awake early Tuesday morning after the election, I watched from my bed as the northward moving sun touched the tops of the trees of the orchard windbreak, then moved down to gild the grass, now turning green after the long hard winter. The red fox, richly furred, slithered by towards his den on the hill after a night's hunting. A cock pheasant crowed, and the early morning chorus of the birds began. It is still country here, in spite of houses that have sprouted on the hayfields, orchards, and pasture land of the old farm.

Tuesday was a moody day. It should have been, I suppose, a day marking a failure, one of many inevitable in a long life. In retrospect, failures loom larger in memory than successes.

There were the enraging failures of childhood: the poem that did not win the prize, the sailboat that capsized just before the finish line, the dropped ball that lost the game, the forgotten lines in the school play, and ah, how prophetic, the defeats in the class elections—yes, more than one.

After each of these episodes, I came slamming up the stairs, banging shut the door of my room. There in a frenzy of rage, I pounded the already battered face of my teddy bear, attacked the cushion with the embroidered owl with green glass eyes and flung it in the corner, swept the books and papers from the desk onto the floor, and turned face to the wall to see the annoying picture of a bland Sir Galahad with his white horse.

There was no such easy release from the failures and agonies of adolescence. Even after all these years, they still bring a prick of pain. There was no anodyne of pills or pot or beer in those long ago days. The failures, the confusion, the uncertainty had to be faced and mastered, cold turkey and without help.

Often, it was touch and go. I remember sitting on the windowsill, three stories up above the brick back yard, my back to the darkened room, trying to decide whether to dive headfirst or feet first. I can remember the crescent moon above the chimney pots, the muffled night sounds of the city, but I cannot remember what it was that brought me to such an edge of despair.

It was only when a steam train whistled far away that I hauled myself away from the open window back into the room and dove shivering into bed.

What I would have missed if I had yielded to the mood of that self-pitying moment.

I have to laugh to recall how I pictured the drama. The finding of the broken body on the bricks, the eulogy of sorrowing relatives and friends, the organ rolling solemnly at the funeral. I would be there, of course, to savor the moment. Imagination stopped short of the graveyard and the cold earth under the stone.

There is a kind of resilience acquired with the passing years. The failures so often turn out to be only a shift of wind that sets the vessel sailing on a new course, along coasts beautiful and exciting, in and out of bays varied and strange.

Oddly enough on Monday night and Tuesday morning, I felt a sense of relief, of excitement. Once again, the wind had shifted. What mysteries, what challenges, what adventure still lie ahead as the old boat sails along shores, still unseen, unexplored?

And so on Tuesday, I busied myself with the typewriter, replacing the dried ribbon and cleaning and polishing the letters that are the symbols of language.

It is the link in the chain of communication that began with grunts and squeaks around the cave man's fire and will end, Heaven forbid, with the soulless clatter of the computer.

My Bed: Like a Boat on a Foggy Sea

My bed, in which I spend too many hours, midnight to beginning dawn, is like a boat on a foggy sea, a little world apart. After the troubled day, when I can leave the things done and not done, there is that wonderful sense of ease, of peace, of the kindly wall of darkness, soft, mysterious, wrapping me like the fog.

And when my eyes become adjusted, and tense nerves and muscles relax like the strings of an abandoned instrument, there is a window on the world outside. From my nest, eye level with the windowsill, I can see the edges of the night world taking shape, the so familiar and reassuring things that are always there, unseen by day and significant by night.

The old Baldwin apple tree, a net of branches, the stout trunk lost in darkness, still flies a few flags of leaves, moving delicately against the passing stars. The neglected fruit still lies in the frosty grass; stepping softly, pausing to look and listen, a deer comes to the tree for a midnight feast. She does not know she shares the night with a watcher in the dark house, but I see her there, a gray shadow, and I hear her crunching, and then she drifts away among the trees.

Once I tended this Baldwin tree, fed it, sprayed it along with all the others, and in the winter with pruning saw and shears, I tried to shape it to my wishes, opening it up for the ladders of the fall picking, barbering the top so that those finest and best apples on the high, sunny branches could be within reach. It is years and years since the saw has sliced through the living flesh under the bark and the heart wood with its secret records of years gone by. The tree has returned to its predestined way of growth, and all the old wounds have healed.

Left to itself, the tree produces quantities of small bright apples, but the seeds are the thing, the vital core, and so what does it matter if the fleshy envelope is small and wormy? The deer, the raccoons, and the squirrels enjoy the fruit and scatter the seeds as they were meant to do. The apple is not essential, it is the seed that counts.... And sleep comes.

The window faces northeast. On still autumn nights, I can hear the waves trampling on the bars offshore. Only with a breath of east wind, and only sometimes, can I hear the individual waves. But when the gale blows, the roar is like a train heard at night, but *this* train comes from nowhere and goes nowhere: it is always there.

Even when the winter northeasters bring lashing rain or whipping snow, I must have the window open just a little bit. The touch of rain on my face wakes me often, and even in the black darkness of the storm, I can see the evergreens on the hilltop tossing and twisting, and hear above all the noises of the storm, the sound of the wind in the evergreen needles.

I am wakeful, too, when it snows. The flakes find their way through the open crack of the window and make a little drift on the floor. And outside there is an exciting whirl and smother, a grayness like a false dawn. The little creatures of the night are all hidden away: the squirrels in the hollow hickory, the fox in his den, and the deer and raccoons in the thick shelter of the evergreens. And I too am in my lair, my warm safe bed, while outside the storm roars in off the Atlantic and beats against the stout little house, built like a ship to ride out the strongest gales.

A vessel on the waves facing north and south becomes polarized after awhile, they say, all her iron fastenings and keel magnetized so that she is like a compass needle. Perhaps sleeping all these years under the north star, I too have become polarized.

I have grown old in my northward facing room, and among the few compensations of advancing years, there is at least freedom from the terrors of my childhood. I can lie quietly in my familiar bed and remember the little girl I once was, who had to take a brass candlestick from the rack in the hall and stumble up the stairs pursued by a monstrous jumping shadow. And finally in the room, there were things lurking in the corners, and though I never dared to look, there was something under the bed, something that would reach out a cold hand to grab my ankle.

Each night, I went through the same ritual, pushing open the south-facing window and letting the candle gutter in the wind. Quick before it blew out-there were two leaps to take from the window to the middle of the floor, and finally, convulsively, the leap to the bed, careful not to put my foot down within a skeleton arm's reach, because it was a dead thing under there, I knew it was, though I had never looked to see.

Now coming home late on a cold and windy night, the little house with its single lighted window and its waiting, patient dog has no terrors. It is a harbor of refuge after a rough passage, a place that waits for me when I am far away.

And if I find myself thinking that someday I shall not come again, I turn on the light and read a few lines until once more, I feel safe under the North star.

The Montreal Express is Early

The Montreal Express came early this year, rumbling through Ipswich in the night, even before the leaves had fallen and before the Hunter's Moon had reached the full. I don't know why the great Canadian metropolis should take the blame for the wicked wind that in fact is born much further to the north, along the ice-clotted shores of the Hudson Bay or in the shadow of the Pole itself.

It was only a trial run last week, a testing of the track, a coming and a going, a warning of bitter nights and days to come when the wind roars in the chimneys and sends snow devils whirling across the frozen marshes.

I am a fair weather sailor, I guess. Not for me the chill Autumn days, the hard breezes, the lead-blue water with running whitecaps. I love the blaze of summer sun, the marshes green as emerald, the gentle tides that fill the river's bank full but not overflowing, the long warm evenings with a whisper of a dying southwester to bring the little red sailboat quietly back to her mooring in the cove.

Last week I stood on the float and watched as northerly gusts whipped the water and the boat twitched nervously at her buoy, swinging in an arc, northwest, north, northeast and back again. I thought, "It's time, once again it's time; summer's ended."

So, the next day, Betsy and I hauled her out, dripping on her trailer, trundled her up to the shed where she will sleep away the winter. Just for reminders she will contain mementos of summer, the can of bug spray, the life preserver cushion for capsizes (never used) and the paddle for auxiliary power when I guess wrong on the failing wind. And of course, the aluminum mast and boom and the metal bladed rudder, all laid away and ready for spring.

The cove looked very empty when she had gone and there was just a gentle breeze. Perhaps it had been a mistake to haul her out so early. We decided to settle for a run downriver and around the island in the motorboat. The beauty of the evening furnished a fresh impression to add to the store that can be hauled out and contemplated before the winter fireplace. When the snow lies piled around the house and the north wind whips the bare trees, it will be nice to remember how the low sun gilded the sand dunes, deserted now, almost the way they used to be.

We ran along the inside beach where maples growing in the sand were crimson and gold, a lighter gold than the marsh grasses shaded with russet and bronze. Then, home around Hog Island, passing first the broken pilings of an ancient pier. Whoever laid them down must have chosen seasoned oak and driven them deep into the mud and glacial till. Each year, there are fewer left after the battering assault of the moving ice, leaning at crazy angles. Once upon a time, so it is said, the hay from the island fields was shipped aboard schooners to feed the horses of Boston.

The old Choate house was in shadow. The pre-Revolutionary builders knew where to site a house so that the winter sun poured in through the small-paned windows, the summer southwester cooled the low-ceilinged rooms, and the rising shoulder of the hill blocked off the bitter blasts of the Montreal Express. I used to go duck hunting there long ago, setting out my block decoys in the creek and crouching motionless among the trunks of the basswood trees that grew along the shore. Even on the coldest days, it was warm there in the sun.

Water birds, unseen in summer, were abroad on that last evening. Cormorants turned their snake-like heads as we passed the pilings where they watched for passing schools of herring. Flocks of ducks came arrowing in from the sea, and from the marshes came the croaking voices of the geese.

We passed the west side of the island, the steep side with the tumble of rocks left by the melting glacier. Here grew the only trees on the once bare slope, a grove of cedar trees, richly green against the dead grasses of winter. They were all of a size, spaced so that each had room to grow into a perfect cone. I used to marvel at them as I sailed by in my yellow dory long ago, and still I wonder if someone planted them there, carefully dropping the seeds into soft spring earth.

Their terrain has been invaded by some of the thousands of pines and firs planted on order of Cornelius Crane who thought it would be nice to change a bare grassy hill into a forest. Fifty years and more have passed, and it is indeed a forest. The little park of cedars is all but swallowed up by bigger trees with an undergrowth jungle of fox grape and sumac.

The sun had set when we tied the motor boat to the float and headed home. Already, the Montreal Express was heading our way with the first chill blasts. . . . And so ended another summer with an earlier than usual foretaste of winter.

Returning from a late fall tour to the inner beach and around Hog Island, 1975; *Ipswich Chronicle* photo

WINTER

... Standing in the yard, under the brilliant stars on the first cold night of the year, I saw the lights of the neighbors' houses and remembered how terribly alone I felt during the war years when nowhere was there a light to be seen. My daughter, Betsy, and I spent those desolate years in our cold ramshackle little house, no fireplace to cheer us on a bitter night. ...

Winter Back Then

As a child, I would have hated this kind of winter. January was supposed to be the month of deep snow, of forts and igloos built in the drifts, of snowball fights at recess, of jingling sleigh bells and the runners of delivery pungs squealing on hard-packed snow on a zero morning. An open winter was a fraud, and even weeks of skating on ponds and frozen meadows could not compensate.

But as I watched last week the tropical rain eating away the meager cover of snow, I remembered another open winter that was a lifesaver, warmer even than this one, the long ago winter of 1932. Here in those dark days of the Great Depression, I found myself back again at home in Ipswich, but how differently from the carefree happy days. My father was dead, the family scattered, and the bank, with its unpaid mortgage, snarled over the old house and fields like a fierce dog with a bone.

Sitting on the front doorstep facing south in the weak autumn sunlight, I was determined that these fields and this old house in which we had all been born would never be lost. The apple orchard and the peach trees would save us all. I never doubted that this operation was my destiny. No one else shared my optimism, but if I was crazy enough to try, why not? What else was there to do?

I remember walking out among the trees, bare now and stark, but in my mind's eye I pictured them in blossom, in leaf, and at last loaded with fruit, the golden apples of the Hesperides. Yes, I thought, the trees so hopefully planted as a haven for retirement would in the end justify
their existence and would save us all.

They had been neglected and had grown wild, thick with interlacing branches and brush. Untended, they would revert to their natural way, perpetuating their species with quantities of tiny apples, envelopes of seeds. The trees had to undergo surgery, and armed with saw and shears, I became the surgeon.

It was lonely in the big empty house with only the fog for company. We lived in the kitchen, cooked, ate, read, slept, never venturing into the cold rooms haunted by memories of happier days. At dawn, we were up and doing, and as the sun rose far away on the southern horizon, we were out among the trees. At sunset, exhausted from sawing, pushing the ladder around, hauling out and stacking the cut branches and brush, we came back to the house, supper and bed, the dog collapsed and snoring behind the stove after a day of barking, running, and chasing rabbits.

The days passed, one by one by one. The brush piles grew under the trees, and as I saw progress and neatly trimmed branches resulting from my labors, I was encouraged, filled with hope, and though weeks passed with only the dog to talk to, I was seldom, hardly ever, sad. Whatever would I have done, I have often wondered, if that first year had been a normal winter.

Instead, week after week, snow held off, and day after day, it was warm enough to work outdoors in shirtsleeves. January merged into February, the sun became higher and warmer, the days longer. Row after row, the older trees were finished and bordered with piles of brush. I could hardly believe that I had done all that myself. Last to be done were the peaches; being small trees, they were easy.

I had planned to haul away and burn the brush in March so that all would be clear for the first spray in early April. The giant Fordson tractor with cleated metal wheels had squatted in the barn all winter, and with my usual careless optimism, I expected it would start when called on, even though I was no great hand with engines. It had to be hand cranked, but I had run it in the past in apple picking vacations. But when I came to start it, I could not even turn it over and found that last fall's hired man had driven it into the barn empty of oil and had left it, seized up, dead.

Do you remember that tractor, Jim Gaudet? Nearly fifty years later, I still remember how you helped me out, working on your own time with only a promise of payment in the fall.

The years in the orchard taught me more than "can do" in growing apples. I learned about the kindness and generosity of many different kinds of people, and somehow we all managed to survive the Great Depression of the thirties together.

It was a time to try the soul. We learned to help each other. It strengthened us, grizzled old-timers that we are now. We managed without social services until Roosevelt came along with his "socialistic notions." I wonder if today's easy living generation would do as well as we did.

But, reliving those years in memory, I see that there was a pattern to them — the grand design of the seasons: awakening, unfolding, opening, and becoming dormant: the life cycle of birth, growth, maturity, and death.

It seems to me that the closer people are to the natural cycle, the more firm their belief in immortality, in another spring and flowers.

Winter Breakfasts

I was shocked to read recently that only about one-fifth of the students eat breakfasts before coming to school. How ever do they last out the morning, I wondered, thinking of the abundant breakfasts of my childhood?

To be sure, the school buses come early, but we also rose before dawn in those long ago childhood winters; why, I can't imagine, except that people down Maine where my father came from went to bed with the birds and rose with the first chirp. Nine o'clock was Crockett bedtime, and at 6:15 came *bang, bang, bang,* the knocking at the door. Woe to the kid who pulled the covers over his head and snuggled down for another forty winks. My father invaded the bedroom, hauled all the covers off the bed, and dragged them away, leaving the pajam'd child shivering with a quick bed to make instead of a quick smooth and tuck-in.

Most of my childhood winters were spent in Boston, except for the longed-for weekends in Ipswich on the farm. I would wake to the sound of wooden snow shovels scraping on brick sidewalks, a lovely hollow sound that signified snowball fights and pung rides through the city streets. Next came the milkman's pung, jingling up the alley, the runners squealing, a sure sign of an icy morning.

He did not stop at our door. We drank milk and yellow cream from the farm at Ipswich and anointed our toast with butter from the churn; the eggs came by mail in metal traveling boxes. What this cost, no one figured out, but our own milk and cream, arriving by train, were better for us.

Peering out from under the covers on a winter morning, I could see the brick walls and the gutter and copper ventilators of the houses across the valley, laced and filagreed with snow, with more snow filtering down between the buildings. All the ventilators pointed to the northeast, and I could hear the muffled horns of steamers in the harbor. More snow, a blizzard: good! How I wished I was with Grandma in Ipswich, snowed in on Argilla Road.

Time to rise and shine, time to pull on those hated long johns, folding the knitted cuff which still made a lump under the long stockings over my ankle; the long johns hooked onto what we called a "waist" with dangling garters. Over this went a wool school dress. No matter how cold the room, hair had to be brushed and pigtails braided before the dress was put on-on account of the hairs, you know: my mother could always tell when I cheated when she pulled a long fine hair from the back of my plaid dress.

Although many things of the childhood years, interwoven in the mind's eye with those later, have been forgotten, I can still see my Boston bedroom and the wicker chair with a cushion that I thought was simply beautiful, an embroidered larger than life-sized owl with real eyes of green glass, and the reproduction of Sir Galahad with his white horse: the knight pure in heart was nasty, but the horse was nice.

The only other art work was a lithograph of Jesus, a child in a nightgown with a lion and a lamb miraculously being friends together. I liked that. There was a bureau with untidy drawers. My clothes smelt queerly because buried underneath were my prize collections of cigarette pictures: baseball players, actresses, boxers that came in Murads, Sweet Caporal, and Virginia Straights, and which were traded among the kids after they had been begged from the cabmen on the corner and from other adult smokers.

I did my homework in the wicker chair, leaning against the owl sitting next to my bed. This was convenient because I could scale the book I was reading under the bed and snatch up a textbook whenever I heard an investigating adult approaching in the hall outside. I was a skinny kid, my long stockings always wrinkled no matter how tightly I cinched them to the garters.

Remembering those breakfasts, I can't imagine why I was so thin. First, there was a baked Ipswich apple with cream: "Don't take a bath in it," my father warned as I tilted the pitcher. Then, there was a big bowl of oatmeal with more Ipswich cream, of course, and West Indian brown sugar, coarse granules that melted into pure molasses. Next, there were eggs from Ipswich; those that had arrived cracked were fried, the sound ones were boiled — two always with bacon or ham that was good and salty from our own pigs. Coffee was not for children except occasionally as a treat in the form of a soaked lump of sugar. We had milk, of course: lakes, rivers, oceans of milk. On Wednesday and Sunday mornings, we had baked beans and pie for breakfast; on Sundays, there was a horrid concoction called brown bread brewis made from leftover-from-Saturday brown bread soaked in milk. My father loved it, we children hated it, but children in that remote period of time ate what was set before them or they didn't eat at all.

This was how prosperous city children ate, with dinner and supper accordingly, but still I remained scrawny, much to my mother's distress.

It was a long time before I realized that not all children ate this way, and it came as a terrible shock when one day I hopped off a pung in the wilderness of the South End and saw a ragged woman with a shawl over her head picking through a garbage pail at the back door of a rooming house, then putting things in a paper bag. I returned to Marlborough Street close to tears, and told my father about it, and said that I wished somehow I could give that woman my brown bread brewis.

The Good Old Days

Sentimentally, it is a fine thing to look back on what are known as the good old days. Every time I do so, I get quite a response from people who join me in becoming dewy-eyed at the thought of jingling sleigh bells and roaring fires in the fireplace and from kids who say wistfully, "Gee, it must have been fun to live then."

But Sunday afternoon and Monday morning with the glass at zero and the north wind whirling drift devils of snow across the frozen marshes, I was glad indeed to live in the age of the four-wheel drive, oil heat, and diesel power. The fireplace, so inefficiently sending half its heat up the chimney, was more for cheer and comfort than for warmth, and the snow shovel was for opening paths and clearing a way to the bird feeder, rather than for digging out a road to the world of people and civilization. It was a long cold ride to town in the days of the horse and sleigh, with the wind whooping across the open fields and the roads filled in solid with unploughed snow from stone wall to stone wall. We used to cut out through the fields where the snow had blown thin and the frozen grass poked out through the crust.

All very fine to think about: but how cold were the feet in the hay in the bottom of the sleigh, how numb the hands clutching the frozen reins, and how sharply the fingers of the wind probed through the pores of the mackinaw and flannel shirt before the days of windbreakers.

How wonderful to lie toasting under an electric blanket and hear the ploughs go rumbling by and the jeep pushing and panting as it cleared the snow out of the driveway. The shovel work that remained was only play, not work. How soft we have become! But on a bitter blowing day, it is like biting on a sore tooth to remember how it once was.

My life, like *omnis gallia,* divides itself into three parts. The first part was the time before World War I, with coal stove in the warm kitchen and a barn full of animals down here on the farm. The discomforts did not bother us children, and being snowed in was an adventure. We thought it odd when parents and grandparents complained and worried.

Then came part two of my life, mostly the seemingly endless Depression days when there were armies of men lining up at the town hall for jobs shoveling out the roads. I remember seeing at least twenty five men working in the drifts between Northgate and Argilla Farm in those terrible winters of the thirties when the snow was so deep that it had to be shoveled out in stages.

I have an indelible picture of those tiny little figures digging for dear life in the smother: it was dig or freeze. I remember thin, worn overcoats and one quite old man with no gloves and a long icicle hanging from his mustache. I had finished my own lonely stint of digging and had traveled on snowshoes to see how the road work was coming and how soon I could coax my weak old car to town. Not that I needed anything or could afford to buy it if I did, but just to get out: I felt myself going stir-crazy in a cold kitchen with only a dog for comfort. I'll bet there were few people who understood Admiral Byrd's book *Alone* any better than I did, how there is a disintegration of the mind that comes with being constantly cold and with no one to talk to.

On Sunday afternoon, looking out of the living room window towards the north, while the wind drove the blowing snow rattling against the house, I recalled how a friend from Newfoundland told me that when she was a child, she used to dig down in March to see if the earth was really there under all that snow. I remembered sitting for hours huddled on a sofa in the kitchen during the winter of 1933-34 with the dog curled up beside me, motionless, while the snow blew around, drifting deeper and deeper by the window where the garden used to be. Among the few random thoughts that floated through my mind, I recall only wondering if the snow would ever melt, or if this was the age of the glaciers returning.

Somehow, we all lived through those days, and spring came again. There is nothing in all the world so wonderful as the first thaw, the drip, drip, drip of the downspout, and the mild damp southwester blowing.

It was not all beer and skittles in those days-no beer and mighty few skittles, whatever they are.

And now comes part three, the present day when no one is truly hungry or cold and when the only people who want to shovel snow are some of the more ambitious school kids out to make a dollar. In Depression times, a whole family lived for a week on eighteen dollars and thought themselves lucky to have it. There are the sharecroppers in the South, the dispossessed African-Americans of Mississippi, and people in the slums and ghettos — but not here, not here in Ipswich.

Now what do we do, turn up the electric blanket another notch and snuggle down, forgetting? Or spend some minutes or hours in idle recollections? Or turn our memories and experiences into such action as we are capable of taking?

Skating

You won't find the name of Goodale's Pond on any of the old maps. The space it occupies at the foot of Sagamore Hill was formerly a tongue of salt marsh fed by a tiny creek until way back before the turn of the century, Dr. Joseph L. Goodale created the pond by building a gravel dam across the creek at the narrow neck of the marsh. There was an abundant supply of gravel nearby, and farmers were glad to rent out their horses and wagons to the city doctor for a little hard cash; after all, you had to expect fancy notions from these newcomers to town!

The pond was started before I was born, but I remember discussions of it at home and questions on whether the shallow water would not add even more to the abundance of mosquitoes, and whether the fine crop of bullrushes that sprouted all across it was really such an asset to the landscape.

It was true that there were running springs all through that bit of marsh, and the pond was still further fed by the runoff from the surrounding hills which at that time was open pasture land and bare of trees. The gravel dam was low and leaky, and the pond was for years just a shallow spreading puddle, but the dam was added to, bit by bit, to make the handsome little body of water that now looks as though it had always been there.

Almost from its beginning, the pond was a great place to skate, even though it was open to the north wind and bitterly cold. I can remember driving all the way down from Boston in our open car with only isinglass curtains, arriving chilled and frozen for a Sunday afternoon skate. It took more than a cup of cocoa with Grandma to warm us up after an hour or so tottering around on bended ankles.

Those were the days of detachable skates, when children's winter boots had a heel plate, and the front end of skates clamped to the sole and fastened with a key which I used to wear around my neck on a string. The skates had a way of becoming unfastened in a fast game of shinny, resulting in bone-shaking spills.

Straight ahead, I was a fast and clumsy skater, but I fell on the corners and tripped over my big feet when skating backwards. I can remember sitting shivering on a muskrat house, admiring the skill of neighbor-caretaker, Dan MacLeod, who had learned to skate when he was a boy during the long winters of Nova Scotia, and who could do figure-eights, circles, and leaps, all with incredible ease on the same kind of skates I myself wore.

Only the other day, I was talking with a friend about my age about skating on the river, and we were wagging our heads about the good old days as elderly folks like to do.

"Kids today have to have a rink to skate on, and someone to clear the ice when it snows. They'd rather stand on the corner or ride in a car," he said.

"We used to make our own fun," he concluded, and so we did indeed.

We made an iceboat for the pond; it was crossed and braced by two-by-fours, and we used three old shoe skates for runners and the mast and sail from my yellow dory. It was too fast for the little pond: we would be at the end before we had gotten up speed. Then, we tried skate sailing with a cotton triangle, cross-braced with bamboo poles.

This was the great sport on the frozen Charles River Basin in Boston where you could sail from the West Boston Bridge to Harvard Bridge, beating to windward along the Tech shore, and running before the breeze along the Back Bay side.

It was a cold but exhilarating sport and hard on the ankles as you leaned against the sail and went flying over the ice. The pond was also too small for this, and so we went back to games of shinny or tag. As we grew older, there was night skating under a full moon with a bonfire on the ice, the logs and coals melting down and hissing while the fire burned on top.

I had one of those twinges of lost youth remembered the other night as I came by Goodale's Pond just at sunset and saw the ice smooth as glass and all pink in the light of the afterglow as the sun went down. I stopped the car and looked and listened, and then I heard the sound of ringing skate blades in the still air. Far up towards the dam, I saw a child's figure and a running black dog. It gave me the queerest feeling. Darkness fell, and the skater and dog disappeared from sight. I wondered if they had really been there or whether I had seen a flashback to myself, to the child of long ago with my black dog. Nixie.

Sometimes, I think that everything, like matter, endures: all those golden moments, the gaiety and the sadness, the beloved faces and voices and perhaps as long as they are remembered, they do.

Christmas in Boston

Exploring my memories of long ago is something I indulge in between waking and sleeping as I lie in my bed next to the window and look out drowsily at the blue stars of winter wheeling overhead, or tangling in the branches of the evergreens which I remember as tiny little things that I helped my father plant. Almost more than watching a child grow to man or womanhood, the growth of the trees marks the passing of the years.

In restless America, it is strange, I suppose, to be living still in the place where I was born; but here I am, still in the shadow of the glacial hill that curls like a sleeping animal on the surrounding marshes. Except for one brief time in the Great Depression, when I thought it might all be lost forever, this particular piece of land, where a glacier melted and dropped its load of gravel and stray boulders, has been always here, waiting for me. Happy and full of hope, or sad and filled with pain, I always could find solace, and so it is also here that I can evoke faces and voices that live only in memory.

It was on a recent evening that I recalled the memory of a Boston Christmas long ago before the first war. It was my mother's custom to prepare little gifts for her friends; this was before the days when a card would do. If I had been good-and who wasn't with Christmas approaching?

I was allowed to carry the basket with the gaily wrapped little things: jars of honey from the farm, or cranberries from the sand dunes, or arrangements of bayberries and Christmas berries, which is what we always called those of the black alder.

The pung runner tracks in the street gleamed in the lamplight. The snow was piled in the pocket handkerchief-sized squares of grass which fronted each Back Bay house. Some people had a forsythia bush or a little clipped hedge, and in the next block, there was a Missouri currant; I used to stand sniffing the spicy smell of its yellow blossoms and long for my room in Ipswich with the currant bush under the window.

So, in the blue December twilight, we set forth. We rang the doorbells; my mother laughed and joked with her friends, and we left the little gift in its Christmas wrapping and moved onto the next stop. I was so used to the gay exchanges that it came as a great shock when an old lady opened the door, took her present with hardly a "thank you" and closed the door in our faces. I was stunned: she had not even wished us a Merry Christmas. I remember feeling angry and resentful: no one had a right to feel that way on Christmas-but that was before I knew how fragile a thing is the spirit of Christmas.

In those days, Christmas did not begin at Thanksgiving with the grass still green and some trees still holding their leaves. It was only a few days before Christmas when we went down to Fanueil Hall, my father and I, to choose our tree. The trees had only just come out of the woods and were fresh and fragrant and oozing their sap. There was no radio to blast out Christmas music. In those days, when we were old enough to go out caroling, there were sleigh bells in the streets and real candles in the windows.

Thanksgiving was Ipswich, and Christmas was Boston with its slate roofs and the brick spires and chimneys of the old houses outlined with snow, the scrape of wooden shovels on brick sidewalks, and the mournful horns of ships in the harbor carried on the east wind. Santa came in his sleigh by night: I even heard the jingle of the bells and knew that he was on the roof, coming down the big brick chimney to where our stockings hung limp and empty, to my own blue-ribbed stocking, the longest I could find, and the two smaller ones of my brothers which reached only above the knee where the knickers buckled.

What Santa could not fit into the stockings, he would put on the chair from which the stockings hung. I never thought it odd that he had room for everything for all the Boston children. I was a believer and did not know that there were some children, good children, too, who found nothing in their stockings on Christmas morning.

Not much is left to the imagination anymore, I thought, lying in my bed, recalling those simpler times when all the little children were believers and not confused by Santa on every street corner.

I was just beginning to feel like mother's old friend, sad and soured, when I saw the little kids in Ipswich lining up to see Santa. In their eyes, I saw the same awe mixed with fear, and I felt that whatever we do, we cannot steal the magic and mystery from children. Probably the adults of my childhood were tired, irritated, angry, and worried more often than not, or even sad and lonely, but we just didn't see them that way.

Christmas Memory

It has seemed particularly hard these last years to attain that joyous feeling bubbling up from a full heart that used to be called the spirit of Christmas. For too long, the shadow of the Vietnam War hung darkly over everything, and each evening's news showed how little peace there was on earth. Since then, our innocence seems to have gone, and I wonder sometimes how much goodwill there is among men.

Even if there were something of the old feeling left, it would be hard to maintain it for a whole month. Christmas has been taken over by the business people, and it is hard even for the most eager believer to thrill to Santa Claus' magical sleigh ride from the North Pole over the
rooftops when he has been seen on every street comer and in every department store ever since Thanksgiving. Christmas these days has been watered down and vulgarized, and shoppers no longer seem bright-eyed and happy but appear harried, worried, and, alas, often cross.

There are those of us who can find solace in the memory of other Christmases. In Boston, where many of my childhood Christmases were spent, the snow lay deep on the streets till the warm sun of March took it away: it seemed to snow more in those days.

I can remember stirring in my bed when the 7 o'clock factory whistles blew their melodious chorus. Those morning whistles were our alarm clock, announcing it was time to get up, wash in a chilly bathroom, go down to a big hot breakfast of oatmeal and brown sugar and cream from the Ipswich farm, and eggs from Grandma's henhouse.

Then off to school, walking of course, swinging my books on a strap, scuffling and even fighting with the children from the next block, and arriving with those awful knitted leggings, those ribbed cotton stockings twisted and bunched over the long johns underneath.

The 7 o'clock whistles seemed to blow with a joyous sound on the first day of Christmas vacation. Outside the alley, the snow squealed under the runners of the milkman's pung. The pungs were delivery vans on runners, and they ranged all the way from the stylish ones of S.S. Pierce pulled by fast-stepping dappled gray horses to the firewood and coal pungs lumbering in from the country and hauled by plodding long-furred horses with icicles dripping from their nostrils. These horses were guided by a mackinawed driver who was red faced and red nosed with a ragged mustache, also icicled.

The pungs of Boston provided country fun for city children who rode the runners all over the city and even to the outskirts of Cambridge and Charleston. Groups of children waited on the street corners, the bolder and older dashed out to grab a Pierce pung to go whirling away as the sleigh bells jingled and snowballs flew from the flying hoofs of the horses.

Smaller and less venturesome children rode the slow pungs down the alleys, stopping at the back doors while the driver carried in a basket of kindling or bags of cannel coal, the greasy kind that smoked and bubbled in the fireplace until finally falling apart into a bed of glowing coals. In terra incognita, which was for me the South End, Roxbury, and Dorchester, we switched pungs, and eventually, round about and after many switches, we arrived home again, long past dinner time. Being late was all right because no one worried about children in those days: there was nothing to worry about.

Sometimes we hitched our sleds in a long line behind a pung and rode to the common where we coasted on a hill that did not compare with the bare hills of Ipswich but which was enlivened by fights behind snow forts with the "mockers" from the West End. Or if it was cold enough, we skated on the Charles and learned how to fancy skate from a kindly policeman from Station 16 who had the river duty and who cut figure-eights and did spins and circles, never losing his dignity or his balance; we used to hope that he would fall and sprawl in his blue uniform on the ice, but he never did.

The climax came on Christmas Eve when the stockings were hung, and we all went off to bed to await Santa's coming. We had not seen him every day, but we knew that his reindeer were bringing him through the sky, without danger of collisions with airplanes; except for birds, Santa was the only flying thing in those days. I could swear that on more than one occasion, I heard him on the roof with the stamping of reindeer hooves and the jingling of bells. I snuggled down in bed, knowing that children who peeked might find only a lump of coal in the stocking.

Then the joy of Christmas morning and all the things that Santa brought; how ever did he bring my brother's tool bench down the chimney? Or my wooden stable with all the horses and the little carts and buggies? Ah, that was a Christmas!

The glow of innocence remained for years; it was not till long afterwards that I learned that Mr. Gunderson, the lighthouse keeper in Ipswich, made my stable. In the afternoon, the tree appeared that had been smuggled into the house and in secret decorated with real candles, for which there was always a bucket of water and a broom in the corner for safety's sake.

In just remembering these things, I feel a stirring of the Christmas spirit, and I hope that for all who read these words, there will be happy memories too.

Winter Stars

The gentle sun that warmed our spirit in so many summers shines now on southern beaches, palm fringed islands, and coral seas. All across the Northern Hemisphere, this is the time of trial by frost and ice. The hazy stars of summer burn fiercely overhead in the clear winter skies; all across the northern world, the savage winds blow, and only the oaks still carry their rattling metallic leaves.

I wonder how it is in those little sod-roofed houses of Iceland and in north Norway, how dark it must be now. And has the ice locked the great Russian rivers? All those steamers and barges along the Dnieper, are they all frozen in and quiet?

For years and years before going to bed, it has been my custom to walk out into the yard to take a look at the sky. I still feel the inner trembling of awe that I first felt as child after I learned that the sky was not a great blue curtain pierced with points of light through a myriad of tiny holes, but that it was a vast emptiness through which wheeled other planets chained to other suns, and all turning, turning. . . the stars in their courses.

As a child, I felt myself to be a tiny grain of sand on the beach of the world, and I was frightened that some wind might come to blow me away. I would hurry back into the house which somehow I felt was firmly anchored. Still afraid when I lighted my candle and went up the zigzag staircase, followed by my huge leaping shadow, I went to my bed where I was safe and reassured by the grown-up voices talking in the downstairs sitting room. Outside was the north wind coming over the marshes, over the hill, booming in the chimney, and blowing away across the world. I would curl up tight and small so that nothing could find me and carry me away.

Standing in the yard, under the brilliant stars on the first cold night of the year, I saw the lights of the neighbors' houses and remembered how terribly alone I felt during the war years when nowhere was there a light to be seen. My daughter, Betsy, and I spent those desolate years in our cold ramshackle little house, no fireplace to cheer us on a bitter night. The big old house was empty and dark, sinister under the bare trees. We could hear the sea very plainly from the cottage, and in the quiet nights sometimes, there was a trembling of the earth, and all the windows rattled from the depth charges of the prowling submarines stalking the blacked out merchant ships along the coast.

Somewhere out in the North Atlantic was Bill's ship. I never knew where: the days and the weeks and the months went by with no word, except once in awhile there was a letter all cut and tattered by the censor.

Every now and then, Bill would suddenly appear, tense and strained and very restless, to stay for a few days or a week; then he would be gone again to join another convoy out of New York bound for who knew where or for how long.

Daytimes, there was my job and Betsy's school, but in the lonely nights, I felt all the childhood terrors returning. On one trip, Bill brought back a little dog to keep us company. Trixie came from the gutters of Alexandria in Egypt. She became on the long crossing a ship's dog who had seen the war at firsthand. She barked fiercely at passing airplanes. Bill said she did that on the ship, adding her shrill little voice to all the guns.

Trixie could see things that people could not see, and she used to terrify me when she woke up in the silent house and walked stiff-legged to the middle of the room and stood listening, all the hairs on her ruff on end, following something with her eyes. I sat frozen, clutching a book in my lap, until finally with a low growl, Trixie walked back to her basket, turned round and round, sighed, and settled back to sleep.

And then there was the night when I stood in the yard, listening to the voice of a big owl in the woods. Suddenly, he was quiet, and I heard the rustle of the sea. As I turned toward the house, a puff of wind stirred my hair and fanned my face. When I looked up, startled, I saw a monstrous bird right over my head, his wide wings blotting out the stars. There was no sound of feather, just the disturbed air that made me know that he was there.

As our spinning earth tips to the north, and the days are short and the nights are long, all sorts of things are abroad in the darkness seen only by children, the childlike, and animals. The trolls must be out in Norway along the coast where once the Viking ships were beached waiting for the spring.

When the arctic gales blow across the stony plains of Iceland, the people huddle in their remote farmhouses while the elves tap at the windows, their mocking laughter in the wind.

Across the Siberian tundra and the black earth plains of Russia, across the stripped wheat fields of Alberta and Saskatchewan, snow devils swirl and run before the northern blasts.

Long ago, a child sat before the fireplace and heard the wind booming in the chimney, sucking the flames and smoke up to the stars.

Long ago, a young woman waited, as sea coast women have always waited, for a ship to come into the harbor. And now, overhead, as when the world was new, the winter stars move in their courses, with only the North Star steadfast above the rooftop.

Home

The times are out of joint. Who would expect to see, looking out of the window on the last Sunday of winter, the salt marshes glittering under the high sun, locked in a beginning glacier of ice and topped by a foot of unmelted granular snow? Or the Castle Neck River with only a few leads of arctic blue water between fields and moving pans of ice? Each open spot has its rafts and clots of ducks, and while some ducks swim, others stand on the edges, preening or dozing with one leg tucked into the warm belly feathers.

Where a spring runs down from the sand and snow covered Wigwam Hill, at the old Woodbury farm where the inner beach begins, there is a beaten path of webbed tracks where the ducks waddle up from the river for their sips of fresh water.

Even though the glass on the back porch is pushing zero on Sunday morning, the ducks are swimming in pairs, and the red wing blackbirds are crowding the feeder, vying for seeds with the chickadees, the juncoes, and the tree sparrows who have been faithful visitors all these long months.

In their bags in the kitchen, the potatoes and the onions are sending out their green sprouts. They have more faith than we that it is almost spring. And under the snow, the jonquils and the snowdrops have pushed their green spears through the frozen ground.

I hope that in some attic somewhere are still preserved the journals started more than seventy years ago and kept faithfully by those two scientific-minded members of "Doctor's Row," Dr. Joseph Goodale and Dr. Charles Townsend. Dr. Townsend transferred his observations to two books, *Sand Dunes* and *Salt Marshes and Beach Grass*, books which open one's eyes to things underfoot and overhead and round about as one walks on the beach and through the pitch pine woods of the sand dunes.

I remember watching Dr. Goodale writing in his journal, recording in a thin, spidery, old-fashioned hand his careful observation of the temperature, the direction and strength of the wind, the date on which he heard his first song sparrow and the first redwing, or saw the first crocus, jonquil, or apple blossom. I do not remember that Dr. Goodale did more than keep a record; I do not think he noted the personal emotions roused by country Ipswich that he loved so well.

But Dr. Townsend did write of these emotions, and when I was a child and homesick for Ipswich and the old square house on Argilla Road, I used to get *Sand Dunes* out of the bookcase and curl up on the window seat overlooking the brick sidewalks and piled-up dirty snow of Marlborough Street. That way, I could leave Boston behind and return to the beach, to the wild cranberry bogs, and to the pine groves.

The three original members of "Doctor's Row," as some used to call this part of Ipswich, settled here by choice rather than by accident or birth, and so the doctors, my father included, viewed the countryside with eyes not jaded by the familiar. To others, its original Yankee settlers, the area was known as "Hog Town," but even when I was growing up, it was a long time since many hogs rooted for acorns under the giant red oak trees. The old-time Essex County farmers, however, never had time or inclination to write down their feelings about their surroundings.

I wonder if any of the new people who are coming to Ipswich will put down the kind of roots that those doctors did, so that now the third and fourth generations of their descendants are running over the fields and marshes and sailing their boats in the creeks. The third generation now, from Greece and Poland, who settled in town are equally firmly rooted here.

I doubt really that there will be many new roots. This is the age of wheels and wings, how much I only realized when chatting with fishermen and strollers on a California beach a few years back. Of all the twenty or thirty people with whom I talked that day, not one was a native. They came from Indiana or Montana or Missouri or Ohio, or elsewhere, and thought it very strange that I had been born, raised, and then had remained in Massachusetts, in fact, living still not much more than a stone's throw away from the house in which I was born. I have often wondered whether it is a kindness to a child to bring him up so deeply rooted that a move away is a traumatic experience.

But I guess the whole matter is out of our hands in a shrunken and restless world when whole generations have had to follow the guns and the dollars to places that once were only pink and yellow and green patches on the map.

Still, it is nice to have a place to come home to, a place where you belong. I belong here, and I have not been sorry.

Returning from the last summer sail

Ipswich Chronicle photo, 1978

Printed in the United States
127353LV00001B/29-30/P